—THE—
Horsemaster's
Notebook

FOURTH EDITION

MARY ROSE FBHS

Consultant Editor ISLAY AUTY FBHS

KENILWORTH PRESS

To My Father
W. Robert Rose

Copyright © 1972, 1977, 1988, 1997 Peter Barker Ltd

First published in the UK in 1972
by Kenilworth Press, an imprint of Quiller Publishing Ltd
Second edition 1977
Third edition 1988; reprinted 1991, 1993, 1996
Fourth edition 1997; reprinted 2001, 2003, 2007

British Library Cataloguing-in-Publication Data
A catalogue record for this book
is available from the British Library

ISBN 978 1 872082 92 9

Designed by Paul Saunders
Printed in Great Britain by Bell & Bain

Kenilworth Press

An imprint of Quiller Publishing Ltd
Wykey House, Wykey, Shrewsbury, SY4 1JA
Tel: 01939 261616 Fax: 01939 261606
E-mail: info@quillerbooks.com
Website: www.kenilworthpress.co.uk

Contents

Foreword

by ISLAY AUTY FBHS

The Horsemaster's Notebook is a well-known title and has a reputation of many years' standing. The information it imparts, to both the amateur owner-rider and to the aspiring professional in today's booming horse industry, is invaluable. In this fully updated version, Mary Rose's clarity and simplicity of explanation has been maintained, while including all the relevant changes in the management and care of the 'modern' equine. With systematic and concise text, enhanced by clear diagrams, it will be an essential addition to every horse owner's or career student's bookshelf.

Islay Auty
October 1997

Acknowledgements

The author is grateful to N. Lee Newman DVM (Equine Specialist) for extensive help in making revisions to the fourth edition of this book, and also to Islay Auty FBHS and Catherine Eardley BHSI for their assistance in revising the text.

Illustrations
All line drawings are by Dianne Breeze, except page 116 by D. Diane Lent; pages 83, 98, 132 and 210 by Kenilworth Press; and page 170 by Christine Bousfield.

CHAPTER 1

Horse Psychology

The Nature of the Horse

1. Horses are herd animals. If denied the company of other horses, behavioural problems may develop.
2. They are gregarious and communicate by body language, including eye contact, facial expression, sniffing, ear and head movement, body position, licking and body pressures, vocally and telepathically.
3. All horses are constantly aware of the 'pecking order' or hierarchy amongst them and between themselves and humans.
4. When handling horses be authoritative, quiet, calm and determined. Know that you are No.1 on the ladder.
5. For stabled horses the security of the herd is replaced by the security of the stable, which is associated with food and comfort and exerts a strong 'pull' on the horse. This can be the cause of the 'nappy' horse who is reluctant to leave home. Consider locating the riding area at a distance from the living area.
6. The horse's self-preservation instinct is very strong, and when afraid, nature urges the horse to run away. If confined in a stable a nervous horse stands in a corner presenting his hindquarters to the door ready to defend himself by kicking. Training eventually overcomes fear.
7. Horses are perceptive and sensitive. They sense how you feel and respond accordingly.

The Senses

All senses are more highly developed in horses than in humans.

Sight
- Horses see movement even at a great distance and react to it.

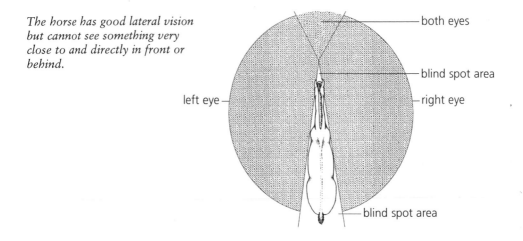

The horse has good lateral vision but cannot see something very close to and directly in front or behind.

- both eyes
- blind spot area
- left eye
- right eye
- blind spot area

- The equine eye cannot change focus from objects close by to objects far away. The horse can only focus by raising or lowering his head. It is therefore important to allow freedom of movement of the head and neck when riding across country or jumping.
- Because of the position of the eyes on either side of the head horses have lateral vision and can see behind them, especially when the head is lowered, but they do not have binocular vision and depth and distance perception are less effective than for a human.
- The horse's pupil takes a full minute to dilate. Therefore a horse moving from bright sunlight into dark shadow is effectively blind for that time.

Hearing

- This sense is highly developed. Large mobile ears rotate to receive sounds from any direction from considerable distance.
- Ear position often indicates horse's feelings. Alert and pricked indicate attentiveness; laid flat back, aggressiveness; half back, anxiety, confusion or relaxation.
- Horses are exceptionally responsive to the tone of the human voice.

Touch

- Touch is a form of communication between horses and also between horses and humans.
- The horse's whiskers are used to touch and evaluate objects which he may not be able to see. In particular, the whiskers help the horse to determine plants and grains. Horses with whiskers removed by clipping may refuse to eat for two or three days because they cannot 'feel' their feed.
- Lips are sufficiently sensitive to separate out powders or granules added to the feed and eat everything else.

Smell
- This sense is more highly developed in horses than it is in humans.
- Plays an important part in the defence system.
- Is used as a means of recognition of other horses and territorial regions; also involved in sexual play.
- Horses are said to be able to detect that a person is afraid by the 'fear scent' they exude.

Taste
- This sense is closely linked to smell.
- Used to determine the suitability and safety of plants and feed.

Sixth Sense
- Horses seem to sense the moods of the rider and reflect them in their behaviour.
- Horses feel, interpret and respond to even slight changes in muscular tension in the rider.

Handling and Training

1. Horses have long, retentive memories, but limited reasoning power.
2. Memory, reward and repetition form the basis of training.
3. Rewards should not always take the form of food. Ceasing to ask is a reward, as are patting, speaking a kind word and finishing work.
4. Know what you want the horse to do and picture him doing it.
5. Speak before approaching or touching a horse.
6. Allow no negative thoughts – 'know' that your horse will respond correctly.
7. Never lose your temper.
8. Be firm and gentle, never rough.
9. Be considerate of your horse's needs.
10. If possible, provide companionship.

Living Arrangements

1. Horses living out at grass 24 hours a day are the most healthy, if properly fed, and suffer least stress.
2. Horses stabled constantly and exercised for only an hour or so a day suffer more colic than those at grass. Stress is known to cause colic.
3. Make living arrangements as near natural as possible. Allowing horses to be outside at night in hot weather and inside during wet, cold weather in winter works very well.

CHAPTER 2

Stable Construction and Fittings

Site

Chief Considerations

When building a new stable or 'barn' the chief considerations to bear in mind are:

1. Dry foundation.
2. Good drainage.
3. Pure air – good circulation, upwind of all nearby housing.
4. Good light. Consider climate – stables should face south if possible.
5. Good water supply.
6. Good access road for delivery of hay etc. and removal of manure, and for vehicles in case of emergency.

Nature of the Soil

1. Best: sub-soil of gravel or deep sand. Gives a firm base with free drainage and dryness.
2. Next best: any rocky formation – e.g. limestone, chalk or granite.
3. Worst: stiff clay, deep loam, or peaty and marshy soils. If buildings must be erected on such soils, sub-soil drainage must be extensively adopted.

Foundations

1. Artificial bases, wider than the intended structure, give stability.
2. Many stable buildings erected today of pole barn or prefabricated structure do not require foundations but careful site preparation is always required. Relevant local authority planning permission must be obtained.
3. If sub-soil water is near the surface, drainage is required to prevent damage from rising damp.
4. In very damp locations, buildings may have to be raised on arches or

piles. Consult knowledgeable contractor.

5. Well-aerated soil provides ready drainage and dry foundation.
6. In site preparation consider the drainage from the stables. A large, shallow, open drain behind the stable is one good method.

Aspect

1. Buildings should be sheltered from most severe prevailing winds.
2. Buildings should not be overshadowed by other structures to the extent of interference with good supply of sunlight and pure air.
3. Buildings are best arranged in echelon or parallel lines, large open squares or L-shapes.
4. Buildings arranged in small enclosures or squares are not good. They permit less free supply of air and give greater chance of contagion when any form of sickness is present.
5. Restoring old buildings is often the best option.

Buildings

Walls – Brick

1. Should be at least 12ft (3.6m) high to give adequate headroom for large horses, 10ft (3.1m) for smaller ones.
2. Should be 1½ to 2 bricks thick and damp-proof.
3. Damp-proofing can be achieved by introducing a 'damp-course' of asphalt, or a layer of vitrified brick, into the wall a little above ground level.
4. Damp-proofing may also be achieved by building double walls with a space in between.
5. The space between double walls is liable to become a refuge for vermin, but does give good protection against dampness from rain beating on exposed brick face. (Brick is very porous.)

Wood or Pole Barn Construction

1. Many varieties of pre-fabricated wood stables are now available.
2. Pole barn construction consists of sinking large poles (or treated wooden posts) into concrete, erecting wood trusses, and covering with sheet metal, Onduline or wood cladding.
3. Complete wooden stalls can be built inside the outer shell giving double-thickness walls and damp-proofing. The interior walls should be of solid tongue-and-groove boards.
4. Barn constructions can be used as an open deep-littered yard for ponies and young horses to winter in, or can be subdivided into stalls or stables either with temporary or more permanent barriers.

5. General considerations of height of walls, slope of roofs and roofing materials are the same as for brick buildings.
6. Pole supports and bottom two or three boards of stalls must be pressure-treated with a suitable preservative.
7. If interior walls are not provided by manufacturer, kicking boards to a height of 4ft (1.15m) should be added to protect horse and outer walls.

The Stable Roof

General Roof Requirements
1. Slope of roof should be at an angle of not more than 45° to the horizon.
2. An ideal roof should maintain an equable temperature in both hot and cold weather.
3. Roof should be durable, noiseless and non-inflammable.
4. Guttering should be fitted to carry away rainwater to drain.

Roofing Materials
1. Shingles: Must be mounted on inner roof of wood. Makes an excellent stable roof, but fairly expensive.
2. Onduline: Similar in appearance to galvanised iron but much better. Durable, quiet and non inflammable. Onduline can melt, however, in very hot climates and is easily cracked during installation, but cannot rust and is reasonably priced.
3. Tiles: Maintain an equable temperature and afford roof ventilation, but are easily broken or loosened and can leak.
4. Slates: Excellent, but also liable to break. Like tiles, make good roofs if kept in regular repair, but should have an under-roofing of boards.
5. Galvanised iron: Not good on its own – excessively noisy, hot in hot weather and cold in cold weather. Now available with fitted insulated sheets or boards. With insulation, or with an inner roof of wood, makes excellent, inexpensive, easily obtained and transportable roofing material.
6. Old buildings may have other types of roof material, e.g. stone flakes are used in some districts where stone is abundant. These are very heavy, clumsy and not recommended. Thatched roofs and tarred felt are noiseless, warm in cold weather and cool in hot weather, but not recommended because of fire risk.
7. Open roofs: Roofs without ceilings. May be closed along ridge or have louvre board ventilation. Louvres consist of two or more overlapping boards, separated from each other by a few inches, and set at such an angle that rain and snow cannot beat in.

Ceilings

1. Flat ceilings are used only when living rooms or lofts are built overhead. Must be airtight to prevent heated air from stable penetrating rooms above. Offer no natural roof ventilation.
2. Sloping ceilings are best. Their construction secures air space and light, and offers ample natural roof ventilation.

Floors

Essential Requirements
1. Floors should be laid on solid foundation, and raised above outside ground.
2. Non-slippery and impervious to moisture.
3. Smooth, durable and should not strike cold to the horse when he lies down.
4. Should slope from front to rear of stall or loosebox. Slope should be only just sufficient to allow drainage.

Materials for Paving
1. For most floors a foundation bed of concrete from 4-6ins. (10-15cm) thick must first be laid.
2. Stable bricks, if thoroughly vitrified or the special non-slippery stable variety, make very good flooring.
3. Concrete: Often used and relatively cheap but not very good as it strikes cold to horses and is very hard on legs. If used it must be given a roughened surface.
4. Asphalt: Often used but not very satisfactory. Too easily affected by heat, and slippery when wet.
5. Clay (or dirt): Does not require concrete foundation. Very good floor but must be re-laid or patched every year to avoid holes.
6. Beware some of the smooth-surfaced, composition floorings which become dangerously slippery when wet.
7. Rubber matting is an expensive flooring but is anti-concussive and can save on bedding.

Dimensions of Stables and Stalls

1. Stables for horses should be 12ft by 14ft (3.6m by 4.25m).
2. Stables for ponies should be 10ft by 12ft (3.04m by 3.6m).
3. Stalls (tie-stalls or standing stalls) should be 5$\frac{1}{2}$ft (1.67m) wide and 11ft (3.3m) long, from wall to heel post.

Ventilation

1. Ventilation is of prime importance
2. Air within building must be changed often enough to keep it pure without allowing draughts to strike the occupants.
3. The body needs a constant and sufficient supply of pure air to enable it to perform hard work and resist the attack of disease.
4. Appearances are not reliable. Unfortunately, horses kept in stuffy, ill-ventilated stables may look fatter and more sleek than those occupying cold, fresh stables. However, experience shows that the latter are better able to undertake hard work and resist disease.
5. If stables smell stuffy, the ventilation is defective and the air should be changed more often.
6. In severe climates stables should be closed in winter. Increased air space per head inside the building will allow sufficient pure air for the occupants.

Draughts and Chills

1. A draught is a current of air moving at such a pace that it produces a feeling of cold when it strikes the skin.
2. The effect of a draught on warm skin is to lower the temperature of the skin surface, reduce circulation and produce chill and shivering.
3. The hotter the skin when horse is exposed to a draught, the greater the danger of a chill.
4. Changing stable air too often will cause a constant in-rush of cold air and keep horses in a perpetual draught.
5. To avoid having to change air too often, ensure sufficient cubic air space per head: 1,500 to 1,600 cubic feet per head is sufficient stable space overall to achieve this.

Temperature of Stable Air

1. Stables ventilated as directed above may be thought to be too cold in winter. Except in extremely severe climates horses usually fare best when the temperature inside the stable is about the same as the temperature outside.
2. If daytime temperatures are below 20°F (-5°C) and probably well below 0°F (-17°C) at night, there may be a case for heating stables artificially, but for most, more moderate climates horses fare better if given extra feed and clothing to maintain body heat and condition.
3. Horses withstand varying temperatures very well. They do not suffer from cold to the extent that humans do because their normal body temperature is 100°F (37.7°C), which is higher than the human normal of 98.4°F (36.8°C).
4. If a horse is hot and tired and left to stand in a cold draught he is

liable to catch a chill and become sick. Always cool tired, hot horses carefully and make sure they are suitably clothed. Do not stand them in cross-ties or stalls but walk them gently, in anti-sweat sheets and coolers, in a sheltered area. Best of all, do not stress or overheat horses in extreme weather.

5. In very hot weather remember that a body is cooled by the passage of air across it. Arrange stables so that a current of air is constantly moving through. Individual fans will help but the air in the whole building must be changed frequently.

Means for Ventilation

1. Doors
   - Stable doors are not a permanent means of ventilation as they are too often kept shut.
   - Where looseboxes have direct access to a yard by an individual stable door, the door should be in two parts. The upper portion can then be hooked back and left open.
   - See also Stable Doors, page 19.

2. Windows
   - Windows are the main inlet for fresh air.
   - If possible, each horse should have a window in his stable. Sufficient light in a stable is very important.
   - Should be arranged along both outer walls of stable, one over each stall or loosebox.
   - Should be hinged from lower edge, or from centre, so they may be opened with an inward slant.
   - Windows should preferably open upwards and inwards so that cold air is directed upwards away from the horse. It will mix with warm air in the top of the stable and prevent draughts across the horse's back.
   - With windows on each side of the stable, those on the leeward side should always be open. In calm weather, those on both sides should be open.
   - Amount of inlet space required per horse is not less than 1ft² (929cm²).
   - Looseboxes should always face south, if possible. Windows should be on same side as the door.
   - The lower edge of the window should be 8ft (2.4m) from the floor.
   - Windows should be fastened by some means which leaves no rope or projection for the horse to play with, or in which to become entangled.
   - Windows should be protected by iron bars on the inside.
   - Sash windows are unsuitable for stables.

3. Louvre Boards
   - Fitted under the ridge of roof they act as outlets for heated, foul air.
   - Should be sufficiently broad and overlapping, and set at an angle acute enough to prevent rain beating in.
   - Should be permanently fixed open. If movable, they will always be shut.

4. Ventilating Cowls and Tubes
   - Foul air can be extracted by means of cowls and tubes constructed so that the wind passes over an upward slant, or through a narrow slit, and creates a continual vacuum below, thus drawing up the foul air.
   - Any patterns which permit birds to nest in them are useless.
   - Cowls and tubes must be of a pattern which allows them to act equally well from whatever direction the wind blows.

5. Fans
   - Extractor or roof fans may be positioned on the ends of stable buildings for use in summer in areas of high heat or humidity.
   - Individual fans, positioned opposite windows in each stall, may be required in hot, stuffy weather. Make sure the horse cannot reach any part of fan, cord or electrical switch.

Direction of Air
1. Direction taken by current of air entering a stable is determined by the slant of the inlet through which it comes.
2. With windows sloping upwards, the air will be thrown up and well over the animals underneath.
3. Air is cooler as it comes in and heavier than the air inside the stable.
4. The cooler air will descend and be spread among the animals on the opposite side.
5. Air is therefore well diffused and slightly warmed before reaching horses and risk of draught is avoided.

Drainage

Requirements for Efficient Stable Drainage
1. A floor which is level from side to side, but sloping sufficiently from front to rear to allow drainage to back of stable.
2. An exit hole, which should be draught-proof, connecting with an open gulley outside.
3. A shallow, open, surface drain behind the walls to convey collected fluid to an outside drain or sewer.

4. Standing should be as level as possible, with any slope being the minimum necessary for drainage.
5. Drain should be shallow. In a long stable, drain should slope from the centre towards both sides.
6. Closed or underground drains, because they are hidden from view, may be difficult to keep clean or even neglected.
7. All drains should be free of sharp angles. A 'trap' should be provided where the stable drainage runs into the outside drain or sewer, to prevent the return of sewer gas.

Stable Doors

1. Doors should be 8ft (2.4m) high and 4ft (1.2m) wide. They should be hinged or hung on rollers.
2. Half-doors, top and bottom portions opening separately, are excellent. Top half can usually be left open for ventilation. Lower half must be high enough to prevent horse from jumping over, at least 4ft 6in (1.37m).
3. Horses like to look out. Therefore grilles are sometimes provided for fastening across the open top half of the door. This prevents biting at passers-by, loosening the top bolt, and checks weaving.
4. Sliding doors should be hung on rollers from above and fitted with large, smooth handles which cannot injure a loose horse.
5. All doors giving direct access to a loosebox should open outwards or slide. If an animal becomes cast in his box near the door, it is then possible to open the door.

Latches
1. Should be strong and easily turned.
2. Should have large, flush handles which offer no projections to injure loose horses.
3. Bolts of loosebox doors of the half-door type should be designed so that horse cannot open them.
4. On loosebox doors of that type, two bolts are necessary, one at the top and one at the bottom. The bottom bolt can be a foot-operated bolt, to save constant bending.

Windows

See under Ventilation, page 17.

Stable Fittings

1. The fewer the better.
2. A ring at breast-level, for tying horse up.
3. Other rings at eye level, for short-racking and for haynet.
4. All rings must be very firmly fitted.

Mangers

1. Should be 3ft 6in (1.06m) from the ground.
2. Should be large, broad and have completely smooth surface and all corners well rounded.
3. A broad, shallow manger is preferable to a deep, narrow one. A greedy horse cannot plunge his mouth deeply into the food and seize large mouthfuls.
4. Rim should be broad enough to prevent horse being able to seize it in his teeth and thus encourage crib biting.
5. Removable rubber or plastic mangers which are placed in loosebox or stall only at feeding times are best – easily cleaned and prevent cribbing.

Hayracks

1. Hayracks fitted above head level are not good. They force the horse to feed at an unnatural level and there is a risk of getting dust and hay seeds in horse's eyes.
2. A deep hay manger at the same level as the manger, which can only be entered from the top, is the most economical kind of hayrack. This hay manger should be narrower at the base than at the top, reducing the risk of the horse banging his knees.
3. Hay may be fed from the ground. This is a natural position for the horse but the method is wasteful. Much hay gets trampled and soiled.
4. Haynets are the most efficient and economical method of feeding hay. They also permit accurate weighing of hay fed. Care must be taken with tying up a haynet safely.
5. To hang a full haynet safely – pull cord tight at top with knot close to haynet. Pass end of cord (doubled) through wall ring at eye level, then through a string of the haynet near the bottom. Pull haynet up as high as it will go and secure with a quick-release knot. Haynet must be hung high to avoid danger of horse getting a leg caught when haynet is empty.

Water Supply

1. Automatic water bowls are efficient and labour-saving. Best type has

closed compartment with ballcock works, or pedal depressed by horse's muzzle to start flow of water.
2. Do not site automatic water bowls near manger or hayrack – they may become blocked with food.
3. If water is supplied in a bucket, a large, hinged ring, about 3ft (90cm) from the ground, preferably in the corner, may be used. The bucket is attached to it with a spring clip. This prevents the bucket being knocked over.

Hay Store

1. Cheapest to buy in bulk at hay-making time.
2. Best store is a separate barn with double doors for loading.
3. Bottom layer of bales should be placed on wooden pallets.

Feed Room

Feed room should be:
1. Suitable size for number of horses in stable.
2. Reasonably central in yard but also easily accessible from road for deliveries.
3. Secure, with concrete floor and solid door which should be kept closed, and locked at night.
4. Properly ventilated, well lit and vermin proof.

General

1. Consult local planning regulations before any conversion or building begins.
2. All fittings, e.g. latches, window fastenings, etc., in a stable must be flush with walls or woodwork, or at least must not offer any projections on which a horse could tear himself.
3. For the same reason, no nails should be driven into the walls.
4. Electric light switches should be placed outside looseboxes in a position where a horse cannot interfere with them.
5. All light switches should be of a special 'stable' type, designed to prevent electrocution should a shod horse seize them with his teeth.

CHAPTER 3

Daily Routine

Horses are creatures of habit and thrive best if cared for according to a fairly strict routine. In their natural environment horses walk and eat almost constantly. They have relatively small stomachs for their size, and very large intestines, which nature has designed to be kept filled most of the time. By keeping horses stabled and shut in for long periods we are providing a very unnatural environment, which can be stressful to the horse.

The following is an ideal routine for horses in training for eventing, for example, where the owner or a groom is around the stables most of the day:

6.30 am Morning stables. Look over horse to ensure he has suffered no injury during the night. Horse should look towards you as he hears you enter stable – if he shows no interest, something may be wrong. Check that he has eaten up his night feed and hay. Check that there are the usual amount of normal-looking droppings in box. Put on headcollar, adjust rugs, water. Feed small quantity of hay to keep horse occupied, and tie him up. Muck out. Pick out feet into muck skip. Throw up rugs and quarter (i.e. brush off stable stains and surface dirt, sponge eyes, nose and dock, brush out mane and tail). Replace rugs.

7.30 am First feed.

9.00 am Remove droppings. Remove rugs and saddle up. Exercise. On return, remove bridle and saddle and allow horse to stale and drink before putting on headcollar and tying him up to groom.

11.30 am Groom. Put on day rugs. Refill water bucket. Second feed. Feed full net of hay. Set fair stable and yard.

4.00 pm Tie horse up. Remove droppings. Pick out feet. Shake up bedding. Remove day rug and rug up with night rug. Fill water bucket.

4.30 pm Remove headcollar. Third feed. Clean saddlery.
7.00 pm Remove droppings and shake up bedding. Refill water bucket. Feed full net – or final ration – of hay. Fourth feed.

This routine is obviously designed for someone spending full time in the stable. A competent person (e.g. BHS Stage III experience or similar) should be able to care for up to four horses under this regime. It must be modified for the horse owner with less available time.

The following is an alternative routine which would be suitable for a pleasure horse in irregular use, where the owner or a groom cannot be present most of the time.

6.30 am Morning stables. Look over horse as described above. Wash out and refill water bucket and feed a small amount of hay to keep horse busy while you muck out. Pick out horse's feet and brush off stable stains if time permits. Feed first grain feed.
9.00 am If you are planning to ride, allow at least one hour after feeding for digestion. If you cannot ride at this time, turn horse into paddock or field to exercise himself.
4.00 pm Bring horse in and pick out feet. Rug up if necessary. Shake up bedding and set fair. Fill water bucket. If horse has had hay or grass available during the day, feed second grain feed. Set the yard fair.
8.00 pm Check round, straighten rugs, skip out. Fill water bucket. Late feed and full net, or final ration, of hay.

Design your own stable routine to meet your particular needs remembering the importance of feeding little and often and at the same time every day. Even if you cannot attend to your horse more than twice each day, make certain that he always has an ample supply of fresh, clean water readily available.

Weekly Duties
- Order feed.
- Muck heap removed (if necessary).
- Clean drains and windows, sweep down cobwebs.
- Wash saddle pads and sweat sheets.
- Wash grooming kit.
- Thorough tack cleaning (take apart).

Annual Duties
- Painting, whitewashing, etc. of stable buildings and fences.
- Winter rugs and blankets washed/cleaned and mended.

- Clippers serviced and blades sharpened.
- Fire extinguishers and smoke alarms serviced.

Stable Tools
Tools required for mucking out horse bedded on:
Straw – 5-prong fork or pitchfork, stable broom, shovel, wheel barrow.
Shavings, sawdust, paper and Aubiose – 10-prong fork, shovel, broom,
   grass rake, wheelbarrow.
Also required under all systems: dung skip – preferably the rubber or
plastic variety, to avoid possibility of injury.

Mucking Out

Straw
1. Consists of removing soiled portions of bedding and droppings,
   sweeping floor, and relaying day-bed or bedding down. Art of good
   mucking out lies in shaking straw.
2. Start at door and throw clean straw to back or to one side of box.
   Shaking causes heavier, soiled straw to fall through prongs of fork
   and ensures maximum saving of straw.
3. Floor must be thoroughly swept all over at least every two days and
   allowed to dry out. Therefore, throw clean straw up to the right wall
   one day and left wall the next.
4. At least once a week disinfect the floor thoroughly, including
   the drain if one is present in the stable, with industrial disinfectant.
5. Replace bedding, shaking well so that straw lies evenly over floor and
   create banks about 18-24ins (45-60cm) high round the walls. Add
   required amount fresh straw – probably about half a bale per day –
   (unless this is done at evening stables). Test depth with fork – it
   should not strike through to floor. The bed should be about 9-12ins
   (23-30cm) thick.

Shavings
Remove droppings and very wet patches with fork. Rake dry shavings
from sides of box to centre to give even depth over floor. Firm up banks.
Add fresh shavings evenly over whole surface.

Sawdust
Treat as shavings. Or rake top 2ins (5cm) of bed into pile, shovel into
potato basket or skip and shake sawdust through. Deposit wet sawdust
and droppings left in basket into barrow. Repeat until all soiled bedding
is removed. Tidy banks and rake surface, but don't dig deep.

Shredded Paper

Treat as shavings. Alternatively whole bed can be shaken up, as straw, but this can be heavy work. Add fresh paper as necessary and remake banks.

Aubiose

Aubiose (dried pulp of the hemp plant) should provide savings in time and labour if managed properly. The bedding works by soaking up liquids in a small area at the base of the bed. The capped layer that forms over this saturated material reduces the chance of wet bedding being mixed in with the dry. The top layers of the bed remain warm, soft and dry for the horse.

1. To create an Aubiose bed, start with a clean stable and add about eight bales (depending on the size of the stable).
2. Dampen the bed by spraying with a hose as this helps the bed to settle and will activate its sponge-like properties. When Aubiose is first used the bed may be sprayed with a weak solution of disinfectant to discourage horse from eating it.
3. Each day remove any droppings and just rake lightly over the top of the bed to keep it level and tidy banks. Every five to ten days (depending on the horse) rake the dry bedding to one side and remove any heavily saturated material underneath. Top up with fresh Aubiose. Average required is half bale/week.
4. Aubiose works equally well on a deep litter system: remove droppings daily and lightly rake the top of the bed to keep its shape. Add fresh Aubiose as required.
5. Disposal: because Aubiose is so absorbent there will be less material removed from the stable thus reducing the problem of muck disposal. Aubiose is made from young plants and will break down rapidly (approx. five weeks) to form a valuable compost.

After mucking out, wash out water bucket, refill and replace in box.

Manure Heap

If limited in size and close to stables, the manure heap must be emptied frequently. If manure is to be stacked and rotted, choose site well away from stables. Make three heaps: (1) the oldest, well-rotted manure ready for garden use; (2) discontinued pile in process of rotting; (3) pile in process of formation. Muck heaps should be close packed (trample, or beat down with shovel) and well squared off – assists decomposition and heat generated inhibits fly breeding. Shavings, sawdust and peat moss are sometimes difficult to dispose of, so ample space is needed well away from stable. Paper bedding may blow around yard and look untidy.

How to tie a quick-release knot.

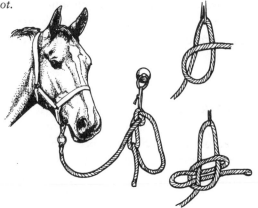

Securing Horses

- Horses are secured in stables by headcollar and rope attached to back 'D' of noseband.
- In 'tie-stalls' secure rope to manger ring or, better, pass rope through ring and secure to 'log'. Log is placed at the end of the rope, so preventing horse getting leg over rope – essential in tie-stalls.
- To 'short-rack' – tie rope to loop of string attached to ring on wall, at eye level.
- For safety, always place a loop of string in all rings and tie rope to string using a quick-release knot.
- To place horse on pillar reins – turn him round in tie-stall and fasten the reins or chains which hang on heel posts to the side 'D's of headcollar.
- Headcollars not made of leather should have leather headband or breakaway buckle to avoid injury if horse pulls back.

Turning Out

Turning horse out in paddock either for exercise or grass.
1. Lead horse to paddock – use long lead rope and both hands.
2. Do not try to out-pull a horse. If horse is impatient and difficult to hold, use quick tug on rope, rather than a steady pull.
3. Never wrap lead rope or reins around hand or wrist. A knot in end of rope avoids it being pulled through hand. Use gloves for safety.
4. Lead horse through gate and turn him round to face the gate. Close gate, then remove lead rope quietly.
5. If turning out for exercise in small enclosed space, remain in centre and 'loose school' horse for five or ten minutes. Many horses simply stand still when turned out alone.

6. Lungeing is often used in place of loose schooling. In this case horse is lunged, either from a headcollar or lungeing cavesson, simply for exercise. Lungeing prevents the possibility of horse rolling in mud.
7. In cold weather put a New Zealand rug on horse.

Exercise and Work

1. Exercise is the procedure of giving a horse sufficient activity to keep him healthy and fit without causing undue exertion or loss of condition. Generally prolonged periods at steady jog on sound, safe going.
2. Work denotes owner riding for pleasure and includes canters, gallops, school work, jumping, hunting and showing, all of which may be expected to cause some effort.
3. Exercise and work must be co-ordinated to produce a fit trained horse.
4. To exercise during periods of heavy frost, snow or ice – lay down circular straw track (good use for muck heap).

Evening Stables

Remove droppings using muck skip, and pick out feet – into skip. Shake up bed if kept bedded down all day, or lay bed, shaking out straw. If shavings or sawdust are being used, add new bedding as required. Wash out and refill water bucket. Feed: if feeding four times, give bulk of hay after fourth feed. Alternatively, give bulk of hay at 5 or 6 pm and return about 8-9.30 pm, water and give late feed. Late watering – filling water bucket late in evening – is desirable. It ensures horse has water during the night. (He will drink after eating hay so bucket must in any case be refilled after final feeding.) Late watering gives opportunity to check that all is well for the night.

General Rules

1. Stick to fixed daily routine whenever possible.
2. Exercise is only exception – vary route.
3. Check horse frequently during day, but allow ample opportunity for real rest and quiet.
4. Train yourself to 'observe'.
5. Speak before entering box or touching horse.
6. Move quietly. Anticipate reactions of horse. THINK.

CHAPTER 4

Bedding

Bedding is necessary for the following reasons:
1. To prevent injury and encourage horse to lie down in comfort.
2. To prevent draughts and to provide warmth around the lower legs.
3. To encourage horse to stale, and to prevent jarring to the feet.
4. As an absorbent or drainage material.
5. As a means of assisting in keeping horse clean and air pure.

Types of Bedding
Bedding may be divided into two categories:
1. Absorbent – preferable where there is no stable drainage. Peat moss, shredded paper, hemp (Aubiose), sawdust and wood shavings.
2. Drainage – used where there is adequate drainage. Wheat straw, barley straw, occasionally oat straw.

Properties of Good Bedding
To fulfil necessary requirements of health, comfort, cleanliness and economy, bedding should be:
1. Dry.
2. Soft.
3. Absorbent of fluids and gases.
4. Clean in use.
5. Easily obtainable.
6. In good condition.
7. Good conductor of heat.
8. Not injurious if eaten.
9. Light in colour for good appearance.
10. Readily disposable.

Effects of Bedding on Horses' Feet
1. Sawdust, tan bark, and peat moss are bad conductors of heat. These

materials can become overheated, soggy and harmful to horses' feet if not properly managed. If the bed is not kept clean and dry, horse may get thrush, leading to canker and contracted heels. However, these types of bedding are good, clean, bright, comfortable and cheap. In clean conditions, horses' feet will suffer no injurious effects.

2. Straw is a good conductor of heat and straw bedding keeps horses' feet cooler and has no injurious effect on them.

Straw versus Other Bedding Materials

Straw
Old straw is better than new – dryer, more elastic (provided it has been well stored). Whatever type is used it should be of good quality – if straw undergoes too much bruising and breaking it loses elasticity and durability.

Wheat Straw
Generally considered the best – light, durable and not usually eaten.

Oat Straw
Sometimes cheaper but less durable. Makes good bedding – disadvantage is that horses often eat it (oat straw has low feeding value).

Barley Straw
Cheapest but inferior in appearance and durability. Beards or 'awns' cause itching and skin irritations, and can cause stamping, kicking and rubbing. Barley straw can cause colic if eaten. Barley straw from a combine harvester is often free of awns and makes fairly good bedding.

Sawdust
1. Inexpensive in many areas. Should be dry and well seasoned.
2. Know which woods are being processed. Nut trees are poisonous and should not be used.
3. Pine sawdust has a deodorising effect.
4. Sawdust may block drains unless precautions are taken in advance.
5. Sawdust is easy to keep clean and light to work but lacks the pleasing appearance of straw.

Wood Shavings
Notes under 'Sawdust' also apply to shavings, but shavings are less dusty. Now available in convenient bales or bags, which makes handling easier. Good bedding. Both shavings and sawdust require constant attention and frequent removal of droppings. Horses do not eat bed and

therefore they are useful for horses with respiratory problems. May also be used very satisfactorily together, when sawdust forms the under layer.

Peat Moss

Comments under 'Sawdust' and 'Wood Shavings' apply also to peat moss, but it is heavier to work, darker in appearance, and requires just as much attention as sawdust. However, peat makes an excellent bed if wet soiled patches are removed frequently and bed forked and raked daily. It is particularly valuable where risk of fire is a consideration. May be dusty when first put down. Disposal sometimes difficult.

Sand

Good bedding in hot, dry climates – gets too cold where there is dampness. A horse can get serious colic from eating sand. Never use ocean beach sand, which horses may lick for the sake of the salt.

Paper

Baled, shredded paper is entirely dust free and useful for horses with respiratory problems. When dry it is light and pleasant to handle; it can be managed like shavings. When wet it can be heavy to work with. Has a tendency to blow around the yard.

Hemp/Aubiose

This is the dried pulp of the hemp plant, baled. Initially expensive but good value, highly absorbent, dust free, low maintenance, and good for the garden.

Combination, Continental or Deep Litter System

Peat moss (or sometimes sawdust) to a depth of 6ins (15cm) may be used as a base with generous bed of straw on top. Droppings are removed frequently but no 'mucking out' is done, instead fresh straw is sprinkled on top of the old bed. Foundation of peat is not necessary and bed can be made entirely of straw. Advantages: warm, horses lie down frequently. Labour saving, very easy to manage. Disadvantages: if sawdust is used as a base, may become heated and maggoty. Needs removing completely once or twice a year and for this a tractor and fork lift are desirable. Horses' feet need very close attention to avoid thrush.

General

Whatever bedding is used it is essential to keep it clean, remove droppings and soiled portions frequently and replace the soiled bedding with a fresh, clean supply. Other bedding materials may be used but caution should be exercised to ensure that they are non-toxic.

CHAPTER 5

Grooming

Grooming is the daily attention necessary to the feet and coat of the stabled horse. The skin is a vital organ and grooming is as essential to a horse's good health as it is to his appearance. Stabled horses are denied the opportunity to live a natural life, to roll and to exercise at will; as a result the skin and the feet suffer unless properly cared for.

Objectives of Grooming

1. To promote health – grooming removes waste products, stimulates the circulation of blood and lymph and improves muscle tone.
2. To maintain condition.
3. To prevent disease.
4. To ensure cleanliness.
5. To improve appearance. Grooming also helps considerably with the 'gentling' of a young horse.

Grooming Tools

- Hoof pick – for cleaning out the feet.
- Dandy brush – for removing heavy dirt, caked mud and dust. Of special value for care of grass-kept horse. Use very sparingly and gently on Thoroughbreds or horses recently clipped. Do not use on head, mane or tail.
- Body brush – for removal of dust, scurf and grease from the coat, mane and tail.
- Curry comb (metal, plastic or rubber) – for cleaning the body brush. The rubber and plastic varieties may be used on horses with heavy coats to help remove caked mud and dirt, particularly in spring when horse is changing his coat. Use gently in small circle, never curry bony parts, i.e. head or lower legs.

■ Circular rubber 'Grooma' – similar to a rubber curry but designed for use on the horse's body to help remove heavy dirt, caked mud and hair when shedding. Comes in a variety of sizes to fit all hands. Horses enjoy the feeling of massage. Use gently in small circles. Avoid bony parts.

■ 'Grooma Mit' – similar idea to circular rubber curry but fits over the groomer's hand and is softer and more flexible.

■ 'Kelly Kurry Comb' – tiny plastic curry designed to fit over the groomer's finger for use on the horse's face.

■ Shedding blade – flexible metal blade with leather handles at each end and one edge serrated to help in removing hair from long-coated horse or pony when winter coat is being shed.

■ Sweat scraper – curved aluminium or plastic blade designed to remove excess sweat or water after you have washed horse.

■ Water brush – for use (damp) on the mane, tail and feet.

■ Sponge – for cleaning eyes, nose and dock. Two are advisable.

■ Wisp – for promoting circulation and for massage.

■ Mane and tail comb – usually of metal; may be used to help comb out tangled manes and tails of grass-kept ponies, but generally used to assist in pulling mane or tail.

■ Stable rubber – linen or cotton towel for final polish after grooming.

■ Electric and/or hand clippers and/or scissors – used for trimming (see 'Clipping and Trimming', page 96).

How to Groom

1. Assemble articles listed above – these should be kept together in a grooming box or wire basket. A bucket of water will also be required.

2. Put headcollar on horse, who must be cool and dry, and remove rugs (if being worn). In stable, short-rack horse; if grooming outside (which is often more pleasant in summer), tie horse up short to a secure ring in the stable yard.

3. Pick out feet with hoof pick. Pick up each foot in turn, remove whatever may be lodged in foot with point of pick, working always from heel towards the toe. In this way there is no risk of the pick penetrating the soft parts of the frog. Clear the cleft of frog and look for any signs of thrush. Tap shoe to see that it is secure, and run tips of fingers around clenches to ensure that none have risen. It is permissible, when picking out the feet, to lift the off feet from the near side. It is correct, when picking out feet, to place a dung skip near enough to allow dirt to fall directly into it. If this is not done, it is necessary to sweep up after picking out feet.

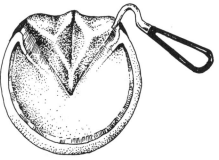

When picking out the feet always work from the heel towards the toe.

4. Using the dandy brush or rubber curry comb, remove all caked dirt, sweat marks, etc. from horse's body. Begin at the poll on the near side and work gradually all over the body, paying particular attention to the saddle and girth region, belly, points of the hocks, fetlocks and pasterns. The dandy brush may be held in either hand and is used with a to-and-fro motion. Avoid using this brush on tender parts of the body. When working on the hind limbs, grasp the tail with the free hand – this not only prevents the horse swishing his tail in your face, but also discourages a ticklish horse from kicking. Never stand directly behind the horse but keep slightly to one side or the other. Never sit or kneel beside the horse to brush his lower legs; always bend or squat.

5. With the body brush, which has short, close-set bristles designed to reach right through the coat to the skin beneath, start grooming in the poll region on the near side. Hold the body brush in the left hand and the curry comb in the right. Stand well back, work with a slightly bent arm and supple wrist and lean the weight of the body behind the brush. The brush is used in short circular strokes in the direction of the lay of the coat, never to-and-fro. After every four or five strokes, clean the brush by drawing it smartly across the teeth of the curry comb, and tap the dirt from the comb out on the floor. When the near side is completed, go to the off side and change hands. Before grooming the off side, throw the mane across to the near side of the neck and brush the crest thoroughly. Continue grooming the off side of the horse and, having finished, groom the mane.

6. Begin at the withers. Insert a finger of the free hand into the mane to separate a few locks of hair and brush the ends of these first to remove tangles. Then brush the roots. Work slowly up the neck, dealing with a few locks of hair at a time.

7. To groom the head, ensure that the horse is turned away from the manger, drop the headcollar and fasten it temporarily around the neck. Dispense with the curry comb and use the free hand to steady the horse's head. Work quietly to avoid injury to the tender parts and bony projections. On completion of the head, replace the headcollar.

8. Finally, brush the tail. Deal with a few locks of hair at a time and start at the bottom of the tail and work up towards the roots to remove tangles gently and avoid pulling out hairs. Do not use the dandy brush on the mane or tail as it removes and breaks the hairs. If the tail is fine, use only your fingers to separate the hairs and remove straw or shavings.

9. Take the wisp, damp it slightly and use vigorously by bringing it down with a bang in the direction of the lay of the coat. Wisping is a form of massage to develop and harden muscles, to produce a shine on the coat by drawing oil from the glands in the skin, and to stimulate the skin by improving the blood supply. Give special attention to those parts where the muscles are hard and flat, i.e. sides of neck, quarters and thighs. Avoid all bony prominences and the tender loin region.

10. Wring out a sponge in the bucket of warm water so that it is left soft, clean and damp. Sponge the eyes first, work away from the corners and then around the eyelids. Wring out the sponge again and sponge the muzzle region, including lips and inside and outside of nostrils, in that order. Using a separate sponge wash the dock region, including the skin of the under surface of the tail. Sponging refreshes a stabled horse and is appreciated greatly.

11. 'Lay' the mane – dip the tips of the bristles of the water brush in the bucket of water and apply flat to the mane working from the roots downwards. Mane is left slightly damp and in the desired position.

12. Wash the feet, using one end of the water brush. Keep the thumb of the hand holding the foot pressed well into the hollow of the heel to prevent water becoming lodged there. Washing the feet is best omitted in cold weather.

13. When hoof is dry, using a small brush dipped in good quality foot dressing/oil, coat the entire hoof with the dressing, starting with the sole and frog, including the bulbs of heels and the wall as far up as the coronet. This not only improves appearance but is good for brittle or broken feet. This is best done two to three times a week.

14. Go all over the horse with the stable rubber to remove the last traces of dust from the coat. Fold the rubber into a flat bundle, damp it and wipe the coat in the direction of the lay of the hair.

15. Replace rugs and put on tail bandage if tail is pulled.

An experienced groom will spend from 30-45 minutes with each horse. A novice will need longer. Thoroughness brings its own reward – a well-groomed horse is not only a pleasing sight but a healthy animal.

Grooming Machines

Many excellent models are on the market. Used intelligently they are a great boon in large stables. The correct method of use is to machine groom every second or third day and to wisp on intervening days.

Sheath Cleaning

Geldings' sheaths should be cleaned regularly, at least every six months. Stallions should be cleaned prior to each covering or, if celibate, every six months.

Smegma, the term given to the build-up of dirt, grit, grime and bodily secretions, accumulates in the sheath of the male horse and is a perfect breeding ground for bacteria. Swelling, infection or ulceration of the sheath and even cancer of the penis has been linked to lack of cleanliness in this area. These common problems can be prevented with good hygiene.

Thorough sheath cleaning takes about 15 minutes and many horses enjoy the process.

Assemble Tools
1. Very mild, pure soap or proprietary brand of cleansing gel designed for this purpose.
2. Rubber gloves. These protect hands from bacteria. Also protect horse from sharp fingernails.
3. Clean sponge or cotton wool. Provides mild abrasion for cleaning tough areas.
4. Bucket of clean, warm water.

Method
1. Horse must be relaxed and may need tranquilliser, or herbal calmer (consult veterinarian).
2. Tie horse in safe, quiet place (wash bay if available).
3. Using plenty of warm water, thoroughly rinse out the sheath. This will remove a lot of loose debris.
4. Thoroughly lather your hands with soap or cleansing gel, then work soap up into the folds of the sheath and take out loose debris.
5. Use as much soap as needed to completely soap up the sheath and leave it on about five minutes. Gently pull the penis out of the sheath and remove loose smegma with sponge or cotton wool.
6. Remove the 'bean' of smegma which collects in the diverticulum, a blind pouch just inside the urethra. This is important as the 'bean' could block the urinary tract and cause real problems.
7. Rinse the sheath and penis thoroughly and repeatedly with lots of clean, warm water. Make absolutely sure that all soapiness is completely rinsed out.

8. Some people like to apply a little vaseline to the sheath after washing, as a lubricant, but this is not really necessary.

How to Make a Wisp

Items Required
1. 8ft (2.4m) length of baling string.
2. Plenty of soft hay.
3. Bucket of water.

Method
1. Fashion a tightly woven rope of hay, using baling string as core, 6-8ft (1.8-2.4m) long. Get a friend to hold one end of string. Take handfuls of soft hay and wet them thoroughly. Twist hay around string repeatedly, adding a handful of hay at each twist, until rope is completed.
2. Make two loops out of your hay rope, one slightly bigger than the other. Use one end of rope for loops so that you have a long tail of rope remaining.
3. Twist each loop in turn beneath the remainder of the rope until it is all used up.
4. Twist the end of the rope through the bottom of each loop and tuck it beneath the last twist.

A properly made wisp should be hard and firm and no larger than can conveniently be grasped in the hand.

Making a wisp.

Bathing a horse

Bathing is not a short cut to good grooming. If a horse is sweaty after work, he will appreciate a bath, and provided he is walked cool first and the weather is warm enough and he can be thoroughly dried, it will do him good.

General Rules
1. Never wash a horse if he cannot be thoroughly dried afterwards (horses are very susceptible to chills).
2. If it is late in the day, or chilly, windy or wet, do not bath the horse. If necessary sponge sweat marks off back, girth area, between hind legs and damp sponge face and base of ears. This spot-washing is much safer than 'hosing off' a horse, as is common practice in many yards.
3. Always walk the horse until he is cool, and breathing normally, before standing him still to bath him.
4. A horse should not be brought back to the stable breathing hard and sweating. His work should be so designed as to include an appropriate length of cool-down at the end. Always walk the last mile back to the stable.
5. Racehorses may arrive back at the yard still blowing and must be walked in hand until they have completely cooled down before being bathed to avoid chilling them.

Method
1. Use warm water and mild soap or special horse shampoo.
2. Thoroughly wet the horse using plenty of warm water. If you have hot and cold water available through the hose at the stable, this is the easiest way to wash the horse. If only cold water is available through the hose, use buckets of warm water.
3. Apply soap or shampoo with a large sponge, going all over the horse's body.
4. Use clear water only on the head, which should be washed last. Never use the hose to spray water at the horse's head – water may get into his ears and cause permanent damage.
5. Rinse horse very thoroughly using plenty of warm water.
6. Remove surplus water with sweat scraper. Do not use sweat scraper on legs below knees or hocks.
7. Sponge up remaining water with a clean, damp sponge. Use this sponge also on lower legs and head.
8. Finally, rub horse as dry as possible with a clean towel; pay particular attention to legs and heels.
9. Walk horse dry in sunshine, if possible, or put on clean anti-sweat sheet and walk dry in sheltered area.
10. When dry, brush horse all over with body brush.

When to Groom

1. Quartering. Done first thing in the morning. Pick out feet. Sponge

eyes, nose and dock. Throw up rugs and quickly brush exposed parts of body. Pay particular attention to removal of stains on flanks, using sponge and water if necessary. Object is to make horse look tidy for morning exercise. Note: quartering is carried out without undoing or removing the roller or surcingle.

2. Strapping. This is the thorough grooming of the animal outlined under the heading 'How to Groom', page 32. Preferably done on return from exercise when the skin is warm, as the pores are open and dust and scurf rise easily in the surface. If, however, horse is fed on return from exercise, allow him time to enjoy his feed undisturbed.

3. Brush-over or set-fair. Done in the evening when rugs are changed and the box set-fair. Pick out feet. Brush over lightly and wisp, if time permits.

The Grass-kept Horse

Some modification of grooming procedure is necessary when horse is kept at grass.

1. Pick out feet.
2. Use rubber curry or rubber 'Grooma' to remove mud.
3. Brush over with dandy brush.
4. Brush mane and tail with body brush.
5. Sponge eyes, nose and dock.

Note: The body brush is designed to remove grease or dandruff and cannot be used efficiently on an animal who rolls every day or has a long coat. The horse kept outside needs the grease in his coat for warmth and waterproofing.

CHAPTER 6

Watering and Feeding

Horses require water and food. Of the two, water is the most essential: horses can survive some time without food, but cannot live long without water.

Watering

Uses of Water

1. Largest constituent of the body. Foal's body consists of 80% water and adult horse 65%-75%.
2. Nutrition is performed by fluids. Without water, blood circulation is impaired and digestive processes impossible.
3. Lime in the water assists in the formation of bone and other tissue.
4. Water is necessary to quench thirst and control body temperature.
5. Water aids excretion.

Quantity

1. A horse drinks between 6 and 10 gallons (27-45 litres) a day.
2. A horse makes 6 gallons (27 litres) of saliva for mastication every 24 hours.
3. A fresh supply of clean water should be constantly available.

Purity

Water given to horses should be fresh, clean and untainted. Running water – i.e. a stream – is best. Moderately hard water contains carbonates of lime and magnesium in addition to traces of common salt. It is more refreshing than soft water. Water that is too hard can produce adverse effects on skin and coat – a harsh coat results but disappears if soft water is used.

Rules of Watering
1. A constant supply of fresh clean water should be always available.
2. If this is not possible, water at least three times a day in winter and six times a day in summer. Water before feeding.
3. If water is not constantly available to horse, allow half to one hour after feeding before watering.
4. Do not warm water artificially, except in winter to keep from freezing; warm to about 45°F-50°F (10°C). Drinking icy water will:
   ▪ Lower consumption of water which will lead to low level chronic dehydration. This can cause increased incidence of impaction colic due to dry hay diet and decreased intestinal fluids.
   ▪ Cause horse to burn calories to heat cold water in stomach to body temperature, thus increasing dietary needs.
   ▪ Cause decreased saliva production. A large amount of digestive enzymes are present in saliva and decreased saliva production can result in poorly digested food.
5. If a bucket of water is left constantly with the horse, change it and swill out bucket at least twice a day, and refill as necessary (probably four or five times a day). Standing water absorbs ammonia and other impurities from the air and becomes 'flat' and tainted.
6. Horses that have been deprived of water should not be given as much as they can drink. Give small quantities frequently until system is back to normal.
7. If horses have unrestricted access to water it should not be necessary to deprive the horse of water before racing or fast work. A full stomach (food or water) presses on the diaphragm and this could restrict breathing, so a large intake of either should be avoided within two hours of competition.
8. During continuous work water every two hours. It is unlikely that you will be able to allow horse to drink while actually hunting, however, but let him drink a small quantity on the way home.

Methods of Watering

Stabled Horses
1. Automatic drinking bowls. Satisfactory if kept clean and tested each day. Should be sited away from manger and hayrack. The main disadvantages are that shallowness prevents horse taking full drink, and groom cannot tell if horse is drinking properly (sometimes an early indication of sickness).
2. Bucket in corner of box. Perhaps the most satisfactory system. Bucket may either be placed on the floor or suspended from special ring at breast height. Bucket should be placed, ideally, in corner away from

manger and away from the door, but within sight of the door. Buckets must be emptied and swilled out and refilled at least twice each day, and topped up three or four times.

3. Water bowl in manger. Satisfactory if bowl is kept clean and full, otherwise may get dirty and clogged with food.

4. Trough in stable yard. Useful for offering a drink to horses returning from work before putting them into the stable. Unsatisfactory as the only means of watering stabled horses as it necessitates taking horse out of the stable to the trough several times a day. Risk of cross-contamination.

Horses at Grass

1. Rivers and streams. These offer a good system of watering horses at grass provided the river or stream is running water with a gravel bottom and good approach. Shallow water and a sandy bottom may result in small quantities of sand being taken into stomach with the water, which will lead eventually to sand colic.

2. Ponds. If stagnant, unsuitable. Other watering arrangements necessary in addition.

3. Field troughs. If filled from a piped water supply troughs provide the best method of watering horses at grass. Troughs should be from 3-6ft (0.9-1.8m) in length and about 18ins (45cm) deep. They must have an outlet in the bottom for emptying so that they can be easily cleaned. Place trough on well-drained land, clear of trees, so that surrounds do not become too muddy and trough is not clogged with leaves. They require attention twice a day during frost and snow. Troughs should be free of sharp edges or projections on which a horse might be injured. If filled by means of a tap, it should be placed at ground level and the pipe from tap to trough fitted close to the side and edge of the trough. A projecting tap near the trough is dangerous to horses. Best means of keeping trough full is an enclosed compartment at one end containing a ballcock apparatus.

Feeding

1. Feed should be stored in secure feed bins and clearly marked. It can also be stored in sacks or bags in bins or on raised pallets, though this is not so satisfactory. Sacks should not be stacked on concrete floor.

2. Feed should be used in the order purchased so new feed is placed at the back.

3. A feed chart giving exact details of the feed for each horse should be displayed obviously, easy to read and kept updated. Details of medications should also be on the feed chart.

4. One person should be responsible for the feed room and for mixing and distributing feeds.

Objectives of Feeding
1. To supply energy for work.
2. To provide material for growth and development, and for repair of body.
3. To put flesh on horse and provide warmth in winter and the energy for cooling in summer.

Groups of Food

1. Proteins – for growth and repair. Proteins are complex organic compounds made up of simpler substances known as amino acids.
2. Carbohydrates – for heat and energy. Cannot replace proteins. Threequarters of all dry matter in plants is carbohydrate. There are two types of carbohydrate in plants:
   ▪ Nitrogen-free extract, includes starch, glucose, fructose and hemicellulose, which are the more soluble and therefore more digestible carbohydrates.
   ▪ Fibre, the woody portion of plants not dissolved by acids and weak alkalis, therefore harder to digest. Fibre stimulates digestive processes and aids in assimilation of digestible matter.
3. Fats – for heat, energy and warmth.
4. Vitamins – all vitamins are necessary and should be available from top quality feed. Horses may be able to synthesise some vitamins in the intestines. Consult veterinarian before adding supplement to avoid causing imbalances. While wheat bran contains satisfactory levels of zinc and copper it is also high in phosphorus and low in calcium. This higher ratio of phosphorus to calcium is also evident in most 'straight' grain feeds. Since the horse's digestion operates most efficiently when the Ca:Ph ratio is in the range of 1.1-1.4 Ca to 1.0 Ph it is advisable not to feed bran in large proportions in the diet.
5. Minerals – horses require calcium, phosphorus, cobalt, potassium, sodium chlorine, copper, iron, iodine, magnesium, zinc and manganese. Mineral deficiency is liable to affect health adversely; however, some minerals fed in high levels may be toxic.

Horse's Requirements

1. Proteins.
   ▪ Essential to plant and animal life. Form the basic components of

every living cell.
- Protein requirements are greatest during growth:
  Foals, 2 weeks to 18 months, require 14% to 16% crude protein.
  Weanlings (6 months old) require 14%-16%.
  One to three years require 10%-12%.
  Adult horses 4 years and over require 8% to 10%.
  Mare in last few weeks of pregnancy 10% rising to 13%.
  Lactating mare 12% to 14%.
- High quality protein from multiple sources (good quality hay, grain, pasture and a few ounces of dried milk for foals and nursing mares) ensures an adequate diet.

2. Carbohydrates.
- Should constitute two thirds of diet.
- Fibre is more easily digested in growing pasture than in hay.
- Early cut hay is more digestible than later cut.
- Young horses require less fibre:
- Foals need less than 6% fibre.
- Yearlings can digest up to 20% crude fibre.
- Adult horses can digest 25% crude fibre.

3. Minerals.
- It is a good practice to provide lumps of rock salt in all pastures, and mineral salt licks in each loosebox or stall.
- Calcium and phosphorus are the mineral elements required in highest quantities because or their importance in bone formation.
- Calcium and phosphorus exist in the body in a ratio of 2 calcium:1 phosphorus.
- Because of the poor absorption of many natural sources of calcium it is generally recommended that horses be fed a ration in the range of 1.1-1.4 calcium:1 phosphorus. Foals should be fed a calcium/phosphorus ratio of 2:1.
- Minerals are indestructible and are found in varying amounts in plants, through the soil and in water sources.

4. Vitamins.
- Horses need vitamins – they act as catalysts in the system to utilise other nutrients and facilitate efficient digestion.
- Vitamins are present in many food sources particularly in fresh green foods.
- Poor storage conditions and poor food preparation can destroy vitamins.
- Seek your veterinarian's advice if you are in doubt as to the availability of sufficient vitamins in your horse's diet. He may recommend

a broad spectrum vitamin/mineral supplement.

▪ Overfeeding supplements or mixing supplements can cause an imbalance which could be dangerous to the horse.

5. A balanced diet will consist of approximately:
$2/3$ carbohydrate
$1/6$ protein
$1/6$ fat
with fibre, vitamins, minerals and water present.

Rules of Good Feeding

1. Keep mangers scrupulously clean. Allow no traces of the previous feed to remain.
2. Feed little and often. Horse has small stomach for his size and the natural way for him to live is with the stomach nearly always two-thirds full.
3. Feed plenty of bulk. Horse has small stomach but large capacity intestine. Hay and grass are main bulk feeds. Adequate bulk is essential for a successful digestive process. Avoid exceeding a maximum ratio of 50% roughage:50% concentrate. Too little roughage can lead to colic. Additional roughage with good caloric level for energy or weight gain is beet pulp.
4. Feed according to: (a) age, (b) work being done, (c) size, (d) temperament.
5. Make no sudden changes in type of food or routine of feeding. All changes in diet must be gradual, spread over several days.
6. Feed at the same hours each day.
7. Feed only clean, good-quality forage. Horses are fastidious feeders. Musty or dusty fodder can prove harmful, causing colic from toxins in the mould or respiratory problems from irritant dust or mould.
8. Feed something succulent each day: grass, sliced carrots, apples, etc.
9. When work starts, digestion slows down. Blood needed to aid digestion goes instead to the lungs. Horses may do quiet work after a small feed, say, 2-3lbs (0.9-3kg), but need complete rest after a large feed, 4-6lbs (1.8-2.7kg), and should not be worked fast when the stomach is full of grass or hay. When the stomach is full the diaphragm (between abdominal and thoracic cavities) presses into the lung space and will restrict breathing if the horse is asked to work hard.
10. The average period of retention of food in the stomach is one to one and a half hours.
11. Always dampen feed.

12. Do not disturb a horse who is eating. Do not feed a hot, tired horse.
13. Do not feed too much at one time – 4lbs (1.8kg) of concentrate (grain) is a large enough feed for the relatively small stomach to cope with at one time.

Amount to Feed

1. Depends on:
    - Whether horse is stabled or at grass.
    - Size – weight is more important than height.
    - Age.
    - Temperament.
    - Work being done.
    - Whether it is summer or winter.
    - What items are available.

2. Rule of thumb for feeding:
    Feed 2½lbs (1.1kg) per 100lbs (45kg) body weight for maintenance. For example, an average-sized 16.0hh horse requires a total weight of 25-30lbs (11-13kg) of food a day. If working hard (hunting regularly) this might be approximately 10-14lbs (4.5-6.3kg) concentrate with 14-18lbs (6.3-8kg) hay per day.

3. Horses are great individualists and each one will vary. A good feeder should have the ability to see which horses do well and which do not and adjust the feeding accordingly. This requires knowledge, patience, observation and a love of and interest in horses.

Times to Feed

Times of feeds will vary from stable to stable according to working conditions. Main rules are:
  - feed little and often
  - always feed at the same hours each day
  - feed regularly – long periods of absence are harmful.
For example:
  first feed before exercise, small feed, 7 am;
  second feed at mid-day, after exercise and strapping, larger feed;
  third feed at night, largest feed.

If it is possible to feed four times a day, give the third feed, a small feed, at 4 pm and the fourth feed, the largest feed, at night.

When Not to Feed

1. When horse is heated after work. Stomach is not then in proper state for digestion of food.
2. If horse is exhausted, after violent exercise. A gruel may be given at this time, as it is easily digestible. Allow horse to rest for an hour or two, then feed.
3. When horse is weakened from long fasting be particularly careful to feed only small quantities. Too much food under these conditions could produce indigestion and, in some cases, gastritis and colic. An over-hearty feed is always harmful. Feed small quantities at frequent intervals.

CHAPTER 7

Feeds and Forage

Types of Hay

Hay is a bulk feed and replaces grass for the stabled horse. Bulk from hay not only aids digestion but is also relatively rich in protein and essential minerals.

There are four basic types of hay:
1. Meadow hay. Cut from permanent pasture. Usually contains a greater variety of grasses than seed hay. Softer and more easily digested than seed hay, meadow hay often contains cocksfoot or orchard grass, sweet vernal, meadow fescue, rye grass and clover. Hay containing any weeds, e.g. docks, thistles, nettles, ragwort, bracken and mares tail, should not be fed. The last mentioned three weeds are poisonous to horses.
2. Seed hay. Sown as a rotation crop it will generally consist of one or two types of grass, e.g. timothy, orchard grass or cocksfoot, Italian rye grass, meadow fescue, alfalfa (lucerne) and possibly a small quantity of clover. Seed hay is hard and generally higher in fibre content than meadow hay.
3. Vacuum-packed hay (haylage). A popular substitute for hay particularly suitable for horses with respiratory problems, since the problem-causing spores that are found in hay are unable to form in these products. Top quality grass is cut, crimped and allowed to wilt. It is not allowed to thoroughly dry as hay would be. The grass is younger than that cut for hay, and it is therefore less fibrous. It is raked and baled, usually within two days and while still wet, and then packaged in strong, airtight plastic bags. This makes a succulent, nutritious substitute for hay. It is more expensive than conventional hay and once the bag is opened it must be used within a day or so or spoilage will occur. Its obvious advantage is that farmers can make

hay when grasses are at their peak, regardless of weather. Haylage may need to be fed in greater volumes than hay because of the high water content, but the concentrate ratio may need to be reduced because haylage has a higher nutrient value than hay.

4. Silage. Cut from young grass and stored at once in a clamp where air is quickly excluded and the grass 'pickles' in its own water content. It is not widely considered suitable for horses, as it is very rich and there is a risk of contamination by the botulism bacteria.

Regardless of type, the properties of good hay are:
1. It should have a good aroma – 'nose'.
2. It should have a sweet taste.
3. The colour of the flowering head should be retained in well-made hay.
4. It should be a good colour – greenish to brownish, but not yellow, which is a sign of weathering.
5. It should be dry but flexible to the touch, bright and clean.
6. It should not be dusty or mouldy.
7. It should contain many of the good grasses, few of the inferior ones, and no bad ones. (See Grasses, page 49.)
8. It should be cut when grasses are at their best – i.e. when they are still young, between the flower and the seed.

Note: New hay, i.e. less than six months old, should be introduced gradually, mixing it with the old hay ration for several days, to enable the horse to adjust. New hay should be stored in a well-ventilated stack so that no overheating occurs.

Quality of Hay

The quality and value of hay depend on:
1. The grasses of which it is composed.
2. The soil in which it has been grown.
3. The time of year when it was cut.
4. The way in which it has been saved, i.e. made.
5. Whether it is first or second cut. Second cut (aftermath) is usually inferior, consisting mainly of leaves and flowering heads. However, a second cutting of alfalfa (lucerne) is often preferable to a first cutting as it will be less stemmy and will have few or no weeds.
6. How it has been stored.

Mowburnt Hay
Hay which has deteriorated due to overheating in the rick is known as

'mowburnt'. It is a yellow or dark brown colour. Cause – baling hay before juicy stems are dry.

Weeds in Hay

The presence of weeds, e.g. docks and thistles, in hay usually signifies an impoverished state of the land on which the hay has been grown (lacking in heart). Avoid hay containing weeds. Poisonous weeds include: ragwort (or ragweed), bracken and mares tail.

Ragwort. A poisonous plant with bright yellow, daisy-like flowers in umbrella-shaped clusters, with jagged leaves.

Grasses

Grasses will vary from country to country and area to area. The best grasses are: timothy, American orchard (cocksfoot), rye grass, sweet vernal, blue grass fescue and meadow fescue. (Do not feed fescue to pregnant mares. It harbours an otherwise harmless organism which can cause abortion or thicken the placenta.) Inferior grasses are: smooth meadow and Yorkshire fog. Bad grasses are: common rush, crab grass, Johnson grass, common meadow barley.

Timothy

Very commonly used for horses and probably the safest hay. Timothy is carbonaceous – fairly rich in carbohydrates and fats but lacking in digestible protein and minerals. Usually free from dust and mould.

American Orchard (Cocksfoot)

Very commonly used hay in North America and similar to timothy in texture and feeding value. Generally well liked by horses. Usually free from dust and mould. Matures earlier than timothy. Second cut similar to timothy.

Alfalfa (Lucerne)

Alfalfa (also known as lucerne) is exceedingly rich in protein and has a high lime content. It is very palatable. Best for horses when it is fairly mature before cutting. Care must be taken not to overfeed alfalfa – about 1/2lb (226g) per day for each 100lbs (45kg) of live weight is safe; i.e. not more than 4-5lbs (1.8-2.3kg) daily.

Clover

Ranks second to alfalfa (lucerne) in feeding value. It is palatable, slightly laxative and has high protein and mineral content. It may be dusty due to inadequate drying of the large trefoil-type leaves. White clover is most commonly used as other varieties are usually coarse and large amounts are wasted. As with lucerne, feed only a limited amount daily. A mixture of clover and timothy hay is a very desirable combination. In the UK clover is usually only a small percentage of the total meadow or seed hay (less than 5%).

Stacking Hay

Hay keeps best if stored in a barn. When carted from the field it will still have a high moisture content.
1. Do not stack tight to the walls or roof.
2. Leave plenty of room for the air to pass through and around the bales to assist in curing.
3. Stack indoors on wooden floor or place wooden boards or pallets on dirt floor, before stacking to avoid deterioration of bottom layer.
4. Stack oblong bales in alternating directions leaving air spaces.
5. If hay must be kept outside, stack on wooden boards or pallets if possible, with spaces between boards for moisture to reach the ground.
6. Never stack on plastic sheeting as this will cause overheating and possibly fire in the stack.
7. Stack may be covered with plastic to keep out rain after it has dried out for several weeks.
8. Remove top layer of bales before covering in case they are wet.
9. Hay which has been baled (as in haylage) in large, sealed, plastics bags can be stored outside.

How to Feed Hay

1. The most natural way for a horse to eat his hay is from the floor. There is a possibility of waste with this method as some hay will be trodden, soiled and not eaten.
2. The most economical and accurate way to feed hay is to put it into a

haynet. It can then be weighed and dampened if required. The disadvantage here is that it is time-consuming and the net must be correctly hung in the stable or it will dangle when empty and create a hazard to the horse. For correct method of hanging, see Chapter 2 'Hayracks', page 20.

3. Many horses appreciate their hay being dampened a little before feeding. The outdated trend of soaking hay for several hours before feeding certainly neutralises most of the injurious spores contained in hay but unfortunately washes out a great deal of the nutritive value as well. It is recommended that hay is immersed in water for 20 to 30 minutes only, which will eradicate any problem from dust or spores but not leach out the valuable nutrients.

Chaff

Chaff is chopped-up hay. Only good hay must be used. Ideally chaff should be cut on the premises as bulk chaff purchased from feedstores may be of inferior quality. Oat straw may also be used for chaff and is sometimes preferred by horses on maximum grain allowance since good hay chaff is too nutritious for the system to absorb. Adding chaff to grain feed ensures mastication. Amount of chaff to be given – approximately 1lb (450g) per feed.

Chaff may have molasses added which enhances palatability and increases nutrient value.

Chopped alfalfa used as chaff is a good source of calcium. Sold in the UK under the name 'Alfa A'.

Hay Substitutes

Grass Cubes
These consist of dehydrated first-quality grass which is steamed, chopped and pressed into cubes approximately 2ins x 1¹/₂ins (50mm x 37mm). These cubes can be fed instead of hay and/or grain. Follow the manufacturer's instructions. Usually about 12lbs (5.4kg) per day per 1000lb (450kg) horse is advised. They are good for horses wintered at pasture. Disadvantage: if fed to stabled horses, cubes are eaten quickly and horses suffer from boredom. Horses often do not like the concentrated grass taste.

Variations on grass cubes are available, for example horse and pony cubes. Horse and pony cubes are an all-round balanced ration for a range of horses and ponies in medium work. Advantages and disadvantages are the same as for grass cubes. Remember to supply plenty of clean fresh water when feeding any dehydrated food. If grain ration is fed in pelleted form, add water to feed when serving.

Bran

This by-product of the milling process of wheat is a bulky, protein-rich concentrate with high salt content. Bran should be in broad flakes, dry and floury, not musty. Fed wet, or as a bran mash, it has a cooling, laxative effect. Bran may be mixed with regular grain ration to slow down the rate of eating and improve mastication, or it may replace the bulk of the grain on workless days.

Bran has a high phosphorus, low calcium balance so must be fed with care, particularly to horses lacking access to calcium-rich foods (e.g. alfalfa, sugar beet). It is expensive and has been outdated by modern chops and molassed chaff.

Oats

Oats are the best energy-giving food for horses. Oats consist of two-thirds carbohydrate, one-sixth protein and one-sixth fat. They are highly nutritious, digestible and palatable.

Oats should be clean, hard, plump, heavy and sweet smelling. Bruising, rolling, crushing or crimping oats exposes the kernel to the digestive juices and aids digestion. After two to three weeks crushed oats begin to lose their value. It is therefore advisable to purchase whole oats and crush them on the premises, as required. Oats may also be fed whole but some may pass through the digestive tract undigested and be wasted. Oats are a good source of phosphorus but deficient in calcium.

Barley

Barley is used in many parts of the world as part or all of the grain ration for horses. Barley is a very hard grain and cannot be fed whole as it will swell in the stomach and usually cause colic. Barley is either soaked overnight and boiled for at least 4 hours, or more commonly, it is fed bruised where the husk is broken, 'micronised' where it is flash heated, or 'extruded' where it is part cooked and reformed in cubes. All these methods improve digestibility of the grain.

Boiled barley fed to a tired horse after a demanding day's hunting or competition is palatable and digestible. Bruised, micronised and extruded barley are all used as alternatives to oats when the horse tends to become too 'sharp' when fed on oats. Barley appears to keep horses calmer, and is also useful for keeping weight on horses who 'run up light' (lose weight easily.)

Wheat

Wheat is not a grain that is commonly used for horses. Bran, a waste product from the milling of wheat, can be useful. (See 'Bran', page 52.)

Maize (Corn)

A feed high in energy value but poor in proteins and minerals. Generally considered too heating and fattening to be fed in large amounts. Small amounts are often added to compound mixes. Should only be fed to weanlings and yearlings in very small amounts as it is deficient in lysine, an amino acid necessary for proper growth. Corn may be fed flaked and it is sometimes used in small amounts in the diet to put condition on 'poor doers.'

Peas and Beans

Very rich in protein, but heating and fattening. Peas and beans are fed split or kibbled, or crushed. Horses wintered out at grass may be fed up to 6lbs (2.7kg) of peas or beans per day with advantage. If mixing peas or beans with grain feed, mix one part beans to two parts oats, by weight. These are not widely used in modern feeding methods.

Steamed/Boiled Food

Barley and oats may be fed boiled or steamed. This softens the grain, increases the palatability, and adds water, which aids in digestion. Boiled or steamed grain tempts a fussy feeder, helps to keep flesh on the horse, and helps to avoid constipation when fresh green food is not available.

Grass Meal

If of good quality may contain 19% protein. Start with small quantity and work up to 1lb (450g) per day. Feed damp, mixed with grain and bran.

Grass meal is not commonly used in the UK. See Grass Nuts.

Dried Sugar-Beet Pulp

Must never be fed dry as choking may easily result and dry pulp will swell within the stomach. Beet pulp should be soaked in plenty of water overnight. Feed mixed with bran and grain. Useful bulk feed for horses doing slower work – helps keep flesh on horses.

Sugar-beet pulp needs to be soaked for 12 hours and used within a subsequent 12 hours. Sugar-beet cubes need to be soaked for 16-20 hours, and used within 12 hours. Soaked sugar beet may need to be used sooner in hot weather when fermentation may begin.

Sugar beet is a palatable, nutritious and economic feed high in fibre and energy. It should be fed with care and with some restriction to horses in hard, fast work. Sugar beet is a good source of calcium.

Horse and Pony Cubes and Pellets

These are a compound of a variety of ingredients, including oats, barley, maize, bran, locust bean, linseed cake, groundnut meal, grass meal, molasses, etc., plus vitamins and minerals. Composition varies according to brand. Cubes may be substituted in part or whole for grain ration and/or hay. Advantages include: ease of transportation; ease of storage; no mixing; ensures standardised, mixed, balanced diet with necessary vitamins and minerals included. Ponies fed cubes are less likely to 'hot up' than those fed on grain. Cubes and compound mixes are now very competitive with regard to price compared to 'straight' feeds.

Disadvantages include: relative expense; danger that their low moisture content may lead to choking unless adequate water is available. Chaff or bran fed with cubes ensures adequate mastication and salivation before swallowing.

Compound Feeds (Coarse Mixes)

Many manufacturers prepare horse and pony feeds ready-mixed and bagged. Composition varies so check labels and feeding values to achieve feed requirements. Advantages: consistent quality, ease of handling and storage, excellent for owner with one or two horses.

Manufacturers provide every type of compound feed for horses in every type of work or lifestyle (e.g. stud mix, competition mix, cool mix, show mix, etc.).

With all prepared, bagged feeds, be sure to feed the correct protein level – most adult horses require only a 8%-10% protein mix. See Chapter 6, page 42.

Succulents

Something succulent, i.e. green or juicy, makes the feed more appetising, gives bulk, provides variety and helps to satisfy the natural desire for grass. Root crops can be very useful especially in winter (carrots, swedes, mangolds).

Green Food
Grass or alfalfa etc. should be readily available in summer and may be fed either in a haynet or chaffed up with hay and added to the feed.

Carrots
Best of all roots. Feed only sound carrots. Feed whole or cut lengthwise. Carrots are cooling and are a natural remedy for some diseases. Carrots are easily digestible and are good for horses with respiratory diseases, coughs and broken wind – 3-4lbs (1.4-1.8kg) per day will tempt delicate feeders.

Mangolds, Swedes and Turnips
Relished by horses, particularly in winter months. Scrub well under running tap, slice lengthwise or feed whole. Begin by feeding 1 or 2lbs (450 or 900g) daily and increase to 4lbs (1.8kg) as horse becomes accustomed to them. Some horses also enjoy parsnips and beetroots.

Compiling a Diet

In compiling a diet remember the ideal proportion of ingredients:
  Carbohydrate, two thirds;
  Protein, one sixth;
  Fat, one sixth.
1. A horse in light work will require about threequarters fibre (hay) to one quarter concentrate (grain, pellets).
2. When fully fit and working hard a competition horse or hunter will require between one third to one half concentrates and one half to two thirds fibre.

3. For fit horses in long-term maintenance work it is safer to maintain a 50% roughage:50% concentrate ratio in the diet. A rise to 60% roughage:40% concentrate for short periods in very hard working horses is viable.

Feed Charts

1. Feeding a small amount of hay before a grain feed is good practice. The bacterial population in the caecum dies very quickly in the absence of food and grows rapidly as soon as horse starts eating.
2. If grain is fed on empty stomach much of it passes through caecum undigested.
3. Sample feed chart for 16hh 1100lb (500kg) competition horse just starting fitness training.

Total weight of feed required: 28lbs (12.75kg)
Concentrates: 8lbs (3.6kg) Hay: 20lbs (9kg)

    7 am: 3lbs (1.4kg) hay
          2lbs (0.9kg) concentrates (grain, coarse mix or cubes)
          handful bran/chaff

After exercise: 5lbs (2.27kg) hay

    12 noon: 2lbs (0.9kg) grain, coarse mix or cubes (nuts)
          handful bran/chaff

    5 pm: 12lbs (5.5kg) hay
          4lbs (1.8kg) grain, coarse mix or cubes (nuts)
          handful bran/chaff
          sliced carrots

---

4. When horse is fully fit 2 months later:

Total weight of feed required still 28lbs (12.75kg) food but concentrates now will be 12lbs (5.5kg) and 16lbs (7.25kg) hay.

    7 am: 3lbs (1.4kg) hay
          1lb (450g) oats (or coarse mix)
          1lb (450g) cubes (nuts)
          1/2lb (225g) bran or 'Alfa A'

After exercise: 3lbs (1.4kg) hay

12 noon: 2lbs (0.9kg) oats
1lb (450g) cubes
1/2lb (225g) bran or 'Alfa A'
handful chaff

5 pm: 10lbs (4.5kg) hay
3lbs (1.36kg) oats
1lb (450g) cubes
1/2lb (225g) bran or 'Alfa A'
carrots, chaff

8 pm: 1lb (450g) oats
1lb (450g) cubes
handful chaff
feed salt daily in the evening feed (approx. 1tbs)

Alternatively the 10lb hay ration could be given at 8pm.

- Make all changes in diet very gradually.
- Divide grain into four feeds and give an extra feed at 8 pm.

Vitamins

Vitamins are necessary in order that the body may utilise food correctly. For example, a diet may be rich in calcium, but the body cannot utilise it unless vitamin D is present. Vitamins are present in most fresh foods but long storage, poor harvesting, fermentation and an overdose of sun will reduce the vitamin values of feed. Vitamin supplements may be necessary for young horses; consult your veterinary surgeon.

Micronutrients

Research shows a strong association between zinc and copper levels as well as calcium and phosphorus levels and ratio, and metabolic bone disease. The best diet for avoiding bone diseases in young growing horses should include alfalfa or alfalfa/timothy mix hay. Additives are available as broad spectrum or specifically directed. Consult your veterinary surgeon.

Salts

Calcium, magnesium, phosphorus and common salt are most important – as is their correct balance. Salts play an essential role in the maintenance of health and development. Common salt plays a vital part in the digestion of protein and a small quantity may be added to the daily diet. Many natural foods are low in salts. Keep salt or mineral lick in all stables and pastures.

Mineral content of basic feedstuffs

	Copper (ppm)	Phosphorus (%)	Calcium (%)	Zinc (ppm)
Alfalfa meal	10	0.25	2.1	35
Barley	7.5	0.4	0.1	17
Beet pulp	12.5	0.1	0.68	1
Corn (maize)	4.5	0.27	0.03	10
Linseed meal	25	0.9	0.4	-
Molasses, beet	18	0.03	0.15	-
Molasses, cane	60	0.1	0.0	-
Oats	6	0.35	0.1	-
Soyabean meal	20	0.65	0.3	27
Wheat bran	25	1.15	0.15	80
Ideal	25	0.6	0.8	80

ppm = parts per million. Chart is calculated on a dry-matter basis.

Note: The chart lists the mineral content on a dry-matter basis of some common feeds. The bottom line is the ideal and recommended level for young, growing horses. Hays vary too widely to be included.

It is obvious that there can be difficulty in meeting the horse's copper needs unless bran is added to the diet. When bringing a ration up to appropriate copper levels, meet or only slightly exceed the recommended level, as copper is highly toxic or even fatal when fed in quantity. If your water system uses copper piping this may provide a significant hidden copper source, so have the water analysed.

Beware of feeding too much bran to growing horses as it is very high in phosphorus and could create an imbalance in the calcium: phosphorous ratio.

Zinc is critical to the function of many other systems in addition to bone and is relatively non-toxic. Aim for levels twice the current recommended level.

Electrolytes

1. Electrolytes balance the fluids and minerals in the blood.
2. Minerals are lost in sweat – electrolytes are of particular concern for horses who sweat profusely.
3. Loss of electrolytes can account for a 30% drop in plasma potassium and a 16% drop in plasma chloride.
4. Endurance and event horses are given electrolytes before and during competitions.
5. Take veterinary advice on which brand to use – some commercial mixtures are too high in bicarbonate and too low in potassium.
6. Dehydration is a common problem in endurance, show and event horses during hot, humid weather.
7. To test for dehydration, pinch the horse's neck skin between finger and thumb – then let go. Skin should spring back immediately showing no sign of fold. If fold remains suspect dehydration.
8. Prevent dehydration by allowing horses to drink whenever they wish, i.e. every hour or so when working.
9. On long rides horses need an average of one gallon of water per hour from the start of work until horse is fully rested.
10. If horse is not properly conditioned he may sweat more and need even more water.
11. Dehydrated, poorly conditioned horses may drink to excess after a long ride, so restrict their water to a gallon (4.5 litres) every 15-20 minutes. Properly conditioned animals usually will not drink too much.
12. Proper conditioning and training will determine the health and success of a horse in competition. No diet can overcome poor training.

Preparation of Food

Bran Mash

Use a metal or plastic bucket. To one third of a bucket of bran add as much boiling water as the bran will absorb. Add 1/2oz (14g) of salt. Stir well. Cover to keep in steam and allow mash to steam until cool enough to feed. Correctly made, the mash should be 'crumble-dry', not stiff nor thin and watery. The mash is more appetising if a handful of oats is added, or some treacle or molasses, or a pint of cooked linseed.

A bran mash is often fed the night before a rest day, to reduce the concentrate intake prior to a day off. However, the change in diet can have a detrimental effect on the gut flora in the large intestine, by disrupting their regular food source. A bran mash has a laxative effect where necessary.

Linseed (Flaxseed)

1. Highly nutritious and rich in protein and oils. May be fed as 'jelly' or 'tea' to improve condition and give a gloss to the coat. Daily allowance is 1/2-1lb (225g-450g) of seed before cooking.
2. Linseed 'jelly'. Cover linseed with water and soak overnight. After 24 hours, add more water and bring to boil. Soaked, unboiled linseed may prove poisonous to horses. Allow to cool. Resulting jelly is then tipped out and mixed with evening feed. Linseed burns easily and should be cooked in an insulated boiler.
3. Linseed 'tea'. Prepare as above but with more water. The water in which the linseed is cooked is very nutritious and is employed with bran to make a linseed mash.
4. Linseed oil meal is also available and may be fed with grains or roughages. Has same properties as cooked linseed. Feed not more than 1lb (450g) mixed with grain daily.

Soyabean Meal

Similar to linseed oil meal and commonly added to commercial feed mixes as protein supplement. Feed in small quantities only (about 1lb or 450g daily). Source of good quality protein – amino acids – lysine and methionine.

Cod Liver Oil

Excellent tonic for debility cases. Beneficial influence on formation of healthy bone. Good preventive for rickets. Feed 1-2 tablespoonsful twice weekly. Cod liver oil possesses a nasty taste and smell and may not be eaten readily. Fed during the winter it provides a source of vitamin D, which might be deficient due to the lack of sunshine. Horse's manufacture vitamin D in the presence of sunlight.

Vegetable Oil

Additional calories can be added by pouring up to 1 cup a day of vegetable oil over grain or hay. This is equal to 3lbs (1.4kg) of grain in energy. Also gives shine to coat.

Milk

May be given with good results to horses in training. Feed either liquid or in powdered form. (Feed up to 1 gallon or 4.5 litres per day, mixed with bran and oats.) Commercially available mare's milk substitute for orphan foals is also good for horses in training. Feed dry with grain mix or liquid prepared as directed on bag. Not commonly fed to adult horses.

Beer or Stout
Good tonic for horses in training. Give two bottles a day up to three days before competition.

Gruel
Made from oatmeal. Palatable and refreshing to a tired horse. Easily digestible. Place a double handful of oatmeal in a bucket. Add a little cold water and stir well. (Cold water prevents lumps forming.) Pour on 1½ gallons (6.75 litres) of hot, not boiling, water and stir again. Offer when cool. Gruel should be thin enough for horse to drink. Boiling water should not be used as it produces a more starchy compound than is suitable for digestion by an exhausted horse.

Hay Tea
Prepared by steeping hay in boiling water and allowing the infusion to cool. Contains valuable nutritional material in the form of mineral salts and other soluble substances.

Warm Water
The oxygen is removed from water by heating and warm water is therefore flat. It is correct to provide artificially warmed water for an exhausted horse as cold water could be a shock to the system. Ice-cold water, also, is not desirable for any horse.

CHAPTER 8

Saddlery

Care

1. Saddlery, also known as 'tack', should be kept clean and in good repair.
2. All tack should be inspected regularly and minor defects remedied. Particular attention should be paid to stitching, which will rot or break before leather. Tack should be wiped daily and the bit washed. At least once a week the tack should be taken apart and cleaned thoroughly.
3. Leather will dry out and crack unless it is kept soft with saddle soap or oil. Glycerine, neatsfoot oil, and Ko-cho-line are good for leather. Neatsfoot oil may rot stitching if over-used and come off on hands and clothing. The best saddle soap contains all the necessary glycerine or oil to keep tack in regular use pliable.
4. If tack is to be stored – cover with Ko-cho-line or leather dressing, cover with brown paper and then place in a linen or cotton bag.
5. Do not wash leather with soda or hot water. Do not place close to artificial heat.
6. Hang up saddle and bridle immediately upon removal from horse. This allows air to get to saddle lining, and avoids possible damage to tack thrown carelessly down.
7. Cleaning tack involves wiping all leatherwork with a damp sponge regularly rinsed with warm water, then rubbing saddle soap well in to all the cleaned leather.

The Saddle

Structure

1. The frame on which a saddle is built is called a 'tree'. It is made traditionally of beech wood, but many modern trees are made of

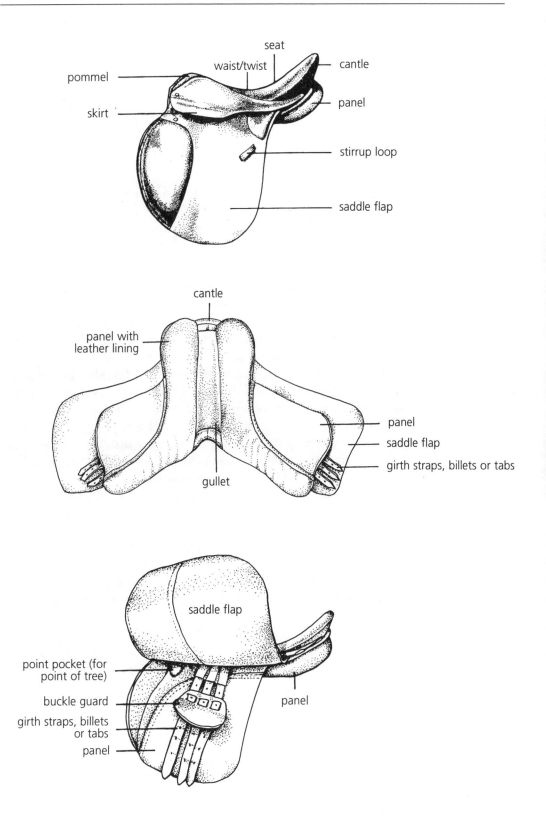

seat

waist/twist

cantle

pommel

skirt

panel

stirrup loop

saddle flap

cantle

panel with
leather lining

panel

saddle flap

girth straps, billets or tabs

gullet

saddle flap

point pocket (for
point of tree)

buckle guard

girth straps, billets
or tabs

panel

panel

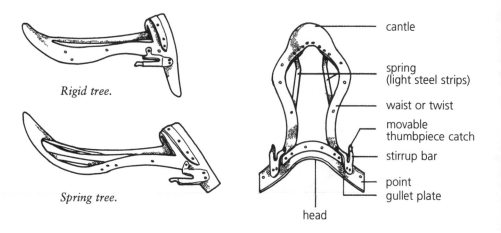

Rigid tree.

Spring tree.

cantle

spring
(light steel strips)

waist or twist

movable
thumbpiece catch

stirrup bar

point
gullet plate

head

laminated wood, bonded under pressure and then moulded. Saddle trees are also made of fibreglass.

2. Trees are either rigid (greater strength and solidity) or 'spring'. Spring trees are arguably more comfortable for the rider but may concentrate weight into one area of the back.

3. The 'spring' in a spring-tree saddle is a thin, flat spring steel strap stretching from the side of the cantle through the seat to the head. Spring-tree saddles are generally used with a numnah to ensure even weight distribution over the surface of the back.

4. The saddle tree may be broken if the saddle is dropped, or if a horse rolls with the saddle on. A broken tree will injure the horse's back. If in doubt, get the saddle checked by a saddler.

5. The saddle should be shaped so that it assists the rider to sit in the central and lowest part. Saddles are made in a huge variety of types, shapes and sizes, in order to cater for the enormous diversity of equestrian sports. A dressage saddle, for example, is made with straight flaps to assist the rider in getting the longest possible leg on the horse, whereas a jumping saddle has flaps cut well forward to accommodate the much shorter stirrup required for jumping.

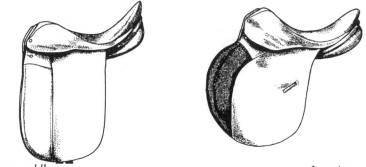

Dressage saddle.   *Jumping saddle.*

6. Saddles may have either a full panel or a half panel. A full panel reaches almost to the bottom of saddle flap and is lined all the way down. A half panel reaches half-way down the saddle flap and has a large sweat-flap.

7. Most stirrup bars are hinged to allow the point to be turned up to prevent stirrup leathers from slipping off when a saddled horse is being led. When the horse is being ridden the points should always be down.

8. Saddles are now also being made of materials other than the traditional leather. Nylon saddles, which cost about one third as much as a leather saddle and do seat the rider correctly on the horse, make sense for riding-school use.

Saddle Linings
Saddles are usually lined with leather. Older saddles may be lined with serge or linen but these materials do not last as long as leather and are rarely encountered today.

Fitting a Saddle (see also Chapter 9)
1. The saddle should be placed just behind the withers and the weight must be evenly distributed on the back muscles.

2. There should be no weight on the loins, and no pressure on the spine (test with rider mounted).

3. There should be one hand's width between the elbow and the girth.

4. The front arch should be neither too low nor too wide. With rider mounted three fingers' width should pass easily under front arch.

5. The front arch must not be too narrow. The withers must not be pinched. When girthed up, cantle should be a little higher than pommel (see illustrations page 86).

6. Movement of shoulder blades must not be hampered.

7. Gullet width and spread of panels should be appropriate to horse's back.

8. Panel must be correctly stuffed. Stuffing should be regulated to give support for the knee and be tilted to prevent rider sliding backwards.

9. Once a year, saddle should be checked by a saddler who will test the tree, stitching, and restuff as necessary. A new saddle will often need checking and restuffing after the first six months of use.

10. The cantle should hold rider's weight without coming down on the horse's back.

Standing and Carrying a Saddle
1. Stand saddle on front arch (pommel). Fold girth to protect pommel from rough ground. Never lean the cantle against a rough surface without protection from the girth or numnah to prevent damage.

2. Avoid placing saddle on the ground if possible. Leather is easily torn and scratched by rough surfaces.
3. If saddle must be placed on ground, put it where it will not be knocked over by people or horses.
4. A saddle should be carried:
   - With the front arch in the crook of the elbow (this allows the bridle to be carried on the same shoulder and leaves other hand free).
   - Along the thigh, with the hand in the front arch.

The above methods prevent injury to the cantle against walls and doorways.

Materials Required for Tack Cleaning

1. Saddle horse.
2. Cleaning bracket suspended from wall or ceiling.
3. Bucket of cold or tepid water.
4. Two sponges: one large one for washing; one for saddle soap.
5. A chamois leather, for drying if necessary. Particularly useful if tack is wet and muddy and excess water is used to remove mud.
6. Bar of glycerine or tin of saddle soap.
7. Two stable rubbers: one dry one to cover the clean saddle, one for drying metal work.
8. Metal polish, and an old cloth for applying it.
9. Burnisher, for rubbing up metal work after using metal polish.

Cleaning a Saddle

1. Place saddle on saddle horse.
2. Remove girths, stirrup leathers and irons, and girth buckle guards.
3. Clean leather lining. Remove all dirt. Squeeze excess water from sponge before use. Only use excess water to wash off mud to prevent scratching the leather. In this case use the chamois leather to dry off tack (never use the chamois dry but always well wrung out). Apply saddle soap.
4. After initial washing of the tack, all small black accumulations of grease and dirt, known as 'jockeys', should have been removed. Never use a sharp instrument to remove 'jockeys'. If difficulty is encountered, rub them off with a small pad of horse hair.
5. Rinse out second sponge and squeeze it as dry as possible. Dip glycerine bar in water and soap sponge liberally. Using circular movements, soap all leather work: panel, girth tabs, sweat-flap, underside of saddle flap, outer side of saddle flap, underside of skirt,

outer side of skirt and seat. Pay particular attention to all stitching –
liberal soaping will keep thread supple and lengthen its life. Do not
use soap on top of dirt.

6. Wash and dry stirrup irons. Clean all metal work with metal polish.
Rub up with burnisher.
7. Cover saddle with dry stable rubber and put away in a dry place.
8. Stirrup leathers and leather girths should be treated in the same way
as the leather parts of the saddle. Clean buckles with metal polish.
9. Before using saddle again, the seat and outside flaps may be rubbed
over with a moist sponge and dried with a chamois, to remove dust
and surplus soap which might stain breeches.

'Putting Up' a Saddle

1. Place saddle on bracket, about 18ins (45cm) long, attached to saddle
room wall at a convenient height.
2. Hang stirrup irons on hook underneath saddle bracket.
3. Hang girth, stirrup leathers, and martingale on hooks alongside
saddle bracket.

Numnahs (Saddle Pads)

1. Made of cotton, felt, sorbo-rubber, sheepskin, or nylon fabric, cut to
the shape of a saddle.
2. Attached to one girth tab on either side, above girth buckle, by a
leather or web loop; or by an adjustable strap round saddle panel.
3. Reasons for use:
   ▪ To rectify badly stuffed or ill-fitting saddle. (If used for this purpose-
   fitting a numnah is an emergency measure and saddle should be
   restuffed or replaced by one that fits.)
   ▪ To protect unfit horse's back.
   ▪ To protect the spine of a jumper (by ensuring it does not contact
   gullet of saddle during jump).
4. Numnah should be slightly larger than saddle. When in place it
should be visible for about 1in. (2.5cm) all round.
5. To avoid pressure being borne on the wither or spine, pull numnah
up into front arch of saddle before tightening girths.
6. Cleaning. If made of sponge or rubber, wash with pure soap or
animal wash. Avoid using synthetic detergents on horses or horse
clothing. If made of felt or sheepskin, dry and brush hard with dandy
brush. Scrub if necessary. Air well and guard against moth damage.
   Some nylon fabric or synthetic sheepskin numnahs may be washed
in washing machine. Use pure soap. Hang out to dry in warm, airy
room.

Felt Saddles or Pad Saddles

1. Made of felt. Sometimes covered, or partially covered with leather.
2. May have a tree forepart, or steel arch, which will help to keep it straight on the pony. Otherwise felt saddles have no tree.
3. Felt saddles often have web girth permanently attached. For safety they should have two straps and buckles, or two web girths.
4. Some felt saddles have 'D's instead of stirrup bars. Safety stirrups (with rubber band at outside) should be employed on these saddles.
5. A crupper may be necessary to prevent felt saddle slipping forward on a fat pony.

Wither Pads

1. Used to prevent pressure of the front arch of the saddle on horse's withers.
2. Made of woollen or cloth material. May be improvised by folding a stable rubber.
3. Wither pads are emergency measures only. Saddle should be re-stuffed, or changed, so that it fits properly.

Girths

Types

1. Leather. Excellent for use on fit horse. May gall unfit horse, even when kept clean and soft. There are many types of straight, shaped and cross-over leather girths, often with elastic at one end. May be covered with sheepskin or nylon girth cover to protect unfit horse.

A leather three-fold girth.

A leather Atherstone girth.

A leather Balding girth.

2. Plain webbing ('Cottage Craft' type). Made from a specially developed, tubular, polyester webbing with a layer of super-fine natural cotton woven onto the inside of the girth. Fully padded, they are comfortable for the horse and provide just the right amount of elasticity to allow freedom of movement. Rot-proof and machine washable, they are an excellent training girth or girth for everyday use. Not advised for strenuous jumping or eventing as they may snap suddenly under pressure. Less expensive than leather.
3. Lonsdale girth. Short girth of leather, nylon or webbing designed for use with long girth billets on a dressage saddle.
4. String girth. Good quality string girths are strong and can prevent galling by spreading the pressure.

Fitting
1. Girth should not be too short nor too long.
2. When drawn up for first mounting, buckles should reach at least to second hole on each side.
3. There should be not less than two spare holes above buckles on each side when girth is tightened.

Stirrup Irons

1. Should be of best quality metal. Hand-forged stainless steel is safest and most satisfactory. Plated metal flakes easily; pure nickel is too soft.
2. Fitting. With the broadest part of rider's foot in the stirrup, there should be half an inch (12mm) clearance at each side. If stirrup is too small rider's foot may be jammed; if too large, foot may slip through.
3. Cleaning. Wash and dry thoroughly. Clean all metals with metal polish and shine with a dry rubber.
4. Safety stirrups. Those most generally used are metal with rubber band at one side. Rubber band must be worn on the outside. Disadvantages – due to being weighted more on one side than the other they do not hang straight. Rubber band may come undone or break.

Safety stirrup.

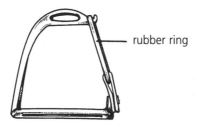 — rubber ring

Snaffle bridles...

...with cavesson noseband

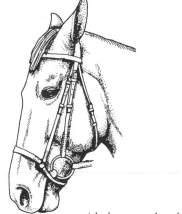

...with drop noseband

...with flash noseband

...with Grakle noseband

Bridles

Parts of a Snaffle Bridle

1. Headpiece and throatlash made on the same piece of leather.
2. Browband.
3. Two cheekpieces, attached at one end to the headpiece and at the other to the bit.
4. Noseband, on its own headpiece (may be plain or raised cavesson, flash, drop or figure eight – see illustrations).
5. Bit – attached to the cheekpieces and reins by stitches, or by studs or buckles if they are required to be detachable. Stitched 'mount' looks best for hunting and showing. Studded 'mount' is useful for exercising as different bits may be attached, and it is easier to clean. Buckled 'mount' is clumsy.
6. Reins – may be plain, plaited, or laced leather with a centre buckle. Reins may also be covered with rubber for better grip when hunting

or jumping, or of 'Continental' type – with leather ends attaching to the bit and webbing with stitched leather stops forming the rest of the reins.

Parts of a Double Bridle

Same as for a snaffle bridle, plus:

1. A sliphead (headpiece without a throatlash) for the bridoon.
2. Two bits – bridoon (small snaffle) and curb bit.
3. Additional pair of reins – bridoon rein is usually slightly the wider; and both reins are of plain leather.
4. Curb chain, attached by a hook on each of the upper rings of the curb bit. It has a special link ('fly' link) in the centre through which the lip strap passes.
5. Lip strap – narrow leather strap, made in two parts, which attaches to the 'D's on either side of the cheek of the bit, to prevent the curb chain from turning over or being lost should it come undone from the hooks.

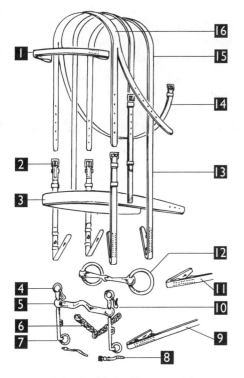

1 browband
2 cheekpiece
3 cavesson noseband
4 curb cheek ring
5 curb bit
6 curb chain
7 cheek
8 lip strap
9 curb rein
10 curb hook
11 bridoon rein
12 bridoon bit
13 cheekpiece
14 throatlash or throatlatch
15 bridoon slip head
16 headpiece

Parts of the double bridle. Assemble as shown, with two buckles on the offside and three on the nearside.

Fitting Headcollars, Halters and Bridles

Care must be taken to ensure that headcollars, halters and bridles fit correctly and comfortably on the horse.

1. The headband should rest flat just behind the ears and hang parallel just behind the projecting cheek bones.
2. The browband should be short enough to prevent the headband from slipping down the neck, but long enough to avoid chafing the base of the ears.
3. The throatlash prevents the headpiece from slipping over the ears but should not be too tight. It should be fitted so that you can place four fingers between the throatlash and the cheek bones, with the head in normal riding position.
4. The noseband (cavesson) should be placed below the projecting cheek bones by about two fingers' width. It should not be tight but should admit two fingers between it and the horse's nose.
5. The flash noseband. This has an extra strap attached to the front of the cavesson which fastens below the snaffle. Should fit snugly but not too tight.
6. Drop noseband. Must be carefully fitted. The front should be well above the nostrils; the back passes under the snaffle and fits in the chin groove. Should be tight enough to prevent horse crossing his jaw, but not so tight as to prevent flexing of the jaw. Used only with a snaffle; never with a double bridle.
7. Rope halters should be fitted to the horse's head and then the attached lead rope should be knotted at the noseband to avoid undue tightening caused by the slip knot.
8. Nylon headcollars are hard-wearing and require less maintenance than leather ones. They come in a variety of colours and are cheap to buy. However, they carry a greater risk of injury to the horse as they will not break under duress. They should be avoided for turning out and for travelling horses. A horse turned out in any headcollar or with its headcollar left hanging on the gate may be seen as an invitation to thieves.

   Note: Check under all headpieces to ensure that they are flat and remember to smooth down the mane. If adjustment is necessary to the noseband headpiece, ease it up at the poll and then ease it down the other side. Stand in front of horse to check that everything is straight, that the bit, or bits, are level in the mouth, and that all keepers are firm – no flapping ends.
9. The snaffle bit should be held in the corners of the mouth by cheek straps of the correct length. If the snaffle is adjusted too low the horse will have to hold it up himself and may draw his tongue back and place it over the bit. This is a very serious fault and hard to correct, but quite easy to avoid by correct adjustment. If the bit is too high in

the mouth it will pull up the corners of the lips. To test that you have the snaffle correctly adjusted, stand in front of the horse facing his head. Place the index finger of your right hand in the left ring of the bit and the index finger of your left hand in the right ring of the bit. Now, gently pull down on the bit and at the same time open the horse's mouth with your right thumb. It will be easy to see if the bit is correctly adjusted. It is also important that the bit is the correct width for your horse's mouth. Use a ruler to measure the mouth. If the bit is too narrow it will pinch the corners of the lips, and if it is too wide it will slide about and possibly bruise the mouth.

10. A double or full bridle consists of two bits: the bridoon, which is like a small jointed snaffle, and a curb bit, a straight bar bit often with a port to allow room for the tongue, and cheek pieces, a curb chain and lip strap.

  ▪ The bridoon is usually half an inch wider than the curb. It fits snugly into the corners of the mouth, making one soft wrinkle but not pulling on the corners of the mouth. Correct width is important.

  ▪ The curb bit lies 1in. (2.5 cm) above the tush of a horse, 2ins (5 cm) above the corner teeth of a mare. It must not be too narrow – or too wide, for the mouth.

  ▪ The curb chain should be twisted right-handed until it lies flat and smooth in the chin groove. Put the base of the link over the near side hook (thumb nail up). The curb chain should come into action when the cheeks of the bit are drawn back to an angle of 40°-50° with the mouth. The fly link (spare ring in centre of chain) should be underneath the chain.

  ▪ The lip strap passes through the fly link (centre ring) of the curb chain. It should be fairly loose. It allows the curb chain to stay flat and holds the chain if it becomes unhooked. It also prevents the horse from catching hold of the cheeks of the bit, and prevents the cheeks of a Banbury-action bit, which are not fixed, from revolving forward and up.

Principles of Bitting

A bit consists of anything passing through the horse's mouth and then, by way of the reins, to the rider's hands.

1. Bits act by applying pressure to the seven pressure points:
  ▪ The tongue
  ▪ The bars of the mouth
  ▪ The lips
  ▪ The curb groove
  ▪ The poll

- The nose (through drop noseband, for example)
- The roof of the mouth (through high port bits which are more severe and should be used with experience and caution).

2. The horse then gives way to that pressure by relaxing the jaw.
3. Immediately, the rider yields the pressure of the hand in acknowledgement.
4. The ability to control a horse via a bit is a learned response. It is accomplished only by a system of correction and reward. When the horse obeys the action of the bit, the rider must reward him by yielding to him at once.

Structure of the Horse's Mouth

To understand how bits work you must understand the structure of the horse's mouth.

1. The jaws, upper and lower, form a longitudinal channel.
2. The bottom of the lower jaw channel is formed by a group of muscles to which the tongue is attached.
3. The top of the upper jaw is formed by the palate.
4. The tongue lies in the channel of the lower jaw, and can move within the mouth cavity while the mouth is closed.
5. The jawbones are covered with a thin layer of flesh and skin – the gums.
6. The teeth, upper and lower incisors at the front of the mouth, then the tushes, in male horses only, and then the toothless part of the jaws, called the bars, follow before the upper and lower molars (cheek teeth).
7. Within the flesh and skin of the bars is a mass of nerves. Once these are destroyed, feeling will disappear.

Action of the Snaffle

The snaffle bit acts on the tongue, the outside of the bars of the mouth, and on the lips or the corners of the mouth.

The Purpose of the Snaffle

Used in conjunction with the rider's body position and weight and soft pressures of the legs the snaffle will raise the horse's head and teach the horse to accept the bit with a still and correct head carriage and a supple jaw.

Types of Snaffle

1. A snaffle is any bit, jointed or unjointed, where the mouthpiece is directly in line with the reins. Its simplest form, as used by the Native Americans, was a rawhide strip which passed through the horse's mouth.

2. Unjointed, half-moon or mullen mouth snaffles, made of rubber, vulcanite or metal are very mild and are often considered the best bits to start a young horse.

3. Jointed snaffles produce a squeezing or nutcracker action in the mouth and are slightly more severe than mullen mouthpieces. However, a rubber-covered jointed snaffle is also a very good bit for starting a young horse. There are many different varieties of jointed snaffle including eggbutt snaffles (which prevent pinching of the corners of the mouth), Dee snaffles (ring is shaped like a D), cheek snaffles, Fulmer or Australian loose-ring cheek snaffles (the loose ring allows more play in the mouthpiece so the horse can mouth the bit and make saliva which relaxes the jaw), German snaffles (thick, mild mouthpiece and wire rings). There are also snaffles with a link or spatula in the centre known as French link bits, which have a lessened nutcracker action.

4. Gag snaffle. Usually a jointed mouthpiece is used. Rounded leather cheekpiece of bridle passes through holes in the top and bottom of the snaffle rings. Has an exaggerated upward, head-raising effect. This is a severe bit and is preferably used with a second rein attached to the bit ring in the normal way, so that the gag rein is only used when necessary.

Action of the Curb Bit

1. On the bars of the mouth.
2. On the tongue.
3. Leverage action on lower jaw dependent on length of cheeks of bit and curb chain.
4. On the poll. Downward pressure achieved by the leverage action when curb rein is used.

Purpose of the Curb

Used in conjunction with the bridoon (snaffle with thinner mouthpiece than described above), curb chain and lip strap to form a double bridle or full bridle.

- Double bridle permits rider to use more refined and imperceptible aids on trained horse. Helps to maintain a relaxed jaw.
- Curb bit should not be used without a bridoon since constant pressure on lower jaw will numb the mouth.

Types of Curb Bit

1. Weymouth bit with sliding mouthpiece is the most common.
2. Weymouth bit with fixed mouthpiece action is more direct.
3. Banbury bit – round bar mouthpiece tapered in the centre to allow room for tongue. Mouthpiece fits into slots in the cheek which allows

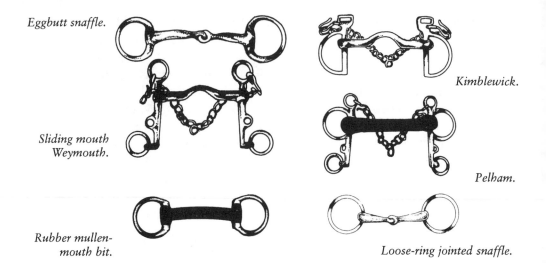

Eggbutt snaffle.

Kimblewick.

Sliding mouth Weymouth.

Pelham.

Rubber mullen-mouth bit.

Loose-ring jointed snaffle.

it to revolve and also to move up and down. Intention is to allow horse to mouth the bit and prevent him catching hold of it.

The Pelham Bit
1. Is a combination of the curb and bridoon in one mouthpiece.
2. Numerous variations of mouthpiece but, generally speaking, action is achieved by pressure on corners of mouth when top rein is used and on the poll and curb groove when bottom rein is used.
3. Sometimes used with leather 'converters' or 'roundings' and only one rein. Apart from the advantage of only one rein in child's hands there is no good reason for using a Pelham this way. Adds to the confusion of a bit already trying to do too many things at once.

The Kimblewick
1. Pelham-type bit – an adaptation of a Spanish jumping bit.
2. Squared eye (as opposed to usual rounded one) allows more downward pressure on the poll.
3. When hand is held low the Kimblewick will lower the horse's head very effectively.
4. Has the advantage of a single rein. Useful bit for children riding rather strong ponies.
5. If overemployed may make horse hang on the bit and the hand.

Causes of Resistance or Evasion

1. Fear and pain, either present or in memory.
   - Tongue over the bit.
   - Going 'above the bit' (horse puts his head up).

- Going 'behind the bit (horse tucks head in).
2. Bit injury or bruised or torn bars.
3. Wolf teeth. (Molar-type teeth with little root, occurring in the upper jaw, just in front of the molars. See 'Wolf Teeth', Chapter 24.)
4. Severe bits.
5. Sharp teeth (when teeth need floating, i.e. rasping, the skin may be pinched between teeth and bit. (See Chapter 24.)
6. Any discomfort.
   - Bit too narrow.
   - Rough edges (watch nickel bits for roughness).
   - Drop noseband wrongly fitted.
   - Browband too narrow, pinching base of ears (horse will shake his head).
7. Horse incapable of doing what is asked (insufficient training).

Cleaning a Bridle

1. Hang up bridle on a hook. Take off the noseband, let out the cheekpieces to the lowest hole. Bridle should be taken apart and cleaned about once a week, when all stitching may be checked.
2. Wash and dry bit or bits. (Remove curb chain to wash and polish.)
3. Wash all leatherwork and dry with a chamois – as described under 'Cleaning a Saddle' on page 66.
4. Polish bits and buckles as described for 'Stirrup Irons' on page 69.
5. Soap all leatherwork, remembering the importance of the underside. Wrap sponge around the straps and rub gently up and down.
6. When cleaning the bridle on the hook, hold it with one hand to keep it taut, and clean with the other. When cleaning the reins, step backwards, away from the hook, to keep them taut. Work downwards, towards buckle. Hang reins on another hook to keep them clean.
7. Put the bridle together, replacing all buckles in their correct holes, with strap ends in their keepers and runners. ('Keepers' are stitched loops; 'runners' are loops that slide up and down.)

'Putting Up' a Bridle

1. Hang bridle on hook. Take buckle in centre of reins in one hand and hold just behind and slightly above noseband.
2. Pass throatlash (long end) across in front of the bridle, round the back, through loop of reins (at buckle), round the front of the bridle again and fasten to its end hole. This gives a 'figure-of-eight' appearance.
3. Put noseband right around the outside of the cheekpieces. Do not

buckle but pass strap end through keepers.

4. Twist curb chain flat and hook across the front of the bit.
5. Bridle may also be correctly 'put up' by passing throatlash directly through the loop of the reins without forming a 'figure-of-eight' and then wrapping noseband around outside of bridle.
6. When 'put up', hang bridle on bridle hanger which is either half-moon or round in shape, in order to keep headpiece the correct shape.
7. If bridle hanger is sufficiently high up, reins may be left hanging straight down tack room wall.

Martingales

1. Standing martingale. A strap attached at one end to the noseband and at the other between the horse's forelegs to the girth, supported by a neck strap. Never attach to drop noseband.
   Purpose: to prevent horse from raising his head beyond the angle of control.
   Fitting: with horse's head up in correct position, place a hand underneath the martingale and push it up. It should just reach into the horse's gullet. A rubber stop should be fitted at the junction between the neckstrap and the martingale.
2. Running martingale. A strap attached at one end between the horse's forelegs to the girth. The other end divides into two straps, each with a ring at the end. The reins are passed through these rings. The martingale is supported by a neck strap. Leather or rubber 'stops' should be used on the reins between the rings of the martingale and the bit. A stop should also be placed at the junction of the martingale

Standing martingale.

Running martingale.

and the neckstrap.

Purpose: to prevent the horse raising his head above the angle of control, or throwing it from side to side.

Fitting: when attached to the girth, take both rings up one side of the horse's shoulder. They should reach to the withers. Note: the neck strap should fit so that it will admit a hand at the withers. The buckle should be on the near side.

3. Irish martingale: Two metal rings connected by a leather strap 4-6ins (10-15cm) long.

   Purpose: to keep the reins in place, preventing them from going over the horse's head. Used mainly in racing.

   Fitting: the snaffle reins pass through the rings, beneath the horse's neck. Should use martingale stops as with the running martingale.

Breastplate

1. Hunting-type breastplate. A neck strap attached to the front 'D's of the saddle on each side of the wither, and to the girth between the forelegs. It purpose is to prevent the saddle from slipping back. When fitted, the neck strap should allow a hand at the withers. The straps joined to the girth and the 'D's should be flat, without strain, when breastplate is in its proper position. If a martingale is necessary as well as a breastplate, attachments for either standing or running martingale can be added to the breast ring.

2. Racing breastgirth. Web or elastic strap fits across the breast and attaches to the girth straps under the saddle flaps. Leather strap across the neck in front of the withers holds the breastgirth in position. Breastgirth must not be fitted so high as to restrict the freedom of the neck.

3. Polo breastplate. Similar to racing type but made of leather. Has a loop set on the inside in the centre of the breaststrap through which the standing martingale passes.

Crupper

Leather strap attached to back 'D' of saddle and passing under tail.

Purpose: prevents saddle from slipping forward.

Fitting: must be put on when girth is loose or undone. Stand close to near hind leg, gather up tail in right hand and pass it through the crupper. Draw crupper well up to top of tail, and smooth all the hairs. Adjust length of crupper so that it steadies the saddle. It should not be so short that it pulls the tail up. Usually used on ponies.

CHAPTER 9

The Back and Saddle Fitting

Parts Concerned
1. Withers.
2. Shoulders.
3. Girth.
4. Loins.
5. Spine.

The Withers

1. Should be well moulded and well clothed at the sides by muscle. The withers of a fat, unfit horse will change shape as he becomes fit.
2. Provide an anchorage for a number of muscles which attach the scapula (shoulder-blade bone) to the body.
3. The height of the withers provides a prominence which helps to give a seating to the saddle. Low, flat withers may cause saddle to slip forwards
4. Withers which extend well back are essential for a well laid-back scapula.
5. Thin, high withers make saddle fitting difficult.

Shoulders

1. Should be of a good length, with ample slope.
2. Degree of inclination of good shoulder, measured from point of shoulder to junction of neck and withers, should be approximately 60°. From point of shoulder to centre of withers (highest point) the angle should be 43°. From point of shoulder to junction of withers and back, the angle should be 40°.

3. The angle formed between the scapula and the humerus, at the scapulohumeral joint, may vary between 110° and 130°.
4. The degree of slope of the humerus is important. It may vary according to relative length of humerus and whether the elbow and forearm are set on well forward or well back. The elbow of the Thoroughbred lies farther forward than that of an indigenous pony.
5. A well-inclined shoulder gives free range of extension and flexion which improves action and increases the potential speed.
6. A well-inclined shoulder provides room for adequate muscular development. Good length of muscle is important.
7. Sloping shoulder is main anti-concussion device within forelimb. It lessens the jar as the weight falls on the forefoot.

The Spine

1. Composed of a chain of bones, each capable of very slight movement both up and down and from side to side.
2. The bony processes growing from the upper part of each vertebra (bone in the chain) form the ridge of the backbone. These processes are the seat of bone trouble which may be found in a sore back.
3. There must be no pressure on the spine from the saddle. Nor must the saddle pinch the spine (press the flesh against the bone). Pinching is not evident for two or three days but eventually causes swelling and possibly an abscess.

The Back

1. Extends from the withers to the quarters. It contains and is supported by 18 thoracic vertebrae, carrying 18 pairs of ribs, and 6 lumbar vertebrae, which lie behind the space occupied by the saddle. The first 13 vertebrae incline backwards and numbers 15-18 and the 6 lumbar vertebrae, incline forwards. The 14th thoracic (or dorsal) vertebra is considered 'the keystone of the arch' since it is the only one standing upright and a good saddle will place the rider in balance with the horse over this optimum point.
2. Back should be shaped in such a way that the saddle will stay on it, and will not slip forward or backward.
3. Should show a definite line and contour. Should never be arched and only slightly concave.
4. A 'roach' back shortens the horse's stride. Gives an uncomfortable ride.
5. A 'sway' back throws an additional strain on the back muscles.

The Ribs

1. Eight pairs of 'true' ribs – attached to the breast bone (sternum).
2. Ten pairs of 'false' ribs – carried by the ten rear thoracic vertebrae and not directly attached to the sternum.
3. The ribs project a few inches on either side of the vertebrae before curving downwards.
4. The weight of the saddle must rest on the muscle covering these horizontal parts, and nowhere else.
5. Some weight can be borne on the slopes of the front ribs which are stouter and fixed into the sternum. If weight is taken too low down – particularly with a slab-sided horse, breathing may be impeded.
6. The girth should not be too far forward, nor too tight, since the ribs behind the shoulder blades are capable of only slight movement as the horse inhales. Leave one hands' width behind the elbow before fastening the girth.

The Loins

1. That part of the back behind the saddle, containing the six lumbar vertebrae.
2. The loins are not protected by any ribs and should not support any weight.

Shoulder Blades

1. The forelegs are fitted to the trunk by large masses of muscle.
2. When forelegs move, shoulder blade bones move.
3. Any constriction by too tight-fitting saddle on shoulder blade bone will affect the stride.
4. To test for constriction – lift foreleg by point of hoof, draw it forward. It should be possible then to get the fingers between the saddle and the shoulder.

Causes of Sore Backs

Pressure. Stops the flow of blood, capillaries die and an area of dead tissue forms.

Friction. The outer protecting scales of skin are rubbed off more quickly than they can be replaced; i.e. excess of wear over production. (Can also happen in the horse's mouth.)

Sites of saddle injuries.

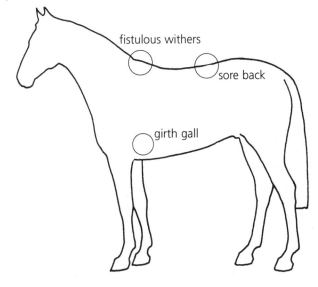

Pressure and friction can be caused by:
1. Poorly fitted saddle.
2. Improper saddling (panel flap turned under or wrinkled, etc.).
3. Dirty saddle lining.
4. Dirty or badly folded saddle blanket or numnah.
5. Careless riding – rolling or lounging in the saddle.
6. Unevenly placed loads.
7. Incorrectly fitted rollers.
8. Poor conformation.

Prevention of Sore Backs
1. Ensure that adjustment of saddle is correct.
   - Withers must not be pinched or pressed upon.
   - Saddle must allow absolute freedom of shoulder blades.
   - Loins should bear no weight.
   - All weight should be borne on the spring of the ribs. No pressure on spine.
   - There should be a clear channel of air along the spine.
2. Keep saddle lining clean.
3. If saddle blanket is used, ensure that it is clean and correctly folded. Saddle cloths and blankets must be very carefully put on or they will press on the spine and at least cut out the channel of air.
4. A wither pad is only an emergency measure. When used it should be pushed up into the arch of the saddle and not allowed to press on the withers or the spine.
5. The rider should saddle up correctly. Place saddle on horse quietly,

well forward of the wither and slide it gently back into position.

6. The rider should mount correctly. Hold the mane in the left hand and the front arch or the far side of the seat of the saddle where it joins the flap with the right hand. Do not put your hand on the cantle. Holding the cantle of a spring tree saddle may twist the spring, upset the balance of the saddle and cause a sore back.

7. Rider should sit in balance in the saddle at all times, to the best of his/her ability.

8. All stable clothing should be kept clean and should be carefully fitted. Rollers should be correctly adjusted to avoid pressure.

9. Before subjecting the horse's back to anything but short periods of pressure, it must be conditioned and hardened gradually.

Types of Saddle Lining

1. Leather. Long-lasting, easy to clean, but can be hard on a back during a long day's hunting.

2. Almost all saddles today are lined with leather but older saddles may be found lined with linen or serge. Linen can be carefully washed and serge thoroughly brushed.

Numnahs (Saddle Pads)

▪ Made of a variety of natural fibres, including cotton, felt and sheepskin and also from synthetic material such as nylon. The latter may cause the horse to sweat excessively and natural fibres are often more acceptable for competition horses.

▪ There is a range of modern numnahs, mostly of synthetic materials but of cellular construction, which claim to dissipate the weight of the rider evenly over the weight-bearing area of the horse's back, while avoiding unnecessary overheating or sweating of the back. Into this category could be placed the 'riser pad' type of insertions, which serve to raise the saddle from either the wither or the seat area of the horse's back, again with the object of better fit and weight distribution. It should be stressed that there is no substitute for a well-fitted saddle which is reguarly checked with regard to the musculature and condition of the individual horse.

▪ Numnahs are usually attached to the saddle by strap(s). Care must be taken to ensure they fit the horse's back and are put on without creases/folds and without pressing on the spine. Can cause overheating of back and predispose it to soreness but are useful on some thin-skinned horses, and for jumping and cross-country riding.

▪ All numnahs should be well mainained by regular brushing to remove hair and accumulated sweat, and by washing according to the type and material of the numnah. A neglected numnah may cause injury or damage to the horse's back.

Care of Back on Removal of Saddle

1. Do not remove saddle immediately if horse is hot or back sweaty.
2. The flow of blood to the parts on which the saddle bears is stopped by the pressure of the saddle. Sudden removal of the saddle causes blood to rush back into the blood vessels and they may be ruptured (known as a 'scalded' back).
3. Slacken the girth and leave the saddle in place for a while, allowing the blood to run slowly back into the blood vessels.
4. After removing the saddle, massage and slap the back gently to help restore normal circulation.
5. Remove saddle mark by sponging with warm water, walking dry and then brushing, if weather is suitable. If sponging is undesirable due to weather conditions, brush saddle mark off when back is dry.
6. If a horse is exposed to hot sunshine with an unwashed, sweaty back, the back may be scalded.
7. The horse changes shape during the period he is in work and the amount of muscle on the back will vary. Saddle padding may have to be altered to accommodate changes in the shape of the back.

Saddle Fitting

Measuring Back for Correct Fit

1. Take a piece of soft lead or stout electric cable 18ins (45cm) long.
2. Shape cable over the withers approximately where the head of the saddle would lie and press well down.
3. Remove cable from horse and trace shape obtained onto a piece of paper, marking which is the 'near' and which the 'off' side.
4. Repeat procedure to obtain a measurement 9ins (23cm) further back.
5. Take a final measurement along the length of the back from the withers.

Trying a Saddle for Correct Fit

- Saddle trees are made in a variety of widths.
- Laminated wood trees are superior to and less expensive than moulded plastic trees.
- Place saddle on horse and fasten the girth. In general, cantle should be a little higher than pommel (see illustrations overleaf), but much depends on the design. If pommel is lower, saddle may be too wide; if pommel is higher, saddle may be too narrow. Consult a qualified saddler for advice, especially regarding specialist saddles.
- Place rider in the saddle then check that there are still three fingers' width between pommel and withers and a clear channel of air through gullet.
- Check that panels lie flat on horse's back, not curved up. Weight

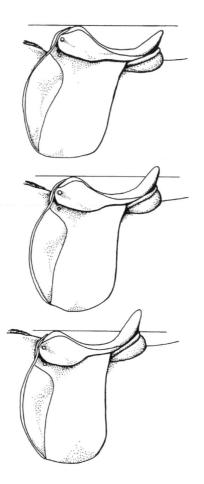

Incorrect. Pommel too high, with too much clearance below it. Deepest point of seat is not in centre of saddle.

Correct. Cantle slightly higher than pommel and deepest point of seat in centre of saddle.

Incorrect. Pommel too low, with too little clearance below it.

should be spread over largest possible area, not concentrated in two points under rider's seatbones.

Treatment of Saddle Sores and Girth Galls

1. Remove the cause. Note causes of sore backs, above. Girth galls are caused by working fat or unfit horse, badly fitted girth, dirt or dried sweat on horse in girth area.
2. Use nylon, cotton, 'Cottage Craft' type or Balding girth on unfit horses. Wrap girth in sheepskin or other non-chafing sleeve, or with gamgee tissue.
3. Stop work. If there is an open wound apply zinc and calamine ointment to take out soreness.
4. Don't allow horse to roll if in danger of opening wound.
5. When skin has healed, apply surgical spirit, methylated spirit or saline solution to harden skin.

10

Boots, Bandages and Rugs

Boots

Purposes
1. Protection of legs from injury by:
   - Blows – jumping fixed fences, etc.
   - Brushing – inside of leg near fetlock knocked by opposite foot.
   - Speedy cutting – inside of leg near knee knocked by opposite foot.
   - Over-reaching – toe of hind shoe striking heel of front foot.
2. Support of tendons of forelegs.
3. Treatment of injuries – i.e. poultice boot etc.
4. Replace lost shoe in competition – i.e. Easy boot.

Types
1. Brushing boots. Many different types. Lighter than polo or speedy cut boots. Protect limbs from injuries caused by brushing or interference by another limb.
2. Knee boot. Skeleton knee cap protects knees of young horse schooling over fixed timber. See also Travelling knee caps, below.
3. Coronet boot. Mainly for protection during polo.
4. Polo boots. Various types, usually similar to brushing boots but 1/4 or 1/2in. (0.6 or 1.25cm) felt. Usually larger than normal patterns with strong elastic insert to give tighter fit and more support.
5. Rubber ring. Anti-brushing device, fitted around coronet usually on one hind leg.
6. Speedy cut boot. Similar to brushing boots but fitted higher on leg. French pattern chasing boot also effective as speedy cut boot.
7. Heel boot. Protects point of fetlock which may come into contact with the ground during fast work or jumping.
8. Over-reach boot. Rubber 'bell'-shaped boot fitting snugly around lower portion of pastern, usually effective in preventing injury due to

Shoe replacement boot.

Over-reach boot.

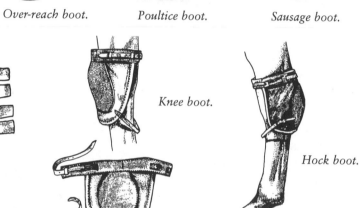

Poultice boot.

Sausage boot.

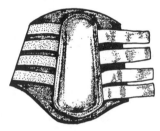

Brushing boot.

Knee boot.

Hock boot.

interference of the hind foot making contact with the heel area of the forefoot.

9. Tendon boot. Made with strong pad at rear shaped to leg. Affords protection from high over-reach and strong support to weak tendons. Usually open-fronted over the shin.

10. Sports support boot for eventing.

11. Hock boot. Thick felt or leather. Protects hocks while travelling.

12. Travelling knee cap. Protects knees while travelling. Must be carefully fitted so as not to hinder knee movement. Hock and knee boots often replaced with travelling boots.

13. Poultice boot. Accommodates foot and bulky dressing in the case of injury to the foot.

14. Stuffed sausage boot. Strapped around coronet it prevents recurrence in the case of capped elbow.

15. Kicking boot. Thick felt. For use on mares during service to prevent injury to the stallion if the mare kicks. Replaces hobbles.

16. Shoe replacement boot, e.g. Easy boot, Shoof. Fits over whole hoof, usually with wire-spring fastener. Made of hard rubber or plastic.

17. Yorkshire boot. A simple brushing boot made of woollen material and fastened with a wide tape. Only suitable for dry conditions.

Materials

Traditionally boots have been made of leather and fastened with small straps and buckles. Leather boots are still available but most are now made from man-made materials with velcro fastenings. If boots or bandages are to be worn during the cross-country phase of a three-day event, do not rely on velcro fastenings alone. Sometimes velcro does not hold if it is wet. It is advisable to use tape over velcro fastenings when competing to ensure security of the boots.

Bandages

General Rules

1. Never apply any one part of the bandage tighter than another. Uneven pressure, especially to the legs, can cause serious, permanent damage to the tendons.
2. Always use Fibregee or Gamgee padding when bandaging legs, for whatever purpose.
3. Do not tighten or pull bandage passing over tendons.
4. Tapes tied tighter than the bandage on a tail bandage may result in hair falling out. Tie tapes with the same tension as the bandage. Most bandages are now available with velcro fastening instead of tapes.
5. When bandaging uneven surfaces, or swollen legs, use plenty of Gamgee or cotton wool underneath.
6. Never leave any bandage in place longer than 24 hours. Most should be removed after 12 hours and replaced, if necessary, for a further 12-hour period.

Purposes, Types, Materials and Fitting

1. Warmth – stable bandages.
   - Used in stable or travelling.
   - Made of flannel or wool, or acrylic.
   - Usually 7 or 8ft (2 or 2.5m) long and 4½ins (11cm) wide.
   - Keep legs warm and encourage circulation.
   - Fitting – start immediately below knee or hock, continue down leg over fetlock to coronet. Must not be too tight.
2. Support – exercise bandages.
   - Also known as pressure bandages.
   - Used during work to support back tendons, reinforce weak or strained tendons, or protect leg from injury (thorns, etc.).
   - Made of crepe or stockinette.
   - Slightly shorter than stable bandages, and 2½-3ins (6-10cm) wide.
   - Fitting – applied over Gamgee or Fibregee with considerable firmness from just below knee to just above fetlock, enclosing

Applying stable bandages.

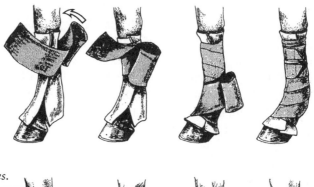

Applying exercise bandages.

sesamoid bones.

(i) Unroll 10ins (25cm) and hold obliquely across outside of leg close to knee.

(ii) Hold roll of bandage close to leg. Take one turn round leg and then allow spare end to fall down outside of leg.

(iii) Bandage neatly down leg over spare end.

(iv) At fetlock, continue to unroll the bandage up the leg as far as it will go.

(v) Secure as for stable bandage – most bandages have velcro closures. Tape should be tied on the outside of the leg. For racing, stitch bandage in place.

- Adhesive tape, 3ins (7.5cm) wide, over bandage, helps keep bandage in place in heavy going.
- Polo-wraps, made of heavy stretch plush fabric with velcro closure, are often used to replace crepe or stockinette support bandages and do not need Gamgee or cotton wool underneath.

3. Poultices.
   - Used to help sprains, and to draw dirt or infection from a wound.
   - If tendon sheath is torn and leg fills, a poultice is effective.
   - Use kaolin, antiphlogistine or Animalintex and prepare according to directions on tin or packet.
   - Poultice should not be applied too hot – should be bearable to back of hand.
   - Cover poultice with oilcloth or plastic wrap to retain heat.

- Bandage securely in place.
- Replace poultice every 12 hours until heat is gone from leg.
- May also be used on open wound to reduce swelling, and draw out infection.

4. Cold water bandage.
   - Used to reduce heat in leg.
   - Made of non-elastic material.
   - Steep in cold water and apply to leg. Change frequently or will become hot-water bandage.
   - Standing horse in running stream for 20 minutes at a time, two or three times a day, or hosing leg, is more effective.
   - Add Epsom salts to cold water to keep bandage cooler.
   - Re-usable ice-packs work better than cold-water bandage. Care must be taken if using ice-packs that the leg is not 'burnt' by excessive cold.

5. Stable bandage.
   - Used to reduce swelling or filled legs, or as a support to the leg adjacent to an injured leg.
   - For warmth in winter for an old horse

6. Pressure bandage, 'Equihose'.
   - Used in stable to reduce windgalls and swelling associated with strained tendons.
   - Stockinette or crepe bandages over Gamgee or Fibregee.
   - Object is to apply an even pressure to disperse swelling.
   - 'Equihose' is an elasticated sock on same principle as surgical stockings worn by humans. Made in three shapes: for tendons, fetlock and hock. Suitable for work or for wear in stable. Gives firm support while maintaining even tension throughout its length. May also be used to hold dressing or poultice in place.

Removing Bandages

1. Untie tapes or pull apart velcro and unwind bandage quickly – pass from hand to hand.
2. Never roll bandage when removing.
3. After removing bandage rub tendons and fetlock briskly with palms of hands.
4. Hang up bandages to dry and air.
5. Do not kneel near horse's legs. Bend or crouch to apply bandages.

Tail Bandage

- Used to protect tail from injury or rubbing during travelling, to improve appearance of tail, and to keep hairs of pulled tail in place.
- Made of stockinette or crepe 2½-3ins (6-10cm) wide.
- Never leave tail bandage on all night.

*How to put on
a tail bandage.*

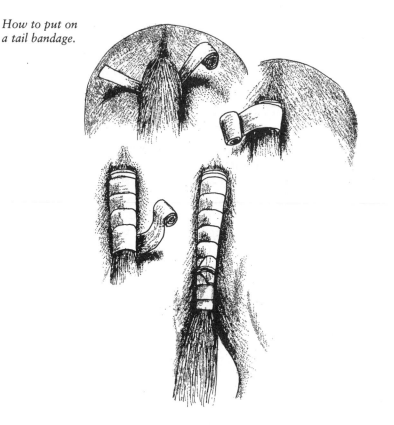

■ Do not apply too tightly and do not tie tapes tighter than bandage
or permanent injury to tail hairs may result.
■ To apply:
(i) Damp tail (never wet the bandage as this may cause shrinkage and
injury to tail).
(ii) Place left hand under tail. Unroll 6ins (15cm) and place under tail,
holding the end in the left hand. Keep the left hand in place until
spare end is secured.
(iii) After making two turns to secure bandage, make next two turns
above to cover hairs at root of tail.
(iv) Unroll bandage evenly down tail and finish just above end of tail
bone.
(v) Gently curve bandaged tail into comfortable position.
■ To remove: grasp bandage firmly near root of tail and slide off in a
downwards direction.

Materials and Fastenings
Bandages are now available in a variety of materials and many bandages
are made with velcro strap fastenings.

Rugs

Types
1. Day rug. Woollen, may be bound with braid.
   Purpose: warmth in stable during day. Maybe used for travelling to a show.
2. Night rug. Traditionally jute with wool lining but now replaced by a range of quilted nylon, cotton and polyester fill which are superior to the conventional jute rug. The best are shaped to fit the horse and have two attached surcingles stitched at an angle and crossing under the horse's belly, and do not require a roller.
   Purpose: warmth in stable at night.
3. Blanket. Woollen, worn under night rug and often held in place with a roller and pad.
   Purpose: extra warmth on clipped horse during cold weather.
4. Leather roller. Used on all above to keep them in place. Day rugs sometimes provided with rollers to match. Rollers are padded on either side of spine to avoid pressure directly on spine. A breaststrap, to prevent roller slipping back, is sometimes required.
5. New Zealand rug. Waterproof canvas, partly lined with woollen material. Also made of treated nylon, padded and lined, e.g. Weatherbeeta. Lightweight versions are available for spring and autumn wear, as are heavy-duty two-layer types for the worst winter weather.
   Purpose: for use on horse at grass. Not designed for wear in stable. Usually provided with attached surcingle and leg straps. Affords protection against wind and rain and may be worn as day rug by stabled horses turned out during day. Sometimes a hood is added.
6. Summer sheet. Cotton, usually provided with fillet string to prevent

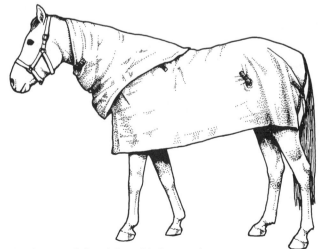

New Zealand rug with hood for added warmth.

Anti-sweat rug.

Multi-purpose rug – wicks moisture away from horse's skin.

sheet blowing up in the wind.

Purpose: protects groomed horse against dust and flies. Maybe used as an extra layer and easily washable lining under wool or nylon rugs.

7. Anti-sweat rug. Open cotton mesh.

   Purpose: used either as sheet or cooler, in summer. May be used under night rug for horse inclined to 'break out' after hunting, etc.

8. Multi-purpose rug. Made from 'breathable', quilted layers of thermal knitted fabric. Designed to wick away moisture from the horse's skin, allowing horse to dry comfortably.

   Purpose: can be used as an anti-sweat rug, after exercise, or any time horse needs to dry off. Useful as a light stable rug, for travelling, or as an extra layer under winter rugs.

9. Quarter sheet/exercise sheet. Generally intended for winter riding,

these are usually waterproof and lined with wool, or sometimes just of wool for warmth. Fluorescent exercise sheets are useful when riding on the roads.

Purpose: to protect clipped horse during exercise. Fitted under the saddle, they should always have a fillet string to prevent rug blowing up in the wind.

10. Under garments/rug bibs – usually of nylon and/or polyester.

Purpose: prevent rugs from rubbing. They keep the underneath of heavier rugs clean.

11. Hoods and neck covers. Can be attached to New Zealands or stable rugs. Made of various fabrics, often matching the rug with which they are worn. Some stretchy Lycra types slip on over the horse's head; others tie with tapes.

Purpose: to keep horses snug and to help keep turned-out horses clean. Also useful when training an unruly mane to lie to one side.

Fitting

Correct fitting of night rug, in particular, is very important. All rugs should be fitted so as to avoid pressure on the spine which may cause damage to the back.

- Rugs with two attached surcingles most satisfactory.
- Separate roller, either leather or web, less satisfactory. Rollers must be carefully fitted and kept well stuffed. Breaststrap prevents roller slipping back and avoids the need to girth up tight.
- To prevent rug from rubbing top of neck, forward of withers and points of shoulders stitch a piece of sheepskin to inside neckpiece and shoulders or use undergarment (bib).

Care

- All clothing should be kept clean, regularly brushed and aired.
- All leather parts need regular oiling or soaping. Metal fastenings should be oiled and covered with film of grease.
- Summer sheets may be washed but leather parts should be removed first and replaced afterwards, or oiled well once dry.
- Winter clothing not required during summer months should first be cleaned, then mended (if necessary), and stored with mothballs, between sheets of newspaper, until required.

CHAPTER **11**

Clipping and Trimming

Reasons for Clipping

1. To keep condition on a horse through winter months by avoiding heavy sweating.
2. To permit horse to work longer and faster without distress.
3. A clipped horse is easier to get clean and dry and therefore less liable to chills.
4. To save labour in grooming. After clipping, adequate clothing must be provided as a substitute for the natural coat. If the horse is not kept warm enough with extra clothing, he will use body fat to maintain warmth and therefore may lose condition and energy for work.

When to Clip

1. First clip usually left till winter coat has set, around early October.
2. Coat continues to grow after clipping. Clip as often as necessary, usually every three weeks until Christmas.
3. Do not clip when summer coat is starting to set – clip only once after Christmas, no later than last week of January.
4. Performance horses may need to be clipped in the summer to prevent sweating.

How to Clip

1. Ensure that horse is dry and well groomed.
2. If possible, clip by daylight. Clipping box must be well lit.
3. Allow horse to become accustomed to the sound of the clippers before actually using them.
4. Before starting, use soap or chalk to mark clipping lines above the legs and around saddle patch. (Saddle the horse and mark under the flap.)
5. Do not push or force clippers through the coat. The weight of the

clipping head provides all the pressure needed.

6. Clip against the coat. Take as much with one sweep as possible.
7. Leave difficult bits to the last.
8. It is useless to continue clipping if horse breaks out (starts to sweat).
9. Application of a twitch may have the effect of making horse sweat. Do not use one unless absolutely necessary.
10. If clippers get hot, stop clipping and switch them off. Continue when they are cool again. Hot clippers will make the horse restless.

Care and Use of Clippers

1. Clippers must always be earthed, with a three-point plug and should be used with a circuit breaker to interrupt the electrical flow in the case of an emergency short-circuit.
2. Arrange all cables so that horse cannot step on them.
3. Keep clippers clean and well oiled. Blades may be run in paraffin or blade wash for cleaning but must be dried and oiled afterwards to prevent rusting.
4. Clean and oil frequently during operation.
5. The tension of the blades should be just sufficient to clip. New blades can be slackened off after they have started to clip.
6. Keep a spare set of sharpened blades to hand.
7. Never clip with dull blades – have them sharpened regularly.
8. When not in use store clippers, cleaned and oiled, in a safe, dry place. Store the blades separately, they should not be left attached to the machine. Blades and head break very easily if machine is dropped or knocked from shelf.

Types of Clipping Machine

1. Hand clippers. Slow and laborious. Useful for clipping whiskers etc.
2. Electric clippers.
   ▪ Motor and clipping head in one. The motor is held in the hand. Power source may be mains, a car battery or battery pack carried round clipper's waist. Advantage: easy to handle, portable. Disadvantage: inclined to overheat and get clogged with hairs.
   ▪ Small hand battery-operated clippers. Good for muzzles, faces and sensitive areas with fine hair. Advantage: quiet and useful for sensitive areas; cordless; some types rechargeable. Disadvantage: not appropriate for large areas.
   Note: All the machines described are made by various manufacturers. The best and most well known are: Wolseley, Hauptner, and Lister.

Types of Clip

1. Full hunter clip. The whole coat is removed. Usually only done the first time of clipping, after which the hunter clip is recommended.

2. Hunter clip. Legs, as far as elbows and thighs, are left unclipped. Leaving hair on legs protects them from cold, thorns, mud and cracked heels. Saddle patch is left unclipped which prevents back becoming sore or scalded.

3. Blanket clip. Suitable for horses being worked lightly. Hair is removed from the neck and belly. A blanket-shaped patch is left on the body.

4. Trace clip. Useful for ponies and horses in light work. Hair is removed from the belly, tops of the legs, and a line half way down the neck and along the flank. Good compromise for ponies living out who must also work and hunt in winter. In most cases they should wear a New Zealand rug in winter if living out.

5. Belly clip or 'neck and tum'. Another useful pony clip. Hair is clipped down the throat and under the belly so that the pony can still winter out with no rug but will not sweat excessively when lightly worked.

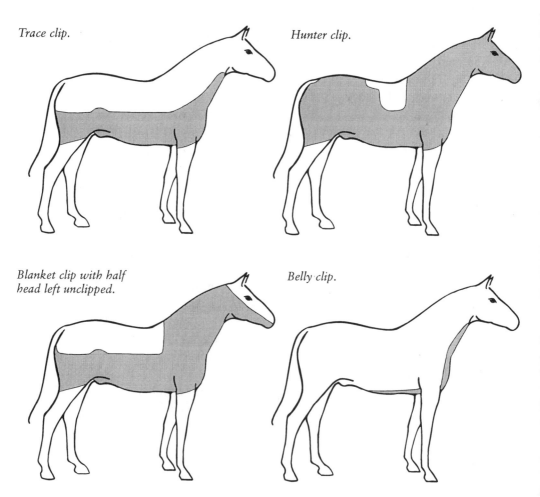

Trace clip.

Hunter clip.

Blanket clip with half head left unclipped.

Belly clip.

Where Not to Clip

1. Whiskers. These are the horse's chief organ of touch. Should be left on except in case of constantly stabled horses, when they may be removed to improve appearance.
2. Ears. Should never be clipped inside. May be clipped level with the lobes. (The hair inside the ears is a protection from cold and a filter for dirt and bugs.)
3. Cat hairs. May be removed with small cordless clippers or by singeing – see below.
4. Heels and fetlocks. May be trimmed with scissors and comb if necessary. (Remember, the horse's 'feather' is the natural means by which water is prevented from collecting in the heels, and causing cracked heels.)

Singeing

This is the removal of long hairs (cat hairs) which appear in various parts of the coat after clipping. A singeing lamp, which gives a small flame, is passed lightly over the body. Lamp must be kept moving in order to avoid burning the horse. This is an old-fashioned and largely unused method of dealing with cat hairs.

Mane Care

Pulling

- To thin an over-thick mane.
- To shorten a long mane.
- To permit mane to lie flat.

Method:

(i) Pull after exercise or on warm day when pores are open.

(ii) Remove long hairs from underneath first. Wind a few at a time around comb and pluck briskly out.

(iii) Never pull the top hair, nor any hairs which stand up after plaiting, as this will form an upright fringe on the crest.

(iv) Never use scissors or clippers on the mane, except to hog.

Hogging

- To eliminate work involved in the care of the mane.
- Also used when horse grows ragged mane which spoils appearance.

Method:

(i) Mane is completely removed with clippers.

(ii) Horse's head should be held low, crest stretched (assistant should stand in front holding ears and gently bring head down).

(iii) Use clippers working from withers towards poll.

(iv) Hogging needs to be repeated every three to four weeks.

(v) Once hogged, a mane takes two years to grow out and may never regain its former appearance.

Plaiting (Braiding)

- To show off neck and crest.
- To train mane to fall on the desired side of the neck.
- For neatness.

Method:

(i) Dampen mane with wet water brush.

(ii) Divide mane into required number of equal parts (usually an even number counting forelock).

(iii) Commence plaiting with first section immediately behind ears.

(iv) Threequarters of the way down the plait take a piece of thread and join into plait.

(v) When plait is completed, loop ends of thread round plait and pull tight.

(vi) Having completed all plaits (which should be approximately equal in length if mane is properly pulled) pass both ends of thread through the eye of the needle and push needle through plait from underneath, near the crest.

(vii) Remove needle. Bind thread tightly round the plait. Cut off spare ends with scissors.

(viii) Plait may be secured with rubber band instead of thread. Loop the band several times round the end of finished plait. Turn end of plait underneath and loop the band round the whole until secure. Plaits are often secured with white tape on dressage horses.

Plaiting the mane.

French Braiding

- To show off neck and crest and for neatness on horse with long mane which must not be pulled, for example Arabian or Andalusian horses.

Method:

(i) Dampen mane thoroughly with wet water brush.

(ii) Starting at the poll, carefully divide three equal bunches of hair and start plaiting, keeping the plait as close as possible to the crest.

(iii) Continuously add in one new section every 2 or 3ins (5 or 7.5cm) if mane is thick; a little farther apart if mane is thin.

(iv) Keep braid as high up on crest as possible but do not pull it too tight.

(v) When you reach the end, at the withers, continue to plait remaining hairs to end, secure with rubber band or thread, and turn end under.

Tail Care

Pulling

- To improve appearance.
- To show off quarters.

Method:

(i) Groom tail well, remove all tangles.

(ii) Start at the dock, removing all the hair underneath. Then work sideways removing hair evenly on both sides of tail.

(iii) Remove only a few hairs at a time with a short, sharp pull.

(iv) The currently popular practice of clipping the hair on either side of the dock is a lazy alternative to pulling and creates an ugly 'butchered' appearance.

Note: do not pull tails of horses or ponies living out as they need full tails as a protection from the weather.

Banging (trimming tail hair at bottom)

- To show off hocks.
- Prevent tail from becoming straggly.
- To prevent tail collecting mud.

Method:

(i) Assistant places arm beneath root of tail.

(ii) Cut off end of tail squarely at the level of the points of the hocks.

A Switch Tail

Continue pulling to half the length of the tail. Allow the ends of the tail to grow to a natural point.

This method of tail plaiting produces a flat central plait. Tightness is essential for a neat result.

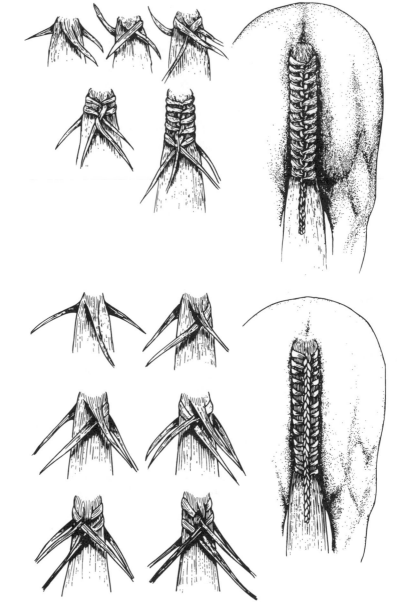

This method of tail plaiting produces a raised central plait. Always take in even-sized strands of hair and finish off neatly.

Plaiting

- Useful alternative to tail pulling.
- Improves appearance without depriving horse of the protection of a full tail.

Method:

(i) Dampen tail with wet water brush in dock region.

(ii) Separate a few hairs on either side of the top of the tail and knot together with thread.

(iii) Separate small bunches of hair on either side and plait in with knot which hangs down centre of tail.

(iv) Continue plaiting downwards in this way, gathering small bunches from either side, for about two-thirds of the length of the dock.

(v) Continue plaiting centre hairs of the tail only to form a free-hanging 'pigtail'.

(vi) Secure the end of the 'pigtail' with thread and loop it back under itself to the point where side hairs ceased to be included. Stitch loop together to form double-thickness plait.

Washing

- To clean tail.
- To improve appearance.

Method:

(i) Groom tail well.

(ii) Using a bucket of warm water, wet tail and work in shampoo. Use fingers actively.

(iii) Change the water and rinse tail thoroughly.

(iv) Squeeze out water gently with the hands and then swing tail to dislodge remaining water.

(v) Using clean body brush, brush out tail a few hairs at a time

(vi) Bandage with clean dry tail bandage.

Note: regular bandaging, after grooming, helps to keep pulled tail in good shape. Do not leave bandage on all night. To protect plaited tail during journey, bandage carefully. Enclose base of tail in an old nylon stocking to keep clean. Remove bandage by unwinding gently, not by pulling off in the usual way.

CHAPTER 12

Vices and Remedies

Kicking in the Box

Causes
1. Boredom – horse likes to hear the noise.
2. Idleness.
3. Irritability.
4. Rats and mice.
5. Parasites.

Remedies
1. Pad box or stall with bales of straw or matting. Play radio in barn – classical music has been proved to be calming. (Unplug radio at night to avoid fire risk.)
2. Line box with gorse (effective for horse who paws or kicks at door with front feet).
3. Hang a sack of straw behind hindquarters.
4. If possible turn horse out to grass for six months – he may forget and overcome habit.
5. Keep horse well exercised. Divide daily exercise into two periods instead of one.
6. If possible, keep horse outside all or most of the time. Horses kept at pasture seldom develop stable vices.

Stamping and Pawing

Causes
1. Same as for kicking, and also
2. Lack of bedding.
3. Impatience, etc.

4. Sign of internal pain or colic. Horse may kick or bite flank in response to pain.

Remedies
1. Removal of cause.
2. Good, deep, clean bed.
3. Some of the remedies for kicking will also help with pawing horses.
4. If colic is suspected, see Chapter 32. If in doubt consult veterinarian without delay.

Biting and Snapping

Causes
1. Mismanagement.
2. Irritation of horse by improper grooming.
3. Feeding of tit bits.
4. Failure to stop playful snapping in early stages – it soon becomes a serious vice.

Remedies
1. Firmness and kindness. Sharp slap on side of muzzle at the crucial moment will usually effect a cure in early stages.
2. Tie up confirmed biters before grooming, to protect groom.
3. Groom carefully and with consideration. Some horses are more ticklish than others. Avoid irritating horse by rough or careless grooming.

Crib Biting and Wind Sucking

Serious vices which constitute unsoundness. Crib biters take hold of projecting object with their teeth and swallow air. Causes damage to incisor teeth and may result in inability to graze properly. Wind suckers arch neck and swallow air, usually without biting on to anything. Swallowing air into the stomach is a common cause of flatulence and colic. Impairs digestion, often prevents horse putting on flesh.

Causes
1. Idleness.
2. Lack of bulk food.
3. Irritation of the stomach which causes a specific craving.
4. Horse may start cribbing by gnawing at manger when being groomed or by gnawing unseasoned wood.

5. Horses may learn crib biting from a stable companion.

Remedies
1. Prevent boredom – divide daily exercise into two periods.
2. Paint woodwork in box or stall with bitter aloes, 'Cribox' or other anti-chew mixture. Cayenne pepper is sometimes effective.
3. If possible, keep horse in loosebox, not tied up.
4. Have rock salt constantly available.
5. Give horse plenty of bulk food. Keep an unlimited supply of fresh, clean water constantly available to him.
6. A broad strap fastened round the thin part of the neck tightly enough to prevent the muscles contracting will help to check wind sucking. (Known as crib strap.)
7. Isolate horses who crib bite or wind suck as other horses are liable to copy them.
8. Recently surgery has been developed in which a small piece of the nerve on either side of the windpipe is removed. This has proved successful if performed before habit is ingrained.

Weaving

A continuous rocking or swaying action of the forelegs followed by a similar action of the head. Weavers cannot rest and deteriorate in condition. Bad cases may become lame. Starts as a habit, develops into a vice and eventually becomes a nervous disease. A horse which weaves cannot be warranted sound.

Causes
1. Boredom.
2. Nervousness – horse may be an intermittent weaver, only actually weaving when someone is in the stable.

Remedies
1. Remove cause, where possible. In case of boredom, apply same remedies as for crib biting. Horses do not usually weave if kept at pasture but may run the fence line if they have no companion.
2. Provide well-bedded loosebox. Encourage horse to lie down.
3. Two bricks, or tyres, suspended over the half-door so that the horse knocks into them first one side, then the other, as he weaves are sometimes effective, as are anti-weaving grille and parallel metal bars fitted to the door.
4. Avoid periods of idleness – or turn horse out to pasture rather than letting him stand in the box.

5. Isolate horses which weave as other horses may imitate the habit.

Refusal to Lie Down

Some horses suffer no apparent harm from refusing to lie down, but legs suffer and will last longer if rested.

Causes
1. Nervousness – strange surroundings, or horse may have been cast.
2. Lack of bedding.
3. If horse is in a tie stall, shank may be too short.

Remedies
1. Put horse in loosebox with deep, clean bed. Try different forms of bedding.
2. Give long, steady work for two or three days.
3. Bring horse in late at night (if he is tired and can once be persuaded to lie down, he may overcome his nervousness).

Eating Bedding and Droppings

A sign of depraved appetite.

Causes
1. Boredom.
2. Lack of bulk food.
3. Lack of mineral salts.
4. Worm infestation.
5. It is normal for foals of 2 or 3 months to eat the mare's droppings and it seems likely they do this to help in gaining beneficial bacteria for the colon.

Remedies
1. Removal of cause.
2. Bed on peat moss or shavings. Mix new and used bedding well.
3. Sprinkle bedding with disinfectant.
4. Horse may have to wear a cradle, or a muzzle.
5. Tie horse up before exercise so he cannot reach bedding or droppings.
6. Consult the veterinarian if habit persists, horse may be deficient in vitamins or minerals.

Tearing Clothing and Bandages

Causes
1. Horse trying to alleviate itching associated with a skin disease.
2. Idleness.
3. Uncomfortable in tight or poorly fitted clothing.

Remedies
1. Examine and treat for skin disease any particular spot horse bites.
2. Paint clothing with some nasty-tasting liquid.
3. Use leather bib hanging from back of head stall, behind lower lip. Or use muzzle.
4. Keep plenty of bulk food and salt available.
5. Be sure clothing is washed in pure mild soap, not detergents, and rinse very thoroughly.

Pulling Back When Tied Up

Causes
1. Fear. Young horse may pull back, feel the headcollar tighten over the poll and around muzzle, become frightened and struggle harder and eventually get free.
2. Past experience that he can free himself this way.
3. Horse kept tied in stall may start pulling back if there is too much slope on the floor. His forelegs are higher than his hind legs and he cannot rest, so he pulls back to alter position and forms the habit.
4. Horse kept tied in stall may start pulling back in order to reach his neighbour in adjoining stall.

Remedies
1. Prevention is better than cure. Never tie a young horse and leave him unattended. Train the young horse to accept being tied up.
2. An additional rope round the horse's neck, provided it is carefully secured so that it cannot tighten, will often help.
3. Use an elastic tie rope.
4. For horse tied in stall, fix a rope across back of stall to come in contact with hindquarters if horse pulls back.
5. Do not tie up – simply loop rope when grooming, etc., so horse does not feel threatened.

CHAPTER 13

Anatomy

To recognise an abnormality it is essential to be familiar with what is normal.

1. Horse comprises a head, neck, trunk, four limbs and tail.
2. The head and neck are freely moving and attached to an almost rigid body.
3. Head contains the brain and the sensory organs – eyes, ears, and nose. Mobility is necessary for their efficient use.
4. Head movement is also important because horses use their mouths as we use our hands, to learn about their environment.
5. The head, through the mouth and nose, provides the passageways for food and air. The continuations of these passageways in the neck are the gullet (oesophagus) and windpipe (trachea) respectively.
6. The frame is made up of a trunk divided into two compartments by the diaphragm, a sheet of muscle attached to the ribs.
7. Front compartment: chest cavity, formed by ribs, contains the lungs and heart.
8. Rear compartment: abdomen, formed by muscles, contains the stomach, bowels, liver, kidneys, bladder and reproductive organs.

Skeleton

1. Basis for whole body.
2. Made up of large number of bones articulated together at joints.
3. Joints are held together by ligaments.
4. A membrane, known as the joint capsule, covers whole joint. Outer layer is thick and acts as a support to the joint; inner layer contains cells which secrete synovial fluid (joint oil) which lubricates.

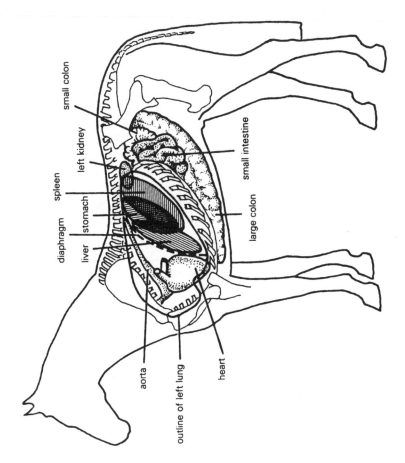

Thoracic and abdominal contents of the horse.

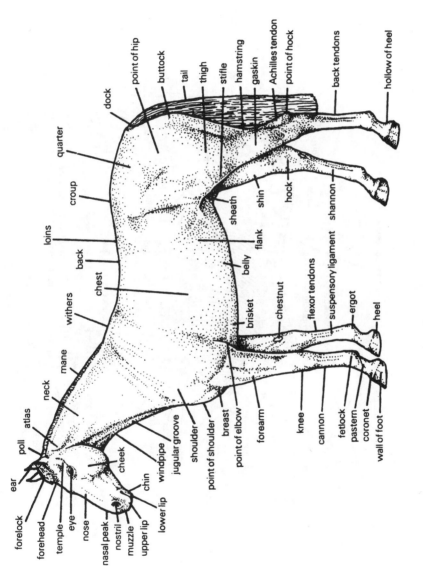

Parts of the horse.

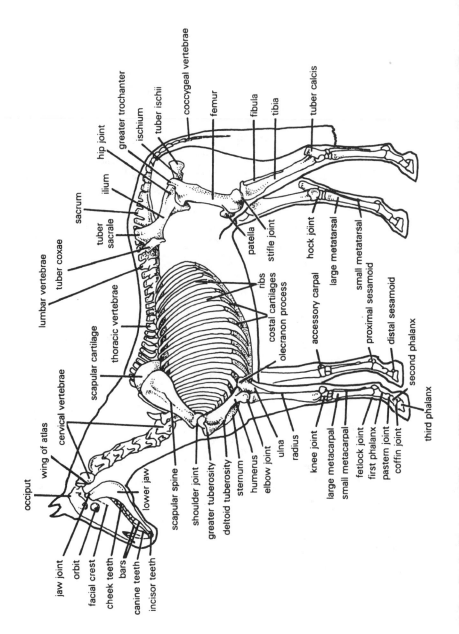

Skeleton of the horse.

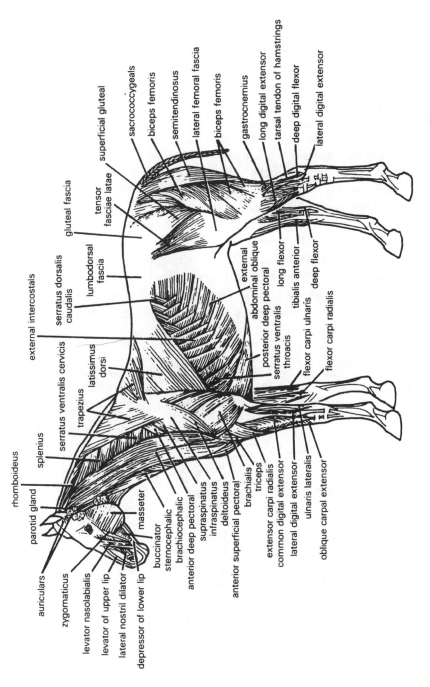

Superficial muscles of the horse.

Muscles

1. Posture cannot be maintained, nor movement occur, without muscles.
2. Muscles run from one bone to another across joints, and by contracting move one bone relative to the other, the movement occurring at the joint.
3. Muscles are distributed in two major groups: flexor muscles which bend the joint and extensor muscles which pull it back into position.
4. During standing, both groups of muscles contract simultaneously to stabilise the joints preventing either flexion or extension.
5. Each limb muscle is made up of two parts:
   ▪ An upper portion (belly), consisting of collections of red muscle fibres capable of great contraction.
   ▪ A lower part, or tendon, consisting of fibrous connective tissue attaching the belly of the muscle to the bone. The tendon transmits the pull of the belly fibres.
6. All muscles are supplied with nerves coming either direct from the brain or from the spinal cord. Impulses are transmitted to the muscle via the nerves to bring about contraction and movement.

   Note: the foot is so important a more detailed description of its structure is found in Chapter 25, The Foot and Shoeing.

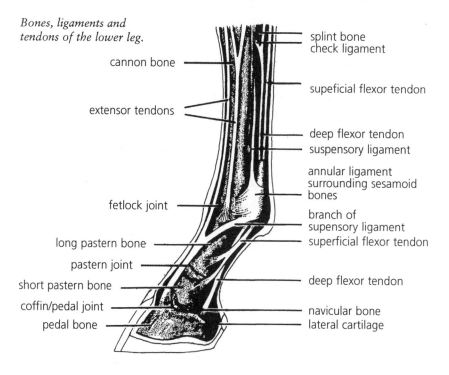

Bones, ligaments and tendons of the lower leg.

cannon bone

extensor tendons

fetlock joint

long pastern bone

pastern joint

short pastern bone

coffin/pedal joint

pedal bone

splint bone
check ligament

supeficial flexor tendon

deep flexor tendon
suspensory ligament

annular ligament surrounding sesamoid bones

branch of supensory ligament
superficial flexor tendon

deep flexor tendon

navicular bone
lateral cartilage

CHAPTER 14

Physiology

The Blood Circulation System

1. The circulatory system is based upon the heart – a hollow, muscular organ in the chest cavity. It pumps the blood around the body. The heart is divided into four separate compartments. (See diagram, page 116.)
2. Blood from the right ventricle goes to the lungs to be oxygenated and then is returned to the left atrium. From there it passes to the left ventricle.
3. Blood from the left ventricle leaves the heart through the aorta and is pumped all through the body in arteries.
4. Arteries repeatedly branch and diminish in size until they become microscopic capillaries.
5. Capillaries permit necessary interchange between blood and tissues. They eventually join up to produce veins, which convey blood returning to the heart, to the right atrium and from there to the right ventricle, and back to the lungs.
6. A horse of average size has approximately 50 pints (28 litres) of blood which circulate through his system every 40 seconds.

Functions of Blood

1. Blood is made up of two main parts: liquid, known as serum; and solid, consisting of red and white blood cells.
2. Serum acts as a vehicle for the solids and also carries the nutritive material, in solution, from the gut to all parts of the body.
3. Serum also carries impurities and waste products which leave the body via the kidneys and the skin.
4. Red blood cells carry oxygen, in solution, from the lungs to all parts of the body and return to the lungs to discharge waste gas (carbon dioxide) and absorb more oxygen.

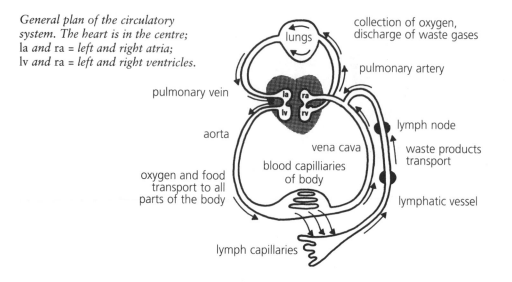

General plan of the circulatory system. The heart is in the centre; la and ra = left and right atria; lv and ra = left and right ventricles.

collection of oxygen, discharge of waste gases

lungs

pulmonary artery

pulmonary vein

aorta

lymph node

vena cava

waste products transport

blood capilliaries of body

oxygen and food transport to all parts of the body

lymphatic vessel

lymph capillaries

5. Arterial blood is bright red and venous blood is dark red because the compound formed between oxygen and the red matter of the cells is bright, but when the oxygen is given off and waste gases absorbed the colour darkens.

6. The white cells of the blood are called leucocytes. They are concerned mainly with fighting disease, both in attack and defence; they destroy bacteria and help heal wounds. Red corpuscles outnumber white by about 500 to 1.

7. Platelets help the blood seal wounds by congealing.

Lymph

1. Lymph is a colourless fluid similar in composition to blood plasma and derived from blood. It directly nourishes tissues and collects waste material from them to convey back to the bloodstream.

2. Plasma constituents exude through the fine walls of the capillaries into the tissue spaces. The cells are bathed in lymph which is then collected and transported in the lymph vessels.

3. The lymphatic system is an extensive system of vessels and their associated glands, widely distributed throughout the body, which plays an important role in the body.

4. Lymph vessels may be compared to the system of blood vessels throughout the body, but instead of containing blood they contain lymph.

5. Unlike blood vessels, the lymph vessels do not form a complete circle. They begin in the extremities and the organs as a system of thin-walled capillaries with blind endings which collect together to form

larger vessels and eventually flow into the large veins close to the heart.

6. Before entering the bloodstream, all lymph passes through one or more lymph nodes (or glands) which act as a filter to the lymph stream.

7. The larger lymph vessels have valves to prevent the backward flow of lymph.

8. There is a continuous flow of lymph, just as there is a continuous flow of blood. Having no special organ, like the heart, to drive the flow, the lymphatic flow is maintained by movement of the surrounding parts, e.g. muscles, tendons, etc. These massage the fluid along the vessels.

9. The purposes of the lymph stream are:
   ▪ To keep in balance the amount of salts and protein in the tissue spaces within the body.
   ▪ To maintain the proper fluid balance within the body.

10. Many conditions and diseases associated with the lymphatic system, e.g. 'filled legs' which subsequently 'walk down', are due to tissue spaces which are over-filled with fluid, and its dispersal by muscular activity which speeds up the flow of lymph.

Digestion

The digestive system starts with the lips and mouth and consists of the organs directly concerned with reception of food, its passage through the body, and the elimination of waste.

1. Lips. Gather food and avoid foreign matter (e.g. pieces of wire, etc.).

2. Incisor teeth. Cut off grazed feed for chewing.

3. Tongue. Helps position food in mouth for mastication by molar teeth.

4. Molar teeth. Reduce food to particle size and mix with saliva to prepare for swallowing. The enzymes in saliva start digestive process.

5. Pharynx (throat). Back of tongue pushes food down into the pharynx. Epiglottis prevents food from entering the windpipe and ensures its passage into the gullet.

6. Oesophagus (gullet). Food is swept down this dilatable tube by a swift peristaltic wave (muscular action).

7. Stomach. Comparatively small, U-shaped, and approximately the size of a rugby football. By contractions of muscles in stomach wall food is mixed with digestive juices. Proteins are acted upon by enzymes and converted into peptones.

8. Small intestine (about 70ft (21m) long, 2-3ins (2.5-7.6cm) tube). Digestive process continues. Divided into three sections: duodenum

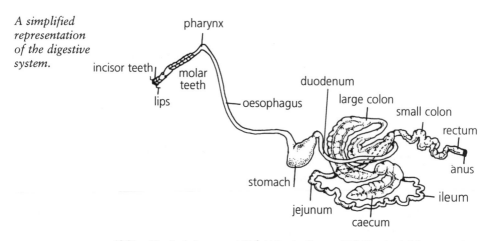

A simplified representation of the digestive system.

(39ins/1m), jejunum (60ft/18m), ileum (7ft/2m). Addition of protein-splitting enzymes. All protein reduced to amino-acids which bowel can absorb. Carbohydrate digestion starts. Sugars and starches broken down to glucose and absorbed. Stems of hay and other roughage are passed on to the:

9. Caecum a 3ft (90cm) long blind sac 8-10ins (20-25cm) in diameter. Bacterial population in the caecum has power to break down cellulose and convert it to fatty acids which are absorbed and passed to liver and converted to glucose if needed for energy.

10. Large colon. Food passes from caecum (at same end and near where it entered) into large colon. More bacterial action takes place. Food now composed of the indigestible fraction of intake and has most of moisture removed. It progresses to:

11. Small colon and rectum. Here it is formed into the boluses we recognise as horse droppings.

Notes

1. Mastication deteriorates with age because teeth become irregular.
2. The sweet smell of food and the motion of the jaws encourage saliva, which plays a vital role in mastication.
3. Horses should be encouraged to eat slowly. To do this, some bulky constituent such as chaff (chopped hay) may be added to the feed. This causes horse to chew rather than bolt food.

Elimination

1. The waste or unusable material which occurs in varying amounts in food must be eliminated from the body.
2. Any hampering of elimination causes ill health.
3. Soluble waste products are absorbed into the blood with food and

eliminated by the kidneys as urine or by the skin as sweat.

4. Insoluble waste products are eliminated by the bowel as faeces.

5. It is vital to keep all these systems working efficiently at all times.

The Skin

1. The skin is the largest single organ of the horse's body. It should be soft, supple and move freely over the underlying tissue. The coat should shine. The skin has three main functions:
   - To protect the underlying tissues.
   - To stabilise body heat.
   - To eliminate waste products in solution

2. Heat is generated in the body by muscular movement or other activity. It is lost by irradiation from body surfaces and by evaporation of sweat which cools skin surface.

3. Sweating takes place constantly but under normal conditions vaporises immediately and is therefore imperceptible.

4. Increased activity of the system forms greater heat within. The blood vessels to the skin surface expand to radiate heat and to stimulate sweat glands to produce more flow of sweat.

5. In a cold atmosphere the blood vessels to the skin contract, reducing the amount of blood circulating in the skin and sweat glands reduce their output.

6. Expulsion of sweat involves the activation of delicate muscle cells surrounding the ducts or pores. Sweating occurs in response to certain chemical substances circulating in the blood.

7. Under normal conditions a balance between heat production and loss is maintained best when the horse's body temperature is 100-101°F (37-38°C).

8. In abnormal conditions, e.g. an infection, the increased activity caused by the system's fight against the invader raises body temperature above normal but the skin glands do not respond, so the horse's temperature rises.

9. Eliminating waste products in solution with sweat is an essential role of the skin.

10. These channels must be kept open by:
    - Grooming – the massage brings more blood to the skin, stimulates sweat production, opens the pores and therefore increases elimination.
    - Clothing helps to prevent the decrease of sweat and closure of pores to retain heat in a clipped horse.
    - Exercise causes an increase in sweat production, opens the pores and accelerates elimination.

Note

Water is obviously essential to make good the losses that occur through salivation and digestive secretions, and excretions of the skin (sweat) and kidneys (urine). Horses suffer more quickly from lack of water than from lack of food and can become severely dehydrated and develop many intestinal troubles if deprived of water for even short periods of time.

The Nervous System

1. The brain and spinal cord form the central nervous system.
2. Every movement, function or sensation requires interpretation of an impulse by the central nervous system.
3. Every part of the body is plentifully supplied by nerves from the brain or spinal cord.
4. Nerves are of two types:
   - Motor nerves – regulating movement.
   - Sensory nerves – registering sensation.
5. Impulses are transferred by sensory nerves to the spinal cord. They are connected with a motor impulse which is passed out from the spinal cord, down the motor nerves to the muscles.
6. When a horse is tired, stimulation from nerve impulses will be weak or nearly absent.
7. These weak nerve impulses are the cause, for example, of some horses 'breaking out' (starting to sweat) on returning to the stable after hard work. Usually this occurs in nervous horses as a result of fatigue. Nerve impulses to the pores are weak so pores remain partly dilated and excessive sweating occurs. Sweat sheets and wool coolers may help, but horse needs reviving with easily digested nourishment, warm gruel, or 1lb (450g) glucose in warm water, for example.
8. Good horsemastership will prevent fatigue or, when it occurs, will bring immediate relief.

The Endocrine System

Consists of a series of important, hormone-secreting glands situated throughout the body. Hormones, chemicals which directly affect the horse's behaviour, are secreted directly into the bloodstream or the lymphatic system.

The major endocrine glands are:
1. The thyroid. Situated on both sides of the larynx, controls growth

and metabolism.

2. The parathyroids. Small glands close to the thyroid; control levels of calcium and phosphorus.

3. The pancreas. Close to the stomach; secretes insulin which controls blood-sugar levels.

4. The thymus. Situated between the lungs; controls immunity.

5. The adrenals. Close to the kidneys; produce adrenalin, the stimulant that increases the heart rate in preparation for vigorous activity.

6. The hypothalamus – at the base of the brain, activates the automatic nervous system.

7. The pituitary. Located at the base of the brain; together with the uterus and ovaries in the female and testes in the male, produces the hormones which control sexual cycle and activity; also male and female characteristics.

CHAPTER 15

Describing a Horse

Colour

1. Description should mention colour; breed; sex; age; height; marks on head (including eyes); marks on limbs, fore first, then hind, commencing from below; marks on body, including mane and tail; acquired marks, congenital abnormalities, whorls or other features of note, e.g. freezemark or brands.

2. Colour – principal body colours are black, brown, bay, chestnut and grey. Other colour types include palomino, Appaloosa, piebald and skewbald (termed Pinto or Paint in USA). Where there is doubt as to colour, examine the muzzle and eyelids.

Breed

There are nearly 200 recognised breeds and types of horses and ponies worldwide. e.g. Thoroughbred (abbreviated TB), Arab, Andalusian, etc. If of mixed breed or unknown ancestry, substitute type, e.g. hunter, cob, warmblood (usually a Thoroughbred cross).

Sex

- Stallion (entire male horse).
- Mare (adult female).
- Gelding (castrated male).

Age

- Age of horse can be determined from the teeth as described in Chapter 24.
- Thoroughbred racehorses are all aged from January 1st in the northern hemisphere. South of the Equator the age of a Thoroughbred racehorse dates from August 1st. Ordinary horses and ponies are reckoned from May 1st of the year in which foaled.

Ageing terms:
'Foal' – any baby horse up to 1 year although after weaning, usually about 5 months, the term 'weanling' is often used instead.
'Filly' – a female foal, up until two or three years; and a male foal is called a 'colt.'
'Rising' – a horse is said to be 'rising five' when he is nearer five than four.
'Off' – he is said to be 'five off' when he is nearer five than six.
'Aged' –
  ▪ in a sale catalogue means from eight years on up.
  ▪ in a racing catalogue means from six years on up.
'Full mouth' – this is the term employed to indicate that all the incisors are fully erupted – horse is 5 years old.

Height

  ▪ The height of a horse is measured when he is standing on all four legs, on a level, hard surface, head and neck in a straight line with the back.
  ▪ The height is measured from the top of the withers in a perpendicular line to the ground. For accuracy a measuring stick incorporating a spirit level in the cross bar should be used.
  ▪ Height is traditionally expressed in 'hands' (the width of a man's hand). A 'hand' is 4 inches (10.16cm). An animal measuring 14.2hh or under is classified as a pony. All height measurements for competitions and documentation are now expressed in centimetres.

Marks on Limbs

  ▪ Coronet markings – the hair immediately above the hoof is white.
  ▪ Ermine marks – small black or brown marks on white hair surrounding the coronet of one or more feet.
  ▪ Fetlock markings – comprising the region of the fetlock joint and downwards.
  ▪ Heel markings – extending from the back of the pasterns to the ergot.

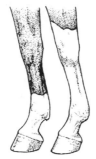

Sock (left) and stocking markings.

- Pastern markings – comprise the area below the fetlock joint and down – may include 'full pastern', 'half pastern', or 'three-quarter pastern'.
- Sock markings – extend to about half way up cannon bone.
- Stocking markings – extend to the region of the knee or hock.
- Acquired marks include injuries, firing, etc.
- Whorl – a circle or irregular setting of coat hairs.

Marks on Head

- Face markings – covering the forehead and front of face, extending laterally towards mouth.
- Muzzle markings – cover both lips and extend to region of nostrils.
- Star markings – appear on forehead (description should include shape, size, intensity and position).
- Stripe markings, extending down the face, no wider than the flat surface of nasal bone. If a continuation of a star – should be described as 'star and stripe co-joined'. If separate and distinct described as 'an interrupted stripe'. Specify whether the stripe is broad or narrow.

Star.   *Stripe.*   *Star and stripe co-joined.*

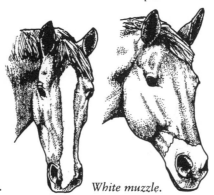

Blaze.   *White muzzle.*   *Snip and lip marks.*

CHAPTER 16

Conformation

1. Conformation – how a horse is put together – is a major factor in soundness of the limbs and often determines the useful lifetime of a horse.
2. Conformation is the key to a horse's movement, and movement often determines value.
3. Poor conformation of the limbs may contribute to certain lamenesses and could determine whether there will be interference of the limbs during movement.
4. Very few horses have perfect conformation, but in selecting a horse conformation should be carefully considered keeping in mind the intended purpose of the horse.
5. Look for a horse which presents a picture of ease and elegance, moves straight and freely, with each leg swinging foward without sideways deviation. He should stand square and balanced with 'a leg at each corner' and should give the appearance of being built 'uphill' with a good top line.
6. Conformation varies among different breeds, e.g. Arabians have a short back in comparison to Thoroughbreds; certain Quarter Horse bloodlines have shorter, heavier bodies and shorter legs than Thoroughbreds.
7. Desirable characteristics of conformation include:
   ▪ A head which is attractive and not too large, broad forehead, large, confident eyes, fine nose and wide open nostrils.
   ▪ Neck that is fairly long and well set into the shoulders. Not too thick, particularly in the throat latch area.
   ▪ Shoulders that are long and sloping, withers well shaped and reaching far back into a short, strong back.
   ▪ Loins should be short and strong. The hindquarters long and broad.
   ▪ The horse should not appear to be too long in the leg. The knees should be broad and flat, the forearm comparatively long and the

Good conformation.

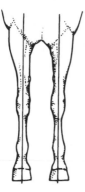

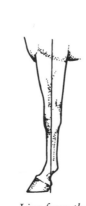

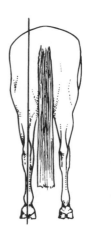

Line dropped from the point of the shoulder bisects the limb.

Line from the tuberspinae of the scapula bisects the limb as far as the fetlock and drops behind the heel.

Line dropped from the point of buttock bisects the limb.

Normal hind limbs from side view.

cannon bone fairly short.

- Viewed from the front, a line dropped from the point of shoulder should bisect the limb.
- The hind leg should be fairly straight, with long, well-muscled thighs and large hocks. Viewed from behind, a line dropped from the point of buttock should bisect the limb.
- The pasterns should be quite long and sloping and the feet well shaped and appropriate in size to the horse.
- The 'bottom line' should appear longer than the 'top line', which will be the case if the shoulder has a good slope.
- The skin should be fine and silky, and the muscles well defined and hard. The head and tail should be carried proudly. The horse should move freely and straight with long, regular strides.

8. If his conformation is good a horse is likely to move well.
9. Usually, a good walker will move well in his other paces. The walk should be long and swinging, with active, rhythmic strides. He should move straight and look better moving than standing still.
10. At trot, the horse should move straight, with roomy, unhurried strides and good rhythm. His joints should be supple and he should step well under his body with his hind feet, taking an equal length stride with each hind leg.
11. Do not expect to find 'the perfect horse' and remember that faulty riding and training can develop the wrong muscles. A horse's shape can be changed totally by correct work.
12. If a horse has most of the good points of conformation, a good temperament and shows quality he is probably a good one.

17

Preventive Medicine

Immunisations

Horses in the UK should be regularly immunised against: (a) **tetanus;** (b) **influenza**. In other countries specific conditions, e.g. rabies, rhinopneumonitis and Potomac horse fever, may require additional vaccination.

Administration

1. Most immunisations currently administered by intra-muscular injection.
2. At 2 to 3 months, foal should receive first dose of tetanus toxoid. Foal is protected by dam's immunity up to 2 to 3 months of age.
3. These shots are often given as a combined dose with a 1cc injection giving the first dose of immunity for tetanus and influenza.
4. A second dose is required 21 to 28 days later. Also 1cc via intra-muscular injection.
5. Annual booster shots are required thereafter, starting the following spring (i.e. about 6 or 8 months after the second dose).
6. Pregnant mares should receive immunisation 30 to 45 days before foaling. This will not only protect the mare but also the newborn foal and removes the necessity of giving newborn foals tetanus anti-toxin.
7. Many regulatory competitive bodies (e.g. BHTA, BHS) make vaccination against equine influenza compulsory for all competitive horses within their discipline. The usual official requirement is for two initial doses separated by 21 to 90 days, with a first booster 150-210 days later, and annual boosters thereafter. A current and fully up-to-date vaccination record for equine influenza is a mandatory requirement for many disciplines of competition in the UK.

8. Consult your veterinarian to set up your immunisation schedule, or if you are in doubt about the status of the horses in your care.

Intestinal parasites

Various types of parasites affect horses:

Stomach Bots
See Chapter 32, Warbles, Bots and Biting Flies.

Ascarids (round worms)
Adults are stiff, white and up to 1ft (30cm) in length. Generally about as thick as a pencil.
Symptoms
- In small quantities, rarely give rise to any symptoms.
- In large numbers may cause loss of condition, stoppage or irregularity of the bowels and intermittent colic.
- Foals from 12 weeks to one year of age are most vulnerable.

Treatment
- All horses over 2 months old should be wormed every 4 to 8 weeks.
- Regular worming is particularly important on breeding farms since the objective is to prevent contaminating the environment.
- Piperazines are effective against ascarids and best administered by a veterinary surgeon via stomach tube. (Tubing best avoided for young foals, better to use paste wormers.)
- First worming for foals should take place at 8 weeks. Use gentle, safe product: telmin, anthelcide, or other benzimadozole product is ideal.
- Ivermectin paste is also effective against ascarids but should not be given to young foals. (May safely be used at 5 months and older. However, if heavy infestation is present, it may be safer to worm first with benzimadozole product and then use ivermectin 30 days later.)

Pinworms (whip worms)
About 1³/4ins (4.5cm) long, very thin; occur in the rectum.
Symptoms
- Horse will rub his tail.
- Sticky discharge will be visible at the anus.

Treatment
- Piperazine, fenbendazone, mebendazole (telmin) and ivermectin are all effective against pinworms.
- Use paper towels or disposable cloths for cleansing the dock area

rather than sponges or towels, which may become contaminated with pinworm eggs and spread infection.

Strongylids – Large and Small Strongyles (redworms, blood worms)

The most harmful of all parasites. Up to ½in. (1cm) long and appear reddish in colour due to the blood they suck. Large strongyles have been well controlled by use of ivermectin. Small strongyles, of which there are many species, are the most dangerous parasites to the horse at all ages. The larval forms may damage blood vessels and intestinal organs. Because of short life cycles and huge numbers of eggs laid, small strongyles are a serious threat, especially where numbers of horses are pastured together.

Symptoms
- Colic, often repeated bouts, is the most common symptom.
- Loss of flesh.
- Anaemia.
- Hollow flanks.
- Dropped belly.
- Dry coat.
- Irregular bowel movements, occasionally diarrhoea.
- Worms may be visible upon careful examination of droppings.
- If in doubt, send sample of dung to veterinary surgeon for microscopic egg count.
- If left untreated horse will suffer excessive debility and eventually be unable to rise.

Treatment
- The benzimadazole group of anthelmintics (wormers), including thiabendazole, oxibendazole, fenbendazole and mebendazole, have all had resistant strongylids develop and are less effective than in the past.
- Ivermectin and pyrantel (Strongid) are the most effective wormers. Strongid is available as a paste for periodic worming, or as granules for continuous daily feeding in areas of high infestation or for foals and weanlings, which are especially susceptible to parasite damage.
- In any worm control programme rotation among different chemical classes of drugs can help prevent the development of resistant parasite populations. The three main classes of anthelmintics are the ivermectins, the pyrantels, and the benzimadazoles. Rotate by drug composition (ingredient) rather than trade name. Changing chemical classes every 6-12 months is sufficient.
- Spring treatment is the most essential to control greatly augmented adult worm population, but it is wise to administer wormer every 8 weeks year round.

▪ Regular worm count should be done on each horse to ensure effectiveness of treatment.

▪ Consult veterinary surgeon for effective rotation of worming medicines and always treat all horses on the property at the same time.

Control of Strongylids

▪ Pay particular attention to animals at grass, mares, foals and young stock.

▪ Dose all animals regularly.

▪ Avoid overstocking pastures.

▪ Mixed grazing is preferable to grazing horses only. Only equines are affected with redworm. Other animals will ingest the eggs and interrupt the life cycle, thus reducing infestation.

▪ Clean pastures by

(i) Removing droppings regularly from paddocks (must be done within 24 to 48 hours to be effective).

(ii) Allowing dung heap to rot thoroughly before ploughing in or spreading as top dressing. Heat of fermentation from properly built and maintained manure pile kills eggs and larvae.

(iii) Ploughing up and cropping for a year or two with a straw crop. Resow with a three-year ley.

(iv) Shut up pastures in turn and crop for hay. Two crops a year may be taken.

Tapeworms

Two species of tapeworm can infest the horse. Adults of both are tiny (0.39-1.8ins/1-3 cm) flat, white worms which attach to intestinal lining near the junction of the small intestine, caecum, and colon, and suck blood.

The tapeworm requires an intermediate host, a tiny insect (mite) which lives in forages and pastures.

Symptoms

▪ May be none, or subtle.

▪ Weight loss.

▪ Colic.

▪ Eggs are not usually seen on faecal flotation.

Treatment

▪ Once annually administer a double dose (twice the normal amount, given all at the same time) of Strongid paste or tube formula.

▪ Can treat in autumn or spring.

▪ Strongid-C (continuous) may be effective in preventing tapeworm development if fed entire time horses are at grass.

CHAPTER 18

Health Indicators

Signs of Good Health

1. Horse alert, head up, ears pricked (back and forwards).
2. Eyes bright. Mucous membrane of the eye salmon pink.
3. Skin supple and loose, coat bright.
4. Droppings should be regular and break on hitting the ground. (Horse passes eight or nine droppings a day which should be greenish or golden brown in colour, depending on the feed.)
5. Body should be well furnished (well fleshed out).
6. Temperature – 100° to 101°F (37° to 38°C).
7. Pulse – 36 to 42 beats minute.
8. Respiration – 8 to 15 breaths per minute.

How to Take a Horse's Pulse

1. Pulse is usually taken where facial artery passes under the jaw on either side.
2. May also be taken at the median artery, which is located in a depression in the centre of the inside surface of the foreleg, level with elbow.
3. The heart can be directly listened to by placing a stethoscope head firmly against the chest wall directly under the left elbow. Horses may have 2 to 4 heart sounds in one 'beat'. Count only the first, loudest 'lub' sound for 15 seconds, then multiply by 4 to get the rate per minute.
4. Pulse should be 36 to 42 beats per minute when the horse is at rest. Pulse will be considerably elevated following stress, but should return to normal within 10 to 15 minutes if horse is rested, providing he is sufficiently fit for the required work.

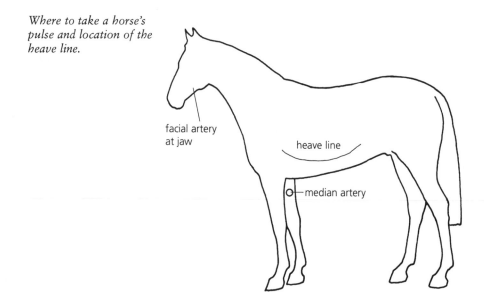

Where to take a horse's pulse and location of the heave line.

facial artery at jaw

heave line

median artery

How to Take a Horse's Temperature

Taken in the rectum. Grease thermometer with Vaseline. Gently raise dock and insert thermometer with rotating action. Leave in position for at least the stated time. Withdraw and read. Normal temperature of a horse is 100°-100.5°F (38°C) and of a foal from 100°-101.5°F (38°-39°C). A rise over 102°F is abnormal and a temperature of 104° or 105°F (40°-40.6°C) may indicate serious disease. Call veterinary surgeon. It is advisable to know your horse's normal temperature when well to be able to calculate the severity of a rise/fall when other symptoms indicate ill health.

How to Take a Horse's Respiration

Watch flanks from behind. Breathing should be even at rate of 8 to 15 breaths per minute when the horse is at rest.

To Test Horse for Soundness of Wind

1. Have horse trotted and cantered in small circle, on lunge.
2. As horse comes close, listen carefully for any noise as he inhales, or exhales.
3. Have horse galloped and then watch flanks.

4. If flanks appear to heave twice on exhalation, or if he has a 'heave line' it could be a sign of some respiratory problem. Seek veterinary advice.
5. Broken wind (heaves) is over-distention and breakdown of air vesicles (alveoli) of the lungs, often caused by allergic reactions to pollens or moulds in forage feeds, or by over-working or straining an unfit horse. There is no cure. In early stages some relief is obtained if all food is damped, the horse is kept reasonably fit and is not overstressed during work. Working the horse from grass or keeping him in an outside airy stable may also help.
6. Broken wind is not considered hereditary.

A Horse in Good Condition

When a horse is physically fit and able to undertake, without strain, the work which he may be required to perform, he is said to be in good condition.
1. Conditioning is a gradual process.
2. Conditioning depends on:
   - Good feeding.
   - Good exercise.
   - Good stable management. (Strapping and wisping.)
   - Attention to detail.

Good Feeding
1. Feed only top-quality forage, best grain and well-cured hay.
2. Feed little and often.
3. Feed at a regular time.
4. Horses brought up from grass should be fed a small amount of concentrate (up to 4lb/1.8kg per day) and hay only for first week or so. Change from grass to dry food should be gradual to avoid a tendency for indigestion and coughing.
5. Increase quantity of concentrates in accordance with increased exercise, as horse gets fitter.
6. Make no sudden changes of diet.

Good Exercise
1. Start with walking exercise. Build up over the first week to 40 minutes a day. After 14 days exercise should be about 1 hour daily.
2. In the third week, trotting can be gradually introduced.
3. Steady trotting uphill is excellent for muscling quarters and improving wind, as the fitness progresses.
4. Gradually increase grain from about 8-10lbs (3.6-4.5kg) with above

exercise, to 10-14lbs (4.5-6.3kg) when horse is in hard work (hunting, showing, etc.).

5. Fat acquired at grass is reduced and muscle develops with long, slow exercise. Do not canter or gallop when horse is fat (fast work is liable to affect wind and damage legs).

6. Horse brought up from grass towards the end of August will be ready for slow cantering in early October, 5-6 weeks into the fitness programme, and should have a gallop or two before the end of October, in preparation for hunting.

7. The gallop would be introduced as an extension of the canter work. A short gallop twice a week (Wednesday and Saturday) in the last two weeks prior to the day's hunting should adequately fitten the horse in his wind.

Good Stable Management

1. Clip as soon as possible. From end of September until end of November clip every three weeks, then once a month. Clip only once after Christmas.

2. Keep horse well clothed – wool blanket under rug.

3. Keep stable well ventilated, but close top half of door at night if very cold.

4. Thorough grooming every day is essential to good health.

5. When hunting, eventing or showing regularly horse needs exercise to maintain fitness. The horse may rest on the day after hunting or showing, though should be led out or turned out to stretch his legs. He will require exercising for 1-1½ hours on other days.

Recognising Lameness

Lameness is usually due to pain. In examining the lame (limping) horse try to avoid causing further pain to the horse.

Lameness can be classified as:

- Supporting leg lameness, where pain results when the injured leg bears weight, e.g. puncture or cut to foot, corns or abscess.
- Swinging leg lameness, where pain results from the movement of a non-weight-bearing part of the limb, e.g. damage to shoulder joint or strained shoulder muscle.

Causes of Lameness – 'Exciting Causes'

- Injury.
- Incoordinate movement.
- Infection.

Contributing Causes
- Poor conformation, e.g. malformed hooves, overlong pasterns, etc.
- Hereditary, weakness or predispositions, e.g. arthritic tendencies.
- Age, e.g. general stiffness.
- State of physical fitness.
- Type of work being done.

Diagnosis
1. Review case history. Before physical examination note: age, recent injuries, physical fitness, current diet, stabling, field conditions if kept at grass, shoeing, acute or chronic (did lameness suddenly happen or has it been exhibited more or less over a period of time), work horse is doing.
2. Examination at rest. Note:
   (i) Obvious injuries, i.e. cuts, bleeding, foreign object in foot.
   (ii) Abnormal stance, i.e. resting, pointing or carrying a limb.
   (iii) Abnormal shape of limb.
   (iv) Irregularities in shoeing eg shoe sprung, loose or missing.
   (v) Old injuries or scar tissue.
   (vi) Feel for heat, swelling or pain on pressure.
3. Examination of horse in motion, done at walk and trot always with a loose head.
   (i) Foreleg lameness is easiest to detect with horse moving towards you, hind leg lameness with horse moving away.
   (ii) At walk the lame leg has support of three other legs, at trot only its diagonal opposite. Lameness is therefore usually more obvious at trot.
   (iii) Foreleg lameness at trot:
      (a) Horse raises head as lame leg comes to ground. Head drops on the sound leg.
      (b) Lameness in both forelegs (e.g. laminitis) shows as short stiff, pottery action with both fore feet kept close to the ground.
      (c) Watch how foot is placed on ground, often a preference for taking the weight on the toe or the heel can be seen.
   (iv) Hind leg lameness at trot:
      (a) The hindquarter of the lame leg will be raised as the lame leg comes to the ground and lowered as the sound leg comes to ground.
      (b) Diagonal lameness may occur, which can be confusing and may result in incorrect diagnosis.
      (c) A hind leg may be dragged to avoid flexing a painful hock (e.g. spavin) or a foreleg may be swung to avoid bending a painful knee.
      (d) Have horse trotted up on hard ground and listen for an irregularity in the footfall, consider the shoeing, position of nail holes, if horse recently shod, foreign bodies in foot, damage to wall,

condition of frog and sole, heat, possibility of abscess in foot.

4. Palpation – feel for heat in foot and tendons (with foot raised). Compare with opposite limb. This takes practice and final diagnosis must be left to veterinary surgeon.

5. Percussion (tap lightly with small hammer) or compression (careful pressure with hoof testers) will show sore or tender area by flinching.

6. Paring – carried out only by veterinary surgeon or farrier, will reveal corns or pus in the foot.

7. The use of special diagnostic techniques, e.g. X-rays, nerve blocks, thermography force plates, and ultrasound, etc. may locate or confirm seat of lameness.

Treatment
Will depend on diagnosis but may include: elimination of infection, rest, electrical treatment, graduated exercise, steroid or other drug therapy, manipulation/physiotherapy, cold laser treatment, surgery, etc.

Conditions that Frequently Cause Lameness
1. In the foot. Foreign bodies lodged in frog, puncture wounds, abscesses, corns, bruised sole, thrush, ringbone, navicular disease, laminitis, pedal ostitis, faults in shoeing (pricked foot or nail bind).

2. In the leg – sprained fetlock, splints, spavin, curb, sprained tendons, check ligament, sore shin, cracked heels, sesamoiditis.

3. Remote – azoturia, rheumatic disease, wobbler syndrome, back injuries, poorly fitting saddle, etc.

CHAPTER 19

Sick Nursing

General Rules of Nursing

1. Good nursing is of primary importance in the treatment of disease.
2. Good nursing implies intelligent appreciation of the minute wants and needs of the patient; and kind, prompt attention to these needs.
3. Quiet is essential and patient should be placed in 'isolation stall' away from other horses, to avoid spread of infection and ensure quiet. Should be a roomy, well-ventilated loosebox. Do not confuse ventilation with draughts.
4. Bed down with plenty of short straw. (Ensures freedom of movement.)
5. Loosebox should have low half-door so patient can lean head over. Especially useful in diseases of the respiratory passages.
6. In cases of infection of the eye and nervous system, the loosebox should be darkened as much as possible.
7. Even in cases of wounds where horse must be tied up, loosebox is preferable to a stall – fresh air will circulate better.
8. Keep patient warm with light woollen clothing. In some areas, on some occasions, when the weather is very cold, the judicious use of artificial heating of the stable may be permitted. Sick horses cannot carry heavy clothing without fatigue, nor keep up body temperature by food. Never use artificial heating at the expense of ventilation. Stable bandages may enhance comfort and warmth.
9. Keep loosebox clean, dry and sweet. Use powder disinfectant to help keep floor dry.
10. Carry out all medication, fomentations, application of dressings, syringing, etc., with great care, at appropriate times as instructed by veterinary surgeon, and keep clear records of treatment.
11. Avoid noise and bright lights during night visits to the patient.
12. If horse is very sick, do not leave him alone. He will derive comfort

from presence of a sympathetic person. Also wise to have attendant on hand in case of crisis.

Warmth

1. Maintain warmth by light, woollen clothing. Bandage legs for additional warmth. Do not put heavy clothing on very weak horse.
2. Warmth may be restored to the body by gentle rubbing with the hands – especially to the legs of the horse.
3. To discover if horse is cold – feel his ears. If they are cold the whole horse is cold. He may also shiver.
4. Clothing should be put on loosely. Loose clothing is easier to wear and warmer than tight clothing.
5. Remove clothing gradually, shake and brush it twice daily. Never have horse completely stripped.
6. If circulation is poor, use a hood for added warmth (see page 95).

Watering

1. Unless instructed to the contrary by the veterinary surgeon, constantly keep in the box a bucket of fresh water at a convenient height.
2. Change water frequently. Even if horse doesn't drink, he will wash his mouth out periodically. In diseases with nasal discharge the frequent changing of the water is even more important. Stale water absorbs stable ammonia and is unpalatable.

Feeding

1. Maintain horse's strength as much as possible by tempting him with small quantities of food at frequent intervals.
2. Food must be suitable for requirements of case.
3. Do not try to force horse to eat.
4. The state of the appetite is a good guide to whether the system requires food or not. When temperature is high, horse is unlikely to eat.
5. Skimmed milk, diluted with water at first, will be taken by most horses.
6. As recovery starts, tempt horse by hand-feeding small quantities of a variety of foods, e.g. green grass, alfalfa, carrots, apples, linseed and bran mash, boiled barley, gruel, linseed tea, hay tea, and milk, etc.
7. Offer only small quantities of these unaccustomed foods and beware of over-indulgence.
8. Do not leave food in manger if refused by horse. Leaving it, even a short while, will dull the appetite.
9. The foods listed above are all laxative. A laxative diet is usually an important factor in restoring condition to a sick animal who is

confined to the stall, but remember also the importance of maintaining nutrition and consult your veterinary surgeon if in doubt about feeding programme for a particular patient.

Salt
Should always be present in some form in the loosebox.

Grooming
Whether to groom will depend on degree of illness. Consult the veterinary surgeon. Hand rubbing is beneficial. If horse is well enough, groom gently, taking care to keep him out of draughts. Do not strip him completely but rather 'quarter' him. Keep him comfortable by daily wiping of eyes, nose, mouth and dock (the latter using a separate sponge).

Exercise
1. Start gradually after all dangers of relapse have passed.
2. Do not start exercise without the authority of the veterinary surgeon.
3. First day – walk across yard and back.
4. Second day – lead out for five to ten minutes. Gradually increase exercise by a few minutes each day.

Bandages (hot fomentations, cold water bandages)
1. Renew hot or cold water bandages every half-hour.
2. Temperature of hot bandage should be no hotter than the hand can bear.
3. Apply above affected part and allow water to trickle down.
4. After application, cover area to avoid chill.
5. Legs may also be cold bathed by hosing, standing in a stream or bucket.
6. Alternate hot and cold applications can be beneficial not only to reduce inflammation, but also to stimulate blood circulation to aid healing.

Removal of Shoes
If horse is obviously to be laid up for a long time, have shoes removed.

Discharge from Nostrils
1. Encourage discharge by feeding from the ground.
2. Small quantity of Vick's vapour rub may be placed in outside nostril.
3. Steaming is beneficial. Place handful of hay in nosebag or corner of a sack; add one tablespoon Friar's Balsam, menthol or oil of eucalyptus; pour on a kettleful of boiling water. Hold mouth of sack or nosebag over horse's nostrils. Steam or inhale until vapours no

longer evaporate (10-15 minutes) 2 or 3 times a day. Avoid over-sensitising the nostril.

Disinfecting after Contagious Disease

1. Scrub stable walls, manger, etc., thoroughly with either: solution made up of two handfuls washing soda to one bucket hot water, or one tablespoonful Lysol to 1 pint (0.5 litre) water, or strong solution of Jeyes Fluid.
2. Wear rubber gloves and scrub thoroughly to remove all dirt and dust.
3. Spray with strong disinfectant to kill all germs.
4. Limewash stable with mixture of one bucket of limewash and 1 pint (0.5 litre) carbolic acid; or wash with 4oz (113g) bleach to 1 gallon (4.5 litres) of water.

Useful Medical Supplies

The following items should be available for first-aid use in every stable or tack room. Store items in box or cupboard in tack room or feed room, clearly marked with the veterinarian's telephone number:

- Veterinary clinical thermometer (in a case).
- Blunt-pointed surgical scissors.
- Gauze bandages – 2ins (5cm), 3ins (7.5cm) and 4ins (10cm).
- 6in. (15cm) Vetrap bandages or similar elastic non-adhesive wrap.
- Flannel leg wraps or 'polo' wraps.
- Roll Gamgee tissue.
- Roll cotton wool.
- Surgical tape.
- Several 1oz (28g) packets of lint, or non-stick gauze pads (Melanin dressings) and normal gauze pads (for cleansing).
- Antibiotic wound dressing, ointment or powder.
- Rubbing alcohol (antiseptic).
- Epsom salts.
- Bottle veterinary embrocation (liniment), e.g. Absorbine or Radiol MR Liniment.
- Oiled silk kaolin paste or packet Animalintex poultice.
- Mild eye ointment or saline drops. Boric acid crystals diluted with water can make mild eye wash.
- Poultice boot.
- Cayenne pepper (put on outside of bandages to prevent chewing) or Cribox.
- Fly repellent.
- Louse powder.
- Cooling lotion (e.g. witch hazel).

- Ice-packs (or hot and cold packs).
- Ordinary table salt (electrolyte replacement).

Prescription Drugs

Certain drugs will only be available on prescription through your veterinary surgeon (marked POM). Some items can be kept in a refrigerator and administered on the advice of, and with the knowledge of, your veterinary surgeon: e.g. Acepromazine (ACP) (tranquilliser) – however, do not use in colic or shock.

No drug should be administered to any injured or sick horse without first checking with a veterinary surgeon by telephone or in person.

Antibiotics

1. Group of substances derived from or produced by living organisms. Act mostly by preventing bacteria from feeding – in consequence, they die.
2. Action is different from antiseptics, which actually kill organisms .
3. New antibiotics are frequently being discovered but those in general use now are: penicillin, trimethoprim–sulfa combinations, gentamycin, and noxcel (ceftiofur). Antibiotics may be in injectable or oral forms, or may be in ointments for topical use in wounds.
4. They are used in treatment of wounds especially to avoid septicaemia following badly infected wounds, or for systemic bacterial infections, especially of the respiratory tract. Antibiotics are not effective against viruses.
5. Antiseptics have a strong cleansing effect but are indiscriminate in destroying live cells and invading bacteria.
6. The coagulating effects of antiseptics prevent the free flow of lymph carrying leucocytes to heal wound.
7. Antibiotics injected into the system combat infections which have already started in the blood. Some have a specific action on certain bacteria.
8. Antibiotics have little or no harmful effects on living tissue and do not coagulate the blood.
9. Antibiotics should not be used at the same time as antiseptics as the action of antibiotics may be destroyed by antiseptics.
10. Antibiotics should only be used on the advice of a veterinary surgeon.
11. Always consult a veterinary surgeon whenever young foals have to be treated with antibiotics as the actions and side-effects may be quite different from those in adult horses. Ask if an oral antibiotic might be appropriate to avoid the trauma of injections.

Effective First Aid

Abrasions
Many abrasions will heal by themselves. The less interference from man the better. Application of home remedies often delays healing.
- Clean wound, trim hair at edges of wound and apply wound powder or ointment (see Cracked Heels below), if minor. If in doubt, leave wound alone and call veterinary surgeon.
- Check horse has been vaccinated against tetanus. If in doubt ask veterinarian to administer a booster injection.

Antiseptics
Salt solution is preferable for cleaning wounds rather than antiseptic. Hydrogen peroxide (mix 1/2 pint (0.28 litre) peroxide with 5 pints/2.8 litres water) can help to flush out and clean a wound.

Colic
A horse with colic usually has to be tubed by veterinary surgeon (tube passed through nose to stomach for administration of appropriate medicine). The veterinary surgeon may inject muscle relaxants and/or painkillers.

Coughs
May be symptom of respiratory disease. Consult veterinary surgeon. For coughs associated with cold, damp all hay. A cough electuary recommended by veterinary surgeon and Vick's vapour rub are useful to have on hand.

Cracked Heels
If minor may be treated with wound ointment, or white Vaseline. If severe or persistent, consult veterinary surgeon. Prevention of cracked heels should include leaving adequate feather over the heels, particularly on horses living at grass, to protect the heel area from wet accumulation. Grease the heels of horses hunting or competing in wet conditions.

Cuts
See Abrasions.

Drugs
Never administer any drug without first consulting your veterinarian – particularly in the case of a sick animal who is already under treatment. You have to be an expert to know the effects of drugs and it is very easy to kill a horse by administering the wrong drug. All drugs are

potentially very dangerous – treat them with great respect.

Eyes
Normal saline solution available for contact lens use is an excellent eyewash, or use boracic (boric) lotion to aid in removal of foreign body from eye. An antibiotic eye ointment recommended by your veterinarian is useful to have on hand. Do not use cortisone ointments when an eye scratch or ulcer is suspected. In case of injury to eye, call veterinarian.

Girth Galls
Treat as abrasions. When healed harden skin with saline solution. Surgical spirit or methylated spirit may also be applied.

Hooves
A biotin supplementation (15mg/day in feed) is helpful for brittle, shelly or poor growing hooves. Raw linseed oil, Cornucrescine, Hooflex, or hoof dressing made up of equal parts pine tar and vegetable oil may be applied. For flaky hooves, put Stockholm tar in frog with newspaper over in stall. Feed corn oil (1 tbspn daily). Iodine and turpentine mixed and painted on soles is helpful for bruises and to harden feet.

Injuries
Help nature, do not hinder it. Redness, heat, pain and swelling all have a function.
- Pain tells horse not to use affected part.
- Swelling immobilises part.
- Heat means more blood is being rushed to area to help in healing injury.
- Never administer pain relievers (i.e. butozolidin) after a wound has been sutured. Horse will feel no pain and will use affected part, possibly pulling out sutures.

Leg Cooling or Reducing
Keep one of the following on hand: Fuller's earth, antiphlogistine, Animalintex, or Aintree Plast powder. For a liquid rub, mix Listerine and surgical spirit 50/50. Many new mineral ice-gels are also now available.

Poultice
Antiphlogistine, Animalintex and/or glycerine and Epsom salts should be kept on hand.

Proud Flesh
Caustic dressing must be applied but caustic materials inhibit healing –

consult veterinarian. Caustic dusting powder may be made up of 3 parts boracic powder, 1 part copper sulphate. Veterinarian may recommend cortisone covered by tight bandage.

Sore Back
Rest, do not ride. Inspect saddle. Apply antiseptic veterinary packs, or cooling lotion. Surgical spirit will harden back.

Strains
Radiol MR Liniment is a useful application. White liniment, antiphlogistine, and Animalintex may also be useful.

Worms
All horses should be on a regular worming programme recommended by veterinary surgeon. See Chapter 17, Preventive Medicine, under Intestinal Parasites, for detailed information. It is useful to have a wormer on hand, such as telmin or ivermectin paste, or another remedy supplied by veterinary surgeon, for emergency or intermittent treatment, or for treatment of new horse.

Thrush
Farrier should trim the frog to allow access of air. Soak affected foot in half bucket of warm water containing double handful Epsom salts, 10 to 15 minutes daily. Then pour antiseptic dressing or Stockholm tar onto affected area. Keep feet and bedding dry and clean.

When to Call Veterinarian

(Also what to do before calling and while waiting for veterinarian.)

1. Take temperature, pulse and respiration. If temperature rises above 102°F (39°C) call veterinarian.
2. Look at mucous membranes – should be salmon pink. Test capillary refill time. Press thumb against gum above incisor tooth. It will blanch. Remove thumb and colour should return immediately. If colour takes longer than 2-3 seconds to return, indicates shock or dehydration.
3. Observe droppings – should be normal in amount, colour, odour and consistency.
4. Has horse urinated? If so, was urine normal? (Clear, yellow no unpleasant or unusual smell).
5. Feel coat and skin – normal, hot and dry, cold and clammy, sweating (if so, where – patchy or profuse)?

6. Is horse nervous, looking at stomach, kicking, trying to lie down, etc.? (Suspect colic.)

7. Is there discharge from eyes or nose. If so, colour and consistency?

The above information should be supplied to veterinarian when telephoning.

CHAPTER 20

Transportation of Horses

Transportation by Air

1. This method now used almost exclusively for racehorses travelling long distances, also for teams of horses attending international events.
2. Air transport is far superior to travel by sea. Journeys take only hours instead of days; horses usually suffer no loss of condition.
3. Cost is high but transport companies now liaise with air charter firms and horses shipped in a full load cost much less.
4. Horses may be lightly tranquillised for travel by air but the advice of the veterinary surgeon should be taken on this subject.

Transportation by Sea

1. Very slow compared to transportation by air.
2. Cost is the same whether one horse is shipped or twenty.
3. Nearly all horses suffer loss of body weight and condition.
4. Horses often subject to coughs and virus attacks during shipping, or upon arrival at their destination.
5. Horses suffer considerable discomfort during rough crossings. On cross-Channel ferry crossings good ventilation is essential. Allow room for lorry ramp to be lowered in the hold.

Transportation by Road

1. Best way to transport horses overland, even for quite long journeys .
2. Preparations must be made in advance for over-night stops during long journeys.
3. Check with veterinarian on paperwork required for your destination

(e.g. negative Coggins (EIA) test (USA and some countries in Europe).

Trailers

- A common form of overland transportation.
- An economic way of moving one or two horses.
- Many trailers are too small in height and width to accommodate large horses comfortably for long journeys.
- Too few drivers of cars really know how to start, stop, turn or back with a horse and trailer.
- Car and trailer can be a dangerous combination.
- Many horses are soured for travel following bad experiences, loading, unloading or in transit in trailers.
- It is essential to regularly check condition of hitch, brakes, lights, connections and floor of trailer.
- Three inches (7.5cm) of straw, sawdust or shavings in the trailer help prevent jarring to legs on long journeys.

Motorised Horsebox

- By far the best method of overland transport for horses.
- Horse has plenty of head room (most important for young and nervous animals).
- Plenty of light and room inside the horsebox.
- Animal is not subjected to the buffeting around often experienced in a trailer.
- Many nervous horses who will not travel in trailers are perfectly happy in horsebox.

Preliminary Preparations for any Journey

1. Check horse for soundness. See that shoes are in good condition.
2. Veterinary examination is advisable to ensure that no contagious disease is present, especially if horse is to be sold.
3. Notify person receiving horse of approximate time of arrival.
4. Prepare equipment required at destination (if travelling to a show or competition).
5. Even for short journeys, e.g. one-day show, take bucket and water in water carrier.
6. If journey is to be long, prepare sufficient hay and feed for entire journey.

Actual Preparations on Day of Departure

1. Clothing will depend on climate, time of year, etc. Cotton sheet with

Dressed for travelling.

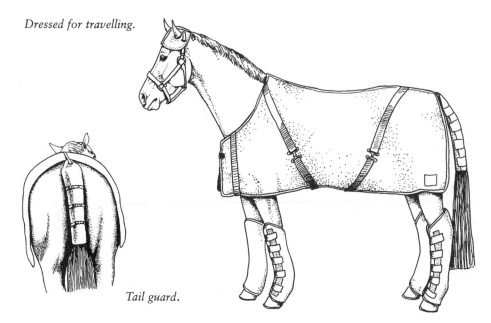

Tail guard.

fillet string may be all that is required. Take rugs, whether worn or not, for use during journey or on return from show, in case they are required.

2. Put on stable bandages, with plenty of Fibregee or Gamgee; or travelling boots.
3. Over-reach boots on forelegs are an added precaution.
4. Knee boots and hock boots are advisable, particularly on long journeys.
5. A tail guard will prevent injury to the tail or unsightly rubbing. For short journeys put on a crepe tail bandage under the tail guard. Do not tie bandage too tightly.
6. Leather headcollar should be worn in preference to rope halter. Should be strong, well fitting, with slightly longer than normal lead rope. If journey is long, pad headcollar with sheepskin where it may rub.
7. If horse is head shy or nervous use a poll guard.

Loading

1. If horse is accustomed to travelling, lead quietly up ramp, secure to ring or bar with normal length of rope, using a quick-release knot, and tie up a net of hay within easy reach.
2. If horse is difficult to load try:
   ▪ Loading stable companion first and follow up the ramp close on his heels.

- Tempting a shy loader with oats. In any case, shy loader should be rewarded with oats as soon as he is in the box and he should continue to be rewarded every time he is loaded until all his fear has been overcome.

- Using two lunge reins, attach one to each side of ramp rail, or on any convenient portion of entrance. Leave lunge reins stretched out on ground with one person ready to take hold of the end of each rein. Lead horse up to ramp quietly and stand him straight. Helpers now pick up lunge reins and walk quietly towards each other and pass each other, so that reins cross over and rest on the horse just above the hocks. Helpers gradually but firmly pull the reins or ropes from the sides so that they tighten behind the horse as he is led forward up the ramp.

- Load really difficult horses wearing a snaffle bridle as well as a leather headcollar. This gives handler much more control in case of horse attempting to rear, run away, etc. Handlers should take the precaution of wearing a hat and gloves for their own safety.

3. When loading horses, everyone present, except the person leading the horse, should stand well behind the line of the ramp and the horse's quarters. Standing in front of the horse's eye is enough to stop even a willing loader and will certainly stop a shy one.

4. Most carriers owning and operating horseboxes are experienced in loading difficult horses and the task may often be safely left to them.

5. During long journeys, arrangements must be made for watering and feeding of horses en route.

6. On journeys taking several days, where overnight stops are not planned, some provision must be made for exercising during short stops. Horses should also be closely watched as some will not urinate in a horsebox. Retention of urine can lead very quickly to serious health problems.

Insurance

1. Special insurance policies are available for the show season, or for short periods of time, to cover horses against show and transportation risks.

2. Most carriers with horseboxes for hire have policies which fully cover any animal against transit risks in their vehicles.

CHAPTER 21

Care of the Hunter

Day Before Hunting
1. Give horse normal exercise for 1-1½ hours.
2. Satisfy yourself that horse is sound. If in doubt, don't hunt. Heat normally comes to a leg before a sprain.
3. Check feet and shoes.
4. Check tack – stitching on stirrup leathers and reins, buckles on girths, etc.

Morning of the Hunt
1. Feed early – 3 to 4 hours before you plan to leave.
2. Muck out and groom in normal way. Try to avoid exciting horse by change of routine or he may not eat.
3. Leave plaiting of mane and tail until horse has finished eating.
4. If a stranger to the district, check the hunting map of the area so that if hacking you can follow bridlepaths to the meet. (Meets marked in red.) Always go to the meet; do not go direct to the covert.

Things to Take with You
1. Money.
2. Piece of string.
3. Clean handkerchief.
4. Folding hoof pick.
5. Pocket knife.
6. Antiseptic cream.

At the Meet
1. If hacking, do not hurry. Arrive at meet with horse cool and quiet.
2. Dismount and slacken girth. Walk horse around. Lead him on the grass and allow him to stale (urinate).
3. Tighten girth and mount. Keep horse on the move if it is a cold day.

4. If travelling to meet by horsebox or trailer, take horse out, tack up and walk and trot about for 20 minutes to loosen him up.
5. Before hounds move off, check girth.

During the Day of Hunting

1. Save your horse in the morning. Don't jump unnecessarily so that horse will still be fresh in the afternoon.
2. Always ride with judgement and spare the horse when possible.
3. At check, dismount, slacken girth, turn horse's head into wind to help him get his 'second wind'.
4. In plough, ride down a furrow. Try to stay on downwind side of hounds – it is easier to hear hounds and they are more likely to turn downwind.
5. If jumping into plough, go slowly – heavy landing may cause over-reach.
6. Ride fence with ditch on take-off side slowly and fence with ditch on landing side faster, to give horse chance to get more spread.
7. Jumping timber, gates, walls or any solid fixed fence, check horse well 40 yards/metres away, then present him to the fence.
8. Never jump on the heels of the horse ahead of you. Riding too close may cause a serious accident if the horse and rider in front fall.
9. Save your horse going uphill. Set steady pace, using good judgement coming downhill.
10. When the horse has had enough, go home.

On the Way Home

1. If going by horsebox or trailer, walk and jog alternately back to vehicle so that horse arrives there cool. Do not load a hot or sweating horse as he will catch a chill.
2. If hacking, walk and trot alternately. Bring horse home dry, cool and as quickly as is reasonably possible.
3. If horse is very tired, walk and lead him the last mile or so with loosened girth. This will help to prevent sore back by allowing circulation to be restored gradually.
4. It is inadvisable to give horse a long drink on the way home. Allow him one or two mouthfuls during hack home or before loading into horsebox or trailer.

On Arrival at the Stable

1. Do not remove the saddle if the horse's back is hot and sweating. Loosen girth and wait until he is dry before removing saddle.
2. On arriving at the stable, give horse a drink of water which has had the chill taken off. After about half an hour he can have more water.
3. Loosebox should be well bedded down ready and haynet hung up

before horse returns. Remove bridle. Throw rugs over horse (inside out if he is still damp), and encourage him to stale by whistling and shaking up the straw.

4. If legs are wet and muddy, put on woollen stable bandages over straw, quite loosely. Pick out feet and check shoes. Check heels for over-reach injury. Leave horse to have a mouthful of hay. Some people prefer to hose/wash mud from legs. If following this method cold water should be used and the legs well dried afterwards to prevent cracked heels.

5. Return in quarter of an hour or so to remove saddle (if horse is liable to roll, stay with him until you remove the saddle). Wisp or massage the back to restore circulation and keep it warm. Ensure all vital parts are dry; if not, dry especially the loins and throat area to prevent horse catching cold.

6. Check horse's ears – they should be warm and dry. If not, rub gently until they are.

7. Perhaps feed bran mash (see page 59). The laxative effect is good for a tired horse and will be appropriate the day before a rest day to help prevent azoturia.

8. When horse has eaten, start to clean him. Only clean the worst off, leave final grooming until morning. The horse is tired and should be left to rest as soon as possible.

9. Remove bandages from legs which should be dry by then. Brush legs, removing dry mud and checking for cuts and thorns (treat any cuts or thorn injuries found).

10. If horse is cool and dry, showing no sign of breaking out, put on night rugs. After he has been in for two hours, refill water bucket and give grain feed. If he is exhausted, feed boiled oats or barley with linseed as they are easier to digest.

11. If it is cold, or horse is exhausted, replace stable bandages (preferably over Gamgee) for added warmth and comfort.

12. Visit horse every hour until he is quite dry. Make sure he has plenty of hay.

13. In clay country, oil horse's belly and inside of thighs lightly with olive oil, neatsfoot oil or liquid paraffin before hunting to prevent clay from clinging. Use Vaseline in heels to prevent cracked heels.

Tack

1. Clean tack that night if possible.
2. Wash thoroughly to remove all mud and sweat. Dry with chamois. Leave to dry overnight. Soap thoroughly the next day.

The Following Morning

1. Undo breaststrap of rug, remove bandages. Trot horse out to discover

any sign of weakness or lameness.

2. Continue normal stable routine. Check horse carefully during grooming for any cuts or thorns overlooked the night before.

3. Exercise should consist of leading out, at walk (in rug if weather is cold) for half an hour or so, or turning out for similar time if horse is regularly turned out.

4. A hunter brought home by 3pm should be fit to hunt one to two days afterwards. If brought home by 5pm he should be fit to hunt four or five days afterwards. If brought in by 7pm he should be fit to hunt once a week.

CHAPTER 22

Care of the Competition Horse

Before the Competition
1. At least a week before a competition all tack and equipment must be checked thoroughly so that any repairs can be made in good time.
2. Shoeing should be up to date with stud holes in place if necessary.
3. Make sure that the horse's vaccinations are up to date.

The Day Before the Competition
1. Organisation is the key. To avoid arriving at a competition without something vital, make a list of all that is needed for horse and rider. The list will be lengthy if there is to be an overnight stay.
2. Remember to take essential items like the horse's passport/ vaccination certificate. Without these entry to a show or permission to compete may be refused.
3. Load your vehicle with the equipment from the list and tick off each item as it is packed.
4. Make sure that your vehicle is secure.
5. Plan your route and travelling times.

The Day of the Competition
1. Allow plenty of time for preparations (e.g. plaiting etc.) and for the journey.
2. To minimise anxiety to the horse, stick to his normal routine of feeding as far as possible. It is advisable to feed at least an hour before the horse will travel.
3. Allow at least an hour on arrival for collecting numbers and assessing the siting of arenas etc. If there is a cross-country course to be walked, more time must be allowed.
4. Remember to take into account each individual's working-in time when calculating your time on the showground.
5. Make sure that a declaration of your intention to take part has been

made to the relevant steward. This may require your tack to be checked.

Care After the Competition

Immediately after finishing a cross-country course or other strenuous test:

- Dismount and loosen the girth.
- Keep the horse moving so that blood continues to circulate well to help cool the horse.
- The priority is to cool the horse and this may require washing him off, particularly on a hot or very humid day.
- If the horse's breathing rate is reducing normally (he gradually stops blowing and is comfortable and at ease with himself) a sweat sheet or similar rug can be put on (this is not necessary on a hot day as the horse will cool more easily without).
- The horse should be quietly walked and after 5 minutes or so his saddle can be removed.
- The horse can be offered small amounts of water at frequent intervals to quench his thirst.
- As the horse cools, his boots and studs should be removed and he should be checked for any signs of injury.
- A fit horse who has competed comfortably within himself should be well on the way to normal pulse and respiration levels within 15 minutes. Continue to check him every 15 minutes until normal values return, which should be within an hour of competing.
- If returning home immediately after competition, the horse may be bandaged to travel and then have a small net of hay for the journey home.
- Assuming that all is well on return, the horse should be made comfortable, checked thoroughly, fed as normal for the evening and left to rest.

Day After Competition

1. The horse ideally should have had a restful night. Any unusual signs should be noted and taken into account (e.g. not finishing the overnight feed).
2. The horse should be thoroughly checked again for any signs of injury which may have arisen overnight.
3. The horse should be trotted up to determine that he is sound.
4. He should preferably be turned out, led out in hand to graze or walked to alleviate any stiffness from the previous day's exertions.

Note: Once a horse is regularly competing, the above routine should become a familiar procedure.

CHAPTER **23**

Roughing Off and Turning Out

General Considerations
1. Object of turning out – to give horse a complete rest and an opportunity to put on flesh after a hard season's hunting, eventing or showing.
2. Before horse is turned out he must be 'roughed off', i.e. prepared gradually, usually about 14 days is sufficient.

Roughing Off

1. Remove one blanket or rug.
2. If top half of the door has been closed, leave open all the time.
3. Gradually reduce the amount of grain fed and increase the amount of hay. When horse begins to feel grain reduction, reduce exercise.
4. Stop thorough grooming. Simply remove stable stains, mud and sweat with dandy brush. Leave the natural grease in the coat as protection against the weather.
5. After a week or 10 days, remove the second rug.
6. If possible, turn horse out in small paddock for an hour or so each day (in New Zealand rug at first, if necessary) to accustom him to being out. All horses when first turned out will gallop and play. If paddock is small and safely fenced, risk of injury is reduced.
7. When horse is roughed off, choose a mild day to turn out completely. Turn out early in the day and check horse at least once during the afternoon. If all is well, leave him out all night. Check him again next morning.

Time of Year to Turn Horses Out
Will depend on climate. In the UK it is not advisable to turn out Thoroughbreds and leave them out at night until first or second week

of May. If horse is an eventer the lay-off time may come in mid-summer. In this case turn horse out at night and bring in to stable during the heat of the day to keep him out of the flies. In areas where the hunting season finishes early due to damage that may be done to crops, rough off early (to save expense) and turn horse out during the day in New Zealand rug. Continue to bring in at night until weather is suitable to turn horse out completely.

Feet

1. If horse has good feet and is being turned out on to good land, shoes may be removed and feet rasped, to prevent horn from splitting, before turning out.
2. If feet are hard and brittle, keep front shoes on and remove hind shoes only.
3. Traditionally, hind shoes were removed and front feet shod with 'grass tips'. This procedure is largely outdated and obsolete.
4. Horses out at grass need their feet trimming once a month. Front shoes must be removed each month and replaced, otherwise toe will get too long and heel too low, causing pressure on the tendons and foot imbalances.

Legs

Bony enlargements, sprained tendons, etc. can be blistered before turning horse out, although the opinion of the vet should be sought as he will advise on current thinking of the value of blistering. The aim of a blister or type of counter-irritant is to produce secondary inflammation to aid healing of certain conditions.

Teeth

Examine teeth for sharp edges. Have them floated (rasped) if necessary. All horses should have their teeth checked by an equine dentist every 6 months.

Choice of Field

1. Choose field where horse has good range rather than small field. In a dry summer, a horse on a good range will come in hard. In a wet summer, if horse is in a small field, he will come in soft and fat.
2. Good safe fencing is essential. Post and rail is best. Ensure that fencing is free of loose strands of wire and broken rails.
3. Ensure that field is free from unnecessary hazards, e.g. pieces of farm machinery which may become half hidden in grass, broken bottles, etc.
4. There must be a plentiful supply of fresh water in the field. Running stream is ideal if sufficiently deep. An automatically filled water

Automatically filled water trough.

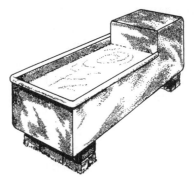

trough is also recommended. Ponds are not generally good – usually stagnant. (In clay country a pond has one advantage, horses stand and walk in the pond and the clay acts as a mild blister.)

5. Horses are gregarious and should not be turned out alone. An old pony makes an ideal companion for a valuable Thoroughbred – or when weaning a youngster.

6. Before turning horse out, feed some green fodder, alfalfa, etc., to accustom stomach gradually to green food. If turning horse into fairly lush pasture, feed him before turning out so that he will be less inclined to overeat on grass. If turning horse on to less good grazing, turn him out hungry so that he will be less inclined to gallop about.

7. The field should have good shade supplied by trees and at least one spot where horse can shelter from wind and rain in the event of summer storms, e.g. good thick hedge on windward side.

Care of Horses at Grass

1. Visit horses turned out to grass at least once a day.
2. Check for injuries, and lameness.
3. Check fences and water supply daily.
4. In the heat of summer, when flies are troublesome, bring horses into the stable during the day and leave with fresh water and small quantity of hay. Turn out at night.
5. Grass is at its best in May and June and horse will not need grain. By the end of July the grass deteriorates and horses still out may need to be given a small grain feed daily.

Bringing Horses Up from Grass

1. After a period of rest, horses should be brought in at least 6-8 weeks before hunting or competitions begin.

2. Feed small grain feed daily for last few weeks at grass.
3. It takes between 6 and 8 weeks to get horses fit for hunting or eventing. If left out too long horses come in soft, without muscle, and if hunted or evented too soon will lose fat without forming muscle and get poor.
4. When bringing horses in, there are three main considerations to keep in mind:
   ▪ Prevention of coughs, colds and sore throats.
   (i) Plenty of fresh air essential. Leave top half of door open.
   (ii) Horse must not be made to sweat during first week in stable.
   (iii) Feed hay well damped. Feed only small quantity of grain mixed with chaff and damp bran.
   (iv) Plenty of walking exercise is essential. As horse becomes fit, slow trotting uphill is an excellent muscling exercise.
   ▪ Prevention of sore backs and girth galls.
   (i) Regular saddle may not fit properly when horse is first brought in. Saddle must not be too tight or pinch.
   (ii) When exercising, stay on level ground at first, or lunge horse to harden before riding.
   (iii) Treat back to speed up hardening process (methylated spirit, salt and water or surgical spirit will harden skin).
   (iv) To prevent saddle rubbing, use a numnah (saddle pad).
   (v) If horse has sore place on back, use felt numnah with a hole cut out to fit over sore area.
   (vi) Harden skin on girth area in same way as back.
   (vii) Use 'Cottage Craft' type girth or sheepskin girth cover for first week or two.
   ▪ Prevention of filled legs.
   (i) Filled legs can be caused by over-feeding. Do not increase grain too quickly.
   (ii) Feed damp hay and damp bran with 3 or 4lbs (1.4 or 1.8kg) oats in two feeds or more, daily.
   (iii) Increase grain ration gradually according to exercise.
   (iv) Feed bran and linseed mash before a rest day. Linseed must be properly cooked – otherwise poisonous. When cooked it forms a jelly and seeds sink to the bottom.
   (v) If legs are filled, consult veterinarian.

Worming

1. Horse should be on a regular schedule of worming every 6-8 weeks. Consult veterinary surgeon for advice in rotating classes of drug used. See Chapter 17, Preventive Medicine – Intestinal Parasites.
2. Paste wormers are most commonly used today, which avoids difficulty of horse not eating whole dose.

Actual Work after Bringing In

1. First week – work on lunge, if horse will lunge in walk and slow trot, for 10 minutes, preferably twice a day. Saddle with numnah (saddle pad) to protect back and girth area from sores. If horse will not lunge quietly, walk out mounted for 10 minutes.

2. Walking exercise, mounted, for second week, starting with 1/4 hour, increasing to 3/4 hour. If convenient, horse may be turned out for an hour or so daily in addition.

3. Third week – walk on hard ground, or road (harden tendons). Slow trotting up and down gentle slopes, gradually increasing distance in succeeding weeks.

4. Fourth and fifth weeks – continue work as in third week and introduce short canters. Gradually increase slow canters.

5. Two weeks later – as canter work develops the stamina, the horse can have a brisk 'pipe opener' at half and then threequarter speed gallop to further develop the fitness, particularly in the wind. These sessions of faster work would usually be carried out twice a week.

CHAPTER 24

The Teeth and Ageing

Types of Teeth

1. Molars – grinding teeth.
2. Incisors – biting teeth.

The horse develops two sets of teeth:
- temporary, milk, or deciduous teeth; and
- permanent or persistent.

Molars
- There are 12 molars in each jaw – 6 each side.
- In temporary dentition only 6 molars – 3 each side.
- Molars form the sides of the dental arch – cheek teeth.

Incisors
- There are 6 incisors in each jaw.
- There are also 6 temporary incisors; these are shed as the permanent incisors come through.
- The incisor teeth are situated in front.

Temporary Teeth
Temporary, or milk teeth, are much smaller and whiter than permanent teeth with a well-defined 'neck'.

Permanent Teeth
Larger than temporary teeth and yellowish in colour.

Tushes or Canine Teeth
- Two in each jaw of adult male. Do not usually occur in female.
- Tushes are situated a little further back in the jaw than the incisors. They occupy the space between the incisors and the molars.

▪ Tushes appear at 3$\frac{1}{2}$ to 4 years and are fully developed at 4$\frac{1}{2}$ to 5 years.

Wolf Teeth

▪ These are molar-type teeth which frequently occur in the upper jaw, just in front of the molars.
▪ Wolf teeth have little root.
▪ They are a remnant of teeth well developed in the Eocene ancestor of the horse.
▪ Wolf teeth may erupt during first 6 months, and are often shed at the same time as the milk teeth behind them.
▪ If not shed, may remain indefinitely, and may cause discomfort and problems when bitting.
▪ Wolf teeth not shed should be removed by veterinary surgeon or horse dentist, as the bit is inclined to catch on them.

The Teeth as Evidence of Age

1. At birth – 2 central incisors may be present, in each jaw. These may not appear until 7 to 10 days after birth. There are 3 pre-molars – cheek teeth – present in each side of each jaw.
2. At 2 months – the lateral incisors are present.
3. At 6 months – the corner incisors appear.
4. At 1 year – all teeth are fully in wear, but corner incisors appear shelly/hollow (little wear on top). There are 4 cheek teeth present: the 3 pre-molars and the first permanent molar, which has just made its appearance through the gum.
5. At 2 years – incisors showing signs of wear. The cup-like cavities on their tables have disappeared. Molars form a better guide. An additional permanent molar has made its appearance. There are now 5 cheek teeth present, 3 temporary pre-molars and 2 permanent. Confusion sometimes arises between a 2-year-old and a 5-year-old. In the case of the male, tushes or canine teeth will be present at 5 years but not at 2 years. The 5-year-old will have 6 molars, the 2-year-old, only 5 molars. The 2-year-old will look young – tail may be shorter.
6. At 2$\frac{1}{2}$ years – permanent central incisors appear.
7. At 3 years – permanent central incisors are in wear. First and second (in position counting from front) molars cut through gums, pushing out first and second temporary molars.
8. At 3$\frac{1}{2}$ years – second pair of permanent incisors, the laterals, appear.
9. At 4 years – permanent lateral incisors in wear.
10. At 4$\frac{1}{2}$ years – third pair of permanent incisors – the corner teeth – are cut. The last two permanent molars (number 3 and 6 in position

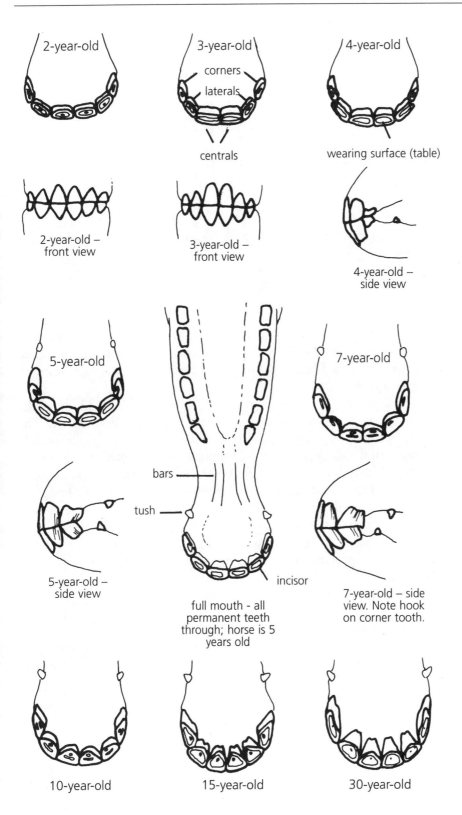

2-year-old

3-year-old

corners

laterals

centrals

4-year-old

wearing surface (table)

2-year-old –
front view

3-year-old –
front view

4-year-old –
side view

5-year-old

7-year-old

bars

tush

incisor

5-year-old –
side view

full mouth - all
permanent teeth
through; horse is 5
years old

7-year-old – side
view. Note hook
on corner tooth.

10-year-old

15-year-old

30-year-old

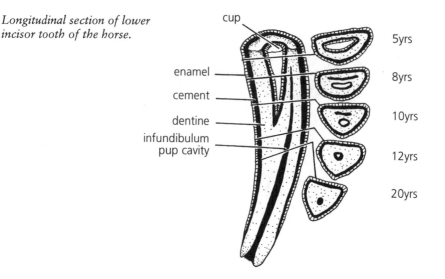

Longitudinal section of lower incisor tooth of the horse.

cup

enamel

cement

dentine

infundibulum
pup cavity

5yrs

8yrs

10yrs

12yrs

20yrs

counting from front) are cut between the ages of 4 and 5 years.

11. At 5 years – central and lateral incisors are in full wear. Corner teeth are well up and the inner and outer edges of their tables are level. Between 4 and 5 years, the tushes or canine teeth will appear in the male horse.

12. At 6 years – corner incisors now in wear. The infundibulum (the mark) of 2 central incisors may have entirely disappeared. The 'dental star' – a brownish or blackish line running transversely between the disappearing infundibulum and the anterior edge of the tooth – may sometimes appear on the tables of the central incisors. This indicates that the tooth has been worn away so as to bring the upper extremity of pulp cavity, filled with dentine, into appearance.

13. At 7 years – the infundibula have disappeared from central and lateral incisors. Dental star may be present in centrals. A hook appears as posterior edge of corner incisors in upper jaw.

14. At 8 years – the hook has gone. The infundibulum has disappeared from all the incisors. Dental star clearly apparent in central incisors.

15. At 9 years – dental star appears in lateral incisors. At 10 to 12 years it is present in all incisors.

16. Shape of tables – tables vary from oval to triangular as horse gets older. Up to 7 years tables are oval, from 9 to 13 years tables are rounder, after 13 years tables are more triangular and have a central pulp mark.

Galvayne's Groove

This is a well-marked, longitudinal groove, appearing on upper corner incisors. Appears as a notch just below the gum at 9 or 10 years and travels down the tooth. When the groove reaches half-way down tooth, horse is 15 years, when it has reached the bottom, horse is 20 years. At 25 groove has disappeared from upper half of tooth, and at 30 it has disappeared completely. Sidney Galvayne, horse expert and author of *The Twentieth Century Book of the Horse*, first drew attention to this groove.

Galvayne's groove.

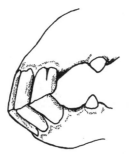

Bishoping
This is the practice of tampering with the teeth to make an old horse appear younger. A false 'mark' is burned into the table of the tooth with a hot iron. Even the most expert bishoper cannot restore the enamel ring which surrounds the infundibular cavity, and which in an old horse, will be absent.

Length and Angle of Teeth
As the table of the tooth is worn out by friction, the alveolar cavity (fang hole), in which the root is embedded, is gradually filled up, so that the tooth is slowly pushed out from its socket. This continues throughout life and therefore, at successive periods, first the crown next the neck, and finally the fang are actually in wear. As the horse gets older, the teeth appear to be longer due to the recession of the gums. The setting of the teeth also becomes more oblique.

The Mark or Infundibulum
A dark depression on the tables of the teeth. It is surrounded by a distinct, narrow ring of enamel which is easily seen and felt. In the new tooth, the mark is broad and deep, but it disappears altogether with age and wear.

The Crown
The portion of the tooth which projects from the gum. It is covered at first with cement but this wears off to leave the enamel exposed.

The Fang
The part of the tooth within the jaw. It is hollow and its cavity (the fang

hole) contains blood vessels and nerves which make the tooth sensitive and also nourish it. The fang hole is gradually filled up with dentine of a lighter colour than the remainder and, when wear reaches this level, it appears on the table as a small white spot in the centre.

To 'Float' (Rasp) Teeth

'Floating' teeth is rasping down the sharp edges and points which may appear periodically. The outer edges of the upper row of molars, and the inner edges of the lower molars, may become sharp with wear and cause injuries to the tongue and cheeks. Teeth should be checked by equine dentist or veterinarian every 6 months. Floating is usually required once a year but some horses may need attention more often.

Black Teeth

A young horse with black teeth probably indicates that the feed is rich in iron.

White Teeth

An older horse with white teeth indicates chalk in the feed.

Gums

The gums recede with age. As they draw back they change the angle of the teeth. The top gum recedes before the bottom gum.

25

The Foot and Shoeing

Structure of the Foot – External

The outside of the horse's foot, or hoof, is made of horn. The outer parts, though constantly growing, are virtually dead matter. This insensitive, horny covering of the sensitive structure of the foot may be divided into:

1. The wall. This is the part seen when the foot is on the ground; it carries the body weight. It is composed of three kinds of horn:
   - tubular horn – resembling fine fibres in appearance. Each tube grows from one tiny papilla of the coronary band.
   - intertubular horn – a glutinous horn substance also secreted by the coronary cushion. It cements horn tubes into solid-looking mass.
   - intratubular or cellular horn – broken-down cells deposited inside the horn tubes. Function is to convey moisture.
   (i) The wall is approximately 1/2in. (1.3cm) thick. It is thicker at the toes than the heels, but does not vary vertically.
   (ii) The wall grows constantly downward from the coronet. It takes 9 to 12 months for a new wall to grow from coronet to toe, and from coronet to heel from 4 to 6 months.
   (iii) The angle at which the front of the wall slopes should be approximately 50° in the front feet and 55° in the hind feet. The important angle to consider in shoeing is the hoof-pastern axis.
   (iv) The outer layer of horn is known as the periople. It is a thin, varnish-like horn which acts as a cover to protect the horn of the wall and prevent undue evaporation of moisture. The periople is secreted from the papillae of the periopic ring which is situated round the upper border of the coronary band and gives the wall a healthy, shiny appearance.
2. The sole. Composed of similar horn to the wall, but is not

constructed for sustaining weight, except at its junction with the wall. The sole, the ground surface of the foot, should be slightly concave and consists of two layers:

(i) Outer, or insensitive sole.

(ii) Inner, or sensitive sole – immediately above the insensitive sole and below the coffin bone. This sensitive sole is therefore between two hard substances and if subjected to undue pressure, it will be crushed and lead to great pain and lameness. Undue pressure may be caused to the sensitive sole by:

▪ Paring of the outer, insensitive sole. Such paring renders the outer sole incapable of protecting the sensitive sole.

▪ Mutilation of the crust (wall) and frog. The sensitive sole feeds the horny sole, which grows from it and is constantly flaking away. Only these flaking pieces should be removed when preparing the foot for shoeing. The sole should not be pared away indiscriminately. A flat sole increases concussion and is more liable to bruising.

3. The frog. The frog is composed more of the glutinous intertubular horn than of the tubular. It is tough and elastic. It only partially supports the coffin bone, which divides into the two processes which extend nearly to the heels. Between these processes is a large space, wherein lies the plantar cushion and below it the frog. This gives the frog great freedom of movement and provides the necessary elasticity of the back portion of the hoof. The frog has five main uses, which can only be fulfilled if it is prominent and well developed:

(i) Shock absorber.

(ii) Anti-slip device.

(iii) Partial support for the coffin bone and especially a support to the navicular bone.

(iv) Heel expander. Every time the frog comes to the ground, it bulges outwards, spreads the heels, and disperses the shock of impact outwards.

(v) Assists in circulation of the blood. Squeezes inner, sensitive parts of foot outwards against insensitive, unyielding horn, thus pumping blood back up veins of lower leg. Lack of pressure on the frog does not cut off blood supply to leg, but does impair it.

Obviously the frog should not be pared, except in the case of disease. With natural use the frog will become strong, and thrive. Without use it will shrink and eventually die.

4. The bars. A continuation of the wall at the heel. They turn inward at the heel and continue alongside the frog to about half way to the point of frog, where they merge in the sole. In preparing the foot for shoeing, the bars should not be pared away. They allow for expansion of the foot as it meets the ground, and assists in shock absorbtion.

5. The white line. A narrow ring or strip of horn between the sole and the wall, and forming the union of the two. It is soft, waxy horn of a lighter colour than the wall and sole.
6. The periople. A thin, varnish-like horn which covers and protects the young horn of the wall.
7. The horny laminae. Thin plates of horn standing at right angles to the interior surface of the wall. They interlock with the sensitive laminae (fleshy leaves) which cover the pedal bone and lateral cartilages, to form a secure union of the sensitive foot to the hoof. Approximately 500 to 600 of each kind of laminae are fitted into each hoof, thus giving a large bearing surface in a compact form.
8. The coronary groove. Runs around the top of the wall. The coronary cushion fits into this cavity. The cavity contains a large number of tiny holes, which are the start of the horn tubes of the wall. The papillae of the coronary cushion fit into these holes, each one carrying on the work of secreting new horn. The wall grows downward from the coronary cushion. Injuries to the coronet may be followed by defects in the horn.

Structure of the Foot – Internal

1. Bones. The foot contains 2½ bones:
   - Coffin or pedal bone. Pyramid-shaped, porous bone. Gives lightness to the foot, affords protection for the nerves and blood vessels it accommodates, and its roughened surface affords ample attachment for the tendons, ligaments and sensitive laminae.
   - Navicular bone. A small, triangular bone, like an elongated sesamoid, situated behind the joint of the pedal bone and the short pastern bone. It acts as a rocker for the deep flexor tendon. Its two rather pointed extremities are connected to the wings of the pedal bone by white, fibrous tissue.
   - Short pastern bone. A nearly square bone to which the superficial flexor tendon and ligaments are attached. It articulates with the pedal bone and the navicular bone and is half inside and half outside the foot.
2. Tendons. There are three tendons in the foot, one in front and two at the back.
   - Extensor tendon. Originates from the muscles above the knee and hock. It runs down the front of the leg, over the fetlock and pastern joints, and is attached to the pointed centre of the upper border of the coffin bone. It straightens the limb and lifts the toe.
   - Superficial flexor tendon, Runs down the posterior surface (back) of the cannon bone. Bends the leg and joints. It is attached to the

Cross-section through the foot.

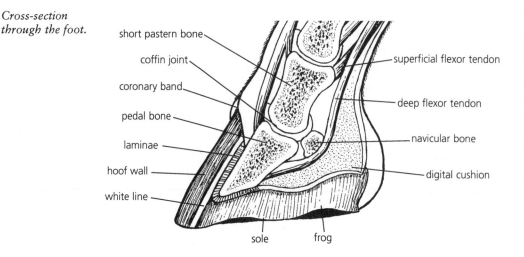

short pastern bone

coffin joint

coronary band

pedal bone

laminae

hoof wall

white line

superficial flexor tendon

deep flexor tendon

navicular bone

digital cushion

sole   frog

upper part of the short pastern bone.

- Deep flexor tendon. Runs down the back of the cannon bone, between the superficial flexor tendon and the suspensory ligament. Bends the joint of the coffin and short pastern bones, passes under the navicular bone, and attaches to the lower part of the coffin bone. The deep flexor tendon is broad and fan-shaped where it passes under the navicular bone and covers the navicular completely, as if passing over a pulley.

3. Ligaments. These hold all bones securely in place and allow only the joints to move. The suspensory ligament occupies the space between the two splint bones and lies close behind the cannon bone. It divides into two strong bands, each of which attaches to the corresponding sesamoid bone. Some fibres pass on over the pastern and reinforce the extensor tendon.

4. The lateral cartilages. Two flat pieces of gristle situated on each side of the foot and attached to the upper edge of the coffin bone. The lateral cartilages stand up above the coronet about half an inch (12mm). They replace bones at the back of the foot, give elasticity to the hoof and reduce concussion. They are the flexible foundation of the wall and with the frog and the plantar cushion assist in expansion of the foot.

5. The plantar (digital) cushion. A wedge-shaped mass of fibro-elastic tissue. It fills the space between the lateral cartilages and the wings of the coffin bone at the back of the foot. The plantar cushion extends forwards beneath the navicular bone. It is similar in shape to the frog. It is a shock absorber, yielding upwards and outwards, forcing the heels apart and dispersing the jar of impact of the foot on the ground.

6. The coronary cushion. A fibrous band between the skin of the leg and the hoof. The flesh-like covering of the band, which is well supplied

with blood, is attached to the upper part of the coffin bone and the extensor tendon. As it runs down the coffin bone, it becomes thinner, and ends in folds, which are the sensitive laminae. The sensitive laminae interlock with the horny laminae of the hoof. There are between 500 and 600 parallel pleats, plentifully supplied with blood. They form a secretory surface which helps to supply the substance to form the horn of the wall.

7. Blood supply to the foot.
   - Blood is carried to the foot through arteries. The large metacarpal artery descends on the inner side of the leg. Just above the fetlock it divides into the digital arteries which then descend towards the wings of the coffin bone, where they divide again to supply the whole foot by means or an arterial circle known as the plantar circle.
   - As a protection to the sensitive foot under pressure, there are no valves in the veins of the foot. The blood is entirely free and is pumped back up the leg by the pressure exerted when the sensitive foot expands on impact with the ground.
   - The volume of blood required by the foot to effect necessary repair is greater than that needed by the brain.
   - The return circulation from the foot to the heart is very important. The health of the foot depends largely on the efficient flow of blood. Each time a horse puts his foot to the ground, pressure from the frog exerts similar pressure on the plantar cushion immediately above it. The cushion is thrust upwards between the lateral cartilages exerting sufficient pressure to squeeze blood out of the venous network and upwards into the veins on the way back to the heart.
   - Blood and nerves give life and sensitivity to the foot.

Shoeing

1. Foot should receive attention every 4 to 6 weeks. If the foot gets too long, the toe turns up and the horse will stumble.
2. Hoof takes from 9 to 12 months to grow from top to bottom, therefore about one-ninth of the foot should be rasped off every month.
3. Test for lameness before taking horse to be shod and also after new shoes are fitted.

To Make the Shoe

1. Many farriers now use ready-made, factory-produced horseshoes. Disadvantages are:
   - Shoes come in set sizes and are not made to each individual foot.
   - Nail holes are all stamped in the same place. This means that nails

are constantly driven through the hoof in the same spots, whereas a good farrier, making his own shoes, will vary the site of the nails.

2. If farrier makes his own shoes he buys the iron in bars, already concave and fullered (broader on the surface which is against the wall of the hoof, and grooved for added grip on the ground).

- Suitable lengths of iron must be cut to make the new set of shoes.
- The iron is made red hot in the fire and then shaped by use of the turning hammer on the anvil.
- Nail holes are 'stamped' and toe clip 'drawn'.
- Usual number of nails is four on the outside and three on the inside. The fewer nails used the better – on a healthy foot only two on each side may be necessary, but on an unhealthy foot up to six nails a side may be needed.

The Shoeing Operation

1. Removal. Old shoe is removed. Using the buffer and shoeing hammer, the clenches are raised or cut off. Using the pincers and starting at the heel, the shoe is levered off the foot.
2. Preparation. Consists of reducing the overgrowth of the wall to its natural length and trimming any ragged pieces from the sole and frog.

- The hoof cutters are used in the case of excessive overgrowth of the wall.
- Normally the 'drawing knife' or 'toeing knife' is used to trim the wall and remove ragged parts of the sole and frog. Undue use of the knife on the sole or frog is harmful.
- The rasp is then used to provide the foot with an absolutely level bearing surface. The rasp is not used on the wall, except to make a nick under the nails before the clenches are turned down. A small piece may be cut from the toe if the shoes are to have toe clips. Toe clips should not be hammered back when on the foot.

3. Forging. This is the making of the new shoe and is described above. The weight and type of iron used will depend directly on the work required of the horse being shod.
4. Fitting. In hot shoeing, fitting is done while the shoe is hot. It is carried, on a 'pritchel', to the foot and held against the ground surface of the foot for a moment. The burning of horn which results shows the extent to which foot and shoe are in contact. Any adjustments necessary to the shoe – or the length of the heels – are then made. In the event that a fire and anvil are not available, the horse must be cold shod. The adjustments which can be made to a cold shoe are limited. Hot shoeing is preferable.
5. Nailing.

- The shoe is cooled by immersion in water.

- The first nail driven is usually one of the toe nails.
- Nails must be driven carefully and must be placed between the white line and the outer edge. A nail too near the white line will cause pressure, or nail bind. A nail driven inside the white line causes a 'prick'.
- Nails should emerge 1½ins (3.75cm) up the hoof.
- Specially designed nails are used and it is important to use the correct size nail.
- The end of the nail which penetrates the wall is twisted off, leaving a small piece projecting. This is called the 'clench'.

6. Finishing.
   - The clenches are smoothed with the rasp and a small 'bed' made for them in the wall.
   - The clenches are tapped down with the hammer or closed with the 'clencher', tightened and given a final rasp to smooth them.
   - The toe clip, or quarter clips, are lightly tapped back.
   - The rasp is run round the lower edge of the wall to reduce the risk of any cracking in the wall.

Foot Balance

Good foot balance is of vital importance to the health and soundness of the horse. Correct balance of the feet is enhanced by the regular services of a good farrier. When considering the natural distribution of the horse's weight over his feet, it is essential to take into account the conformation of the whole limb, and the way in which the horse moves and naturally carries himself. In the simplest terms, ideally the feet should be a pair (front pair and hind pair). A vertical line taken through

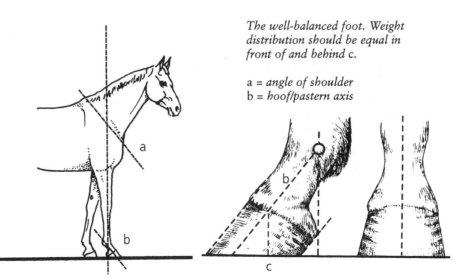

The well-balanced foot. Weight distribution should be equal in front of and behind c.

a = *angle of shoulder*
b = *hoof/pastern axis*

the limb to the floor should equally divide the joints of the limb and the foot itself. Viewed from the side, there should be even distribution over the foot in front of and behind a line taken vertically down from the centre of the coffin joint to the ground. The front wall and pastern should be in perfect alignment (hoof/pastern axis) with an ideal angle of 45-50° to the ground for the front feet, and 50-55° to the ground for the hind feet. The front wall of the hoof and the wall at the heel of the foot should be parallel to each other.

What to Look For in a Newly Shod Foot

1. The shoe should have been made to fit the foot, not the foot to fit the shoe. That is, the wall should not have been rasped away to meet the iron and toe should not have been 'dumped' (see Dumping, page 176).
2. The type of shoe provided should be suitable to the work required of the horse. The weight of iron should be in proper relation to the size of the foot.
3. Correct preparation of the foot is essential. The foot should have been suitably reduced in length at both toe and heel, and evenly on the outside. Correct foot balance is crucial to maintaining soundness and movement.
4. The use of the knife on sole and frog should have been limited to light trimming only. The bars should not be cut out.
5. The frog should be in contact with the ground.
6. Sufficient nails should have been used (normally three on the inside and four on the outside). They should be the right size and the heads should be well-driven home to fill the nail holes.
7. The clenches should be well formed, the right distance up the wall, and all in line.
8. No daylight should show between the shoe and the foot – pay particular attention to the heel region.
9. The heels of the shoe should be the correct length, neither too long nor too short.
10. The place for the clip should have been neatly cut and the clip well drawn and well fitted.

Indications that Re-Shoeing is Necessary

1. There will be a sufficient growth of horn each month for the foot to require trimming even if the shoe is not worn.
2. The foot is overlong and out of shape.
3. The shoe is loose.
4. The shoe has worn thin – in any part.
5. The clenches are no longer close to the wall but have 'risen'.
6. A shoe has been 'cast' – lost.

Plain stamped shoe.   *Hunter shoe, hind.*   *Hunter shoe, fore.*

Types of Shoe

1. The plain stamped shoe. Simplest form of horseshoe. An unmodified bar of iron, shaped, stamped with nail holes and provided with toe clip. Only suitable for horses doing slow work. No provisions against slipping or interfering.
2. The hunter shoe (fullered shoe). Designed for a horse moving fast on grass and stopping suddenly and making sharp turns.
   - Made of 'concave' iron – narrower below than above – to reduce the risk of suction in soft going and to provide a more secure grip on the ground.
   - Ground surface is 'fullered' – provided with a groove for better foothold, provides a 'bed' for the nail heads and reduces the overall weight of the shoe.
   - Heels of the fore shoes are 'pencilled' – smoothed off – to reduce the risk of the heel of the fore shoe being caught by the toe of the hind and torn off.
   - The toe of the hind shoe may be 'rolled' – set back and bevelled off – to reduce risk of injury from over-reaching. Quarter clips are provided instead of toe clip, to allow for rolling, and to reduce possible damage if over-reaching occurs.
   - Traditionally, hunter shoes were fitted with a 'calkin' on the outer heel and a 'wedge' on the inner heel of the hind shoes. These were to provide extra grip. The practice is largely outdated and screw-in studs have replaced the wedge and calkin.
3. The feather-edged shoe. The inner branch of the shoe is 'feathered' – reduced in width – and fitted close in under the wall. Reduces risk of injury from striking the opposite leg. There are no nail holes in the inner branch of the shoe.
4. Grass tips. Thin, half-length shoes, traditionally used on horses turned out to grass to protect the wall and sole from bruising. They allowed the frog to come into full action. Grass tips are not commonly used these days. If horses are turned away unshod, the feet should be regularly trimmed and the application of 'Keratex' hoof hardener will help prevent the horn from splitting.

5. Training plates and racing plates. These are lightweight aluminium shoes for racehorses in training and racing.
6. Aluminium shoes for show horses and eventers are available and useful for some horses with shelly feet. They are usually wider webbed than iron shoes and therefore more protective of the sole. They must be properly forged to fit the horse.
7. Shoes such as heart bar and egg bar are indicated in some cases to improve support, but these should only be fitted after consultation with your veterinarian.
8. Many synthetic shoes are now appearing on the market and have been used with varying degrees of success. Remember that when the unshod foot strikes the ground it slips fractionally forward before stopping. This is one of nature's anti-concussive devices. Many plastic, rubber or synthetic shoes will not allow this slip and can therefore create more conussion than iron shoes. Bar shoes also have a tendency to stop the foot abruptly.

Dumping
This is cutting or rasping back the toe of the foot to make it fit the shoe, instead of adjusting the shoe to fit the foot. This rasping of the surface of the wall removes the surface coat of the wall and exposes the horn. The horn becomes brittle and cracked and the rasped portions inevitably break away in time.

Studs and Stud Nails
Screw-in studs can be used as and when required and are not a permanent feature of the shoe. If studs are required it is sensible to wear two on the shoe, usually the hinds, at the heels, and not just on the outer heel as used to be the case. The farrier can be asked to insert threaded stud holes into the shoes, and these have to be plugged with cotton wool when not in use. Mordax stud nails can also be fitted in the heel region of the shoe. The advantage of these is that they protrude for grip but do not alter the balance of the foot.

Surgical Shoeing
In the past there have been numerous types of surgical shoes designed to give relief to unsound conditions and enable unsound horses to be worked. Unless an unsound condition can be cured so that the animal recovers completely, the horse should not be worked and today the need for surgical shoeing is determined on a case by case basis. If some problem such as brushing, capped elbow, contracted heels, laminitis, navicular disease, sidebone or ringbone is present and special shoeing is required, consult your veterinary surgeon and your farrier to decide on the best shoeing for the individual case.

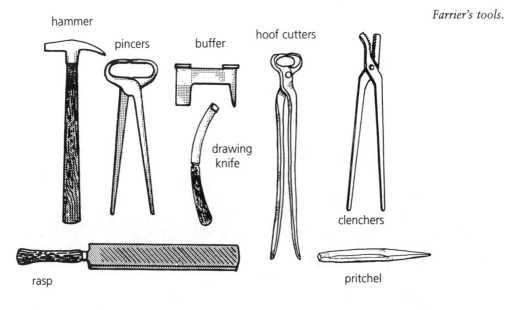

Farrier's tools.

Farrier's Tools

1. Driving hammer. For driving nails and twisting off their points when driven through the hoof. Used in conjunction with the buffer to raise clenches prior to removing a shoe.
2. Buffer. Made of steel, it is about 5½ins (14cm) long. Used for raising clenches.
3. Rasp. About 16ins (41cm) long and three quarters coarse cut and one quarter file cut.
4. Drawing knife. Trimmer, to trim excessive overgrowth of wall.
5. Pincers. Used to remove shoe, easing off from heel towards toe.
6. Hoof cutters. Similar to pincers but with sharp cutting surfaces to remove excessive horn prior to using the drawing knife.
7. Pritchel. Steel instrument with pointed end which fits into nail hole in shoe. Pritchel can then be used as a handle to the hot shoe. Also used in fashioning the nail holes.
8. Clenchers. Shaped a little like pincers but with a flat, cross-cut head to grasp the clenches and close them to the hoof wall.

CHAPTER 26

Diseases and Ailments of the Foot

Pricks in Shoeing

Causes
1. Pricked foot – nail is driven at the wrong angle and penetrates the sensitive part of foot.
2. Nail bind – nail is driven too close to the sensitive part of the foot but does not actually penetrate it. This may cause a bulge of the horn on to the sensitive structures which causes great pain.

Symptoms
1. Lameness and localised tenderness over the site of the nail track.
2. A nail bind may not be noticed at once. Lameness may take days to appear. A prick usually causes more instant pain.
3. Heat is usually present in the foot.
4. There may be a low-grade lameness, which gradually becomes more acute as infection develops in the foot. The resulting build-up of pus and inflammation causes pressure and increased pain and heat in the affected foot.

Treatment
1. Each nail should be withdrawn and examined for moisture on the nail or oozing from the hole. The foot is a closed box and infection within the sensitive parts causes an inflammatory reaction, pain, and, usually, pus formation. As the pus increases the effects of pressure mount since it has no outlet.
2. When the offending nail has been found, the hole should be pared out to release the pus and allow constant, free drainage.
3. Apply hot, antiseptic poultices. Poultices (or hot fomentations in a tub) relieve pain and congestion and encourage the evacuation of pus.

4. Veterinary surgeon should be consulted immediately and will probably put horse on antibiotics for three days.
5. In cases of nail bind where lameness is slight and the sensitive foot has not been pierced, remove the shoe and if necessary the farrier/veterinarian will pare open the hole. Poultice foot (or apply hot fomentations) for a few days to alleviate any infection. Later the nail hole should be filled with turpentine (which keeps it open and has a hardening effect) or Stockholm tar (if the hole has been pared out). The horse must be rested until sound.
6. All cases of nail bind, pricks in shoeing, or other forms of puncture wounds of the foot will necessitate complete rest for the horse until sound. Check on immunisation status and if tetanus toxoid has not been administered within the preceding four months, horse may require tetanus anti-toxin or tetanus toxoid booster; consult your veterinary surgeon. Put horse on a laxative diet and substitute hay for grain until sound.

Wounds of the Sole and Frog

Causes
1. Punctures caused by stepping on nails, glass, etc.
2. Bruises from stones, hard ground, etc. are fairly common.

Symptoms
1. Lameness – very sudden in the case of a picked-up nail.
2. In the case of bruises to the sole, a flush of colour may be seen on the sole. However, the bruise is not in the horn of the sole but in the deeper, sensitive part of the foot covering the coffin bone.

Treatment
Search foot. Treat as for nail pricks above.

Corns

Corns are bruises to the part of the sole in the angle of the wall and the bar.

Causes
1. May be caused by the structure of the foot – flat feet, weak heels, thin soles.
2. May also be caused by poor shoeing – excessive paring of the sole, cutting away the bars, undue lowering of the heels. All such

seedy toe

seat of corn

mistreatment of the foot tends to weaken the seat of corn and expose it to injury.

3. Front shoes too short – create pressure on seat of corn.
4. Shoes insecurely nailed, or loose shoes due to overgrowth of hoof, may be displaced and cause pressure and subsequently a bruise or corn.

Symptoms

1. Ill-defined lameness – horse going short in front. Corns most usually appear in the front feet but they can appear in a hind foot – poor shoeing could cause corns in hind feet.
2. Severe pain and lameness; heat and tenderness.
3. Lameness increasing with work. Lameness more apparent on turns and corners.
4. The existence of a corn is only known for certain when some of the horn is pared away from the sole around the seat of corn revealing a red spot, varying in size from a pea to a thumb nail.

Treatment

1. The affected area must be pared as thin as possible. If the corn is an old one, discoloration will be near the surface; if it is new, it will be deeper, nearer to the sensitive parts of the foot.
2. If lameness is severe, or the corn is found to be suppurating, the foot should be poulticed, as described above under 'Pricks' on page 178. When using a bran poultice, cover the corn with a pad to prevent bran from entering the wound.
3. In severe cases, as with pricks, there may be swelling of the fetlock joint.
4. All pressure of the shoe must be removed from the seat of corn – use a threequarter shoe.
5. Horse should be rested, and put on a laxative diet.
6. When foot is sound, particular care must be taken in shoeing to ensure that the shoe is the proper length. A leather or rubber pad between the shoe and the sole helps to minimise concussion.

Seedy Toe

This condition arises when cavities form in the soft horn between the inner and outer parts of the wall. An unhealthy secretion of the sensitive laminae prevents them from maintaining union with the insensitive layers. Cavities in the toe area are called 'seedy toe', in other areas of the foot they are called 'separation'.

Causes
1. May be caused by injury to the coronet, which results in some aberration in the horn-secreting mechanism.
2. Pressure from the clip of the shoe, or blows to the wall, may be causes.
3. Irritation or inflammation of the sole due to bruising may be a cause.
4. Inflammation of the sensitive laminae.
5. Scalding with a hot shoe.
6. Bruising, caused by working the horse unshod.
7. Diseased sensitive laminae as a result of laminitis.
8. Not trimming feet sufficiently often. Toe grows too long and will pull apart from underlying laminae.

Symptoms
1. Usually first seen by the farrier when removing the shoe.
2. A hollow cavity is found, filled with a soft, dark, cheesy type of material – broken-down horn.
3. If the hoof is tapped with a hammer it may give a hollow sound.
4. If the cavity extends deep into the foot it may become infected and pus may be produced. In very severe cases the pedal bone can also protrude through the sole.

Treatment
1. The best treatment is to stimulate the growth of new horn and avoid all pressure at the point where the cavity makes contact with the shoe.
2. The cavity should be cleaned out thoroughly and packed with an antiseptic paste, such as BIP (bismuth carbonate – 3 parts; iodoform – 1 part; made into thick paste with liquid paraffin). Packing must be firm. Hole should be plugged with tow and if possible horse shod. Stockholm tar may be used as a packing, or Reducine applied under a pad. Dressing may have to be renewed from time to time.
3. Cornucrescine may be applied to the coronet to stimulate growth of new horn.
4. Special shoeing may be required to take weight off the toe. Injured part must not bear any weight. Consult with veterinarian and farrier

since shoeing will be determined by cause.

5. Turn horse into lush pasture (though not if susceptible to laminitis) – spring grass will often work wonders on the promotion of new horn growth.

Quittor

Causes
1. Direct injury – i.e. a tread.
2. Indirect injury – i.e. following suppuration within the hoof caused by a corn, a prick, etc. The pus produced in such a case follows the line of least resistance and travels upwards to the coronet where it forms an abscess.

Symptoms
1. Pain and lameness.
2. A tender area may be found on the coronet.
3. A tread may be suspected and appropriate treatment applied.
4. If the injury is deep-seated, there will be increasing lameness, heat, swelling and pain as the abscess forms.
5. When the abscess bursts there will be some relief. But the wound will not heal so long as the irritating portion of dead tissue remains within the foot.
6. A quittor can become an aggravated chronic condition. It is advisable to seek veterinary advice for treatment at an early stage.

Treatment
1. If the injury is a simple tread, the pain should be relieved with poultices, foot baths, etc.
2. A raw area may occur due to local death of tissue at the site of injury. In this case, after poulticing, keep wound clean and protected until it heals.
3. If a quittor forms due to a deep-seated injury, treatment is more difficult. Poultice the wound. If damage to the sole can be found, pare away the sole and poultice.
4. Successful treatment depends on removing the dead tissue within the foot, which is often part of the lateral cartilage. This may require an operation and is definitely a case for the veterinary surgeon. Antibiotics will be required.
5. Horse will require complete rest and laxative diet as he will be confined to the stable and lack of exercise may cause constipation. Reduce grain, increase hay.

Thrush

A disease which affects the cleft of the frog.

Causes
1. Excessive secretion from the glands deep in the cleft of frog.
2. Wet and dirt; neglected feet. Feet should be thoroughly picked out and washed or brushed clean at least once each day.
3. Standing on wet, dirty bedding.
4. Lack of use of the frog – incorrect shoeing, no pressure on the frog.
5. Usually seen in hind feet but forefeet may be affected.

Symptoms
1. There is a typical, offensive smell, caused by the bacteriological breakdown of the matter accumulating in the cleft of frog. (Excessive secretion from the skin glands.)
2. There is often a ragged appearance to the frog.
3. Severe cases may cause lameness.

Treatment
1. The frog and its cleft must be thoroughly cleaned. Use a stiff brush and soap and water.
2. Loose and ragged pieces of the frog should be pared away.
3. Soak foot for 20 minutes twice daily in hot water and Epsom salts.
4. In very bad cases it may be necessary to poultice foot.
5. When area is thoroughly clean and dry, pour in some simple astringent antiseptic – e.g. 10% formalin solution, which a pharmacist can prepare, or copper sulphate, Stockholm tar or hydrogen peroxide, all of which will easily seep deep enough to be effective, but must be handled with care.
6. Frog pressure is essential in all cases. Smear Stockholm tar on tow and push it down into the cleft of the frog. Try to keep dressing in place, e.g. wrap hoof with a piece of plastic feed sacking and tape it on well, or leave a poultice boot or an Easy boot on (whilst in stable).
7. Cases of thrush caused by lack of use of the frog must be treated similarly, but in addition the foot must be gradually brought into use.
8. It may be necessary to remove the shoe and gradually lower the heels.
9. Shoeing with a shoe that is thin at the heels, or a bar shoe, may be necessary to bring the frog properly into use again.
10. In mild cases of thrush the horse should continue to work since this will encourage more frog pressure.
11. If ground is dry, turn horse out. This achieves constant pressure on the frog and also provides the horse with green grass which promotes

the growth of healthy horn.

12. If horse must be kept in, provide him with cod liver oil daily. This will also help promote the growth of healthy horn.

13. Preventive measures include stable cleanliness and frequent attention to the feet, including washing with disinfectant.

Canker

Canker is a chronic disease affecting the horn-secreting tissues of the foot. It is a foul-smelling, morbid condition, which starts at the sensitive frog and involves the sole, frog, and sometimes the wall.

Causes
1. Not known, but it is often attributed to neglected thrush.
2. May arise from injuries to the foot, or from the downward extension of grease from the heel.
3. It may be attributable to some systemic or constitutional upset.
4. It may be attributable to invasion of the part by bacteria or some organism.
5. Bad hygiene favours the onset of the disease.

Symptoms
1. First sign is usually a greyish-white, offensive discharge.
2. A soft, spongy swelling of the sensitive frog and sole develops and the horny covering breaks up.
3. The horn that is secreted is soft and cheese-like in texture.
4. The horn-producing power of the affected parts is ultimately destroyed. A thick flesh growth with a foul smell appears in its place.
5. Usually canker is not painful and diseased horses may walk sound.

Treatment
1. Canker must be treated at once to be successful. Those cases which have extended beyond the frog are very hard to cure.
2. Treat as for severe thrush.
3. Call the veterinary surgeon at once as an operation may be necessary, and antibiotics will be required.
4. Treatment is likely to be long and tedious.

Laminitis (also called Founder or Fever of the Feet)

Painful state of congestion affecting the vascular system within hoof. The congested tissues provide ideal conditions for invading organisms and inflammation of the sensitive laminae often follows. The original attack is always acute and may be entirely relieved with no permanent ill effects. If the disease progresses to the point where changes in the structure of the foot occur, the result is known as chronic laminitis. Laminitis may involve two feet or all four; usually it affects both forefeet.

Causes

1. Extreme stress, e.g.:
   - Excessive work, especially if horse is unfit.
   - Concussion; long journeys, long, fast driving or riding (particularly if the sole and frog have been cut away, impairing the shock absorbency of the foot).
   - Heredity or malconformation – wide, flat feet and weak horn. Extremely easy keepers (tendency towards hereditary hypothyroidism, especially common in Arabian, Quarter Horse, Morgan, or pony breeds).
   - Idleness and lack of exercise especially if fed on a diet well beyond the maintenance requirements.
   - Debilitation diseases – e.g. influenza, which weakens the action of the heart.
   - Difficult foaling or retained placenta – which may cause general disturbance of the vascular system.
   - Undue weight placed on one or more feet, e.g. horse in pain as a result of accident to one limb may place unusual amount of weight on the other leg (front or hind). If continued for a long time this may give rise to a state of congestion and ultimately laminitis in the weight-bearing limb. Always support both legs (front or hind) with bandages if one is injured.
   - Standing about in very cold or wet weather when sweating.
2. Ingestion of excessive carbohydrates, e.g.:
   - Too much spring grass – grass laminitis often affects small ponies who will eat without ceasing as long as they are able. Keep ponies in during the day and only turn out to grass at night.
   - Digestive disturbance – high feeding, too much grain (especially heating grain, barley, wheat, beans, etc.).
   - Ingestion of large amounts of cold water by an overheated horse.

Symptoms

1. In acute laminitis attack is sudden, with acute pain and lameness; horse can hardly be made to move. Signs of grain founder usually do not appear for 12 to 18 hours after ingestion.
2. Heat may be present in front part of feet, over the sole, the wall and the coronary band. Tapping the affected foot, or feet, lightly with a

hammer gives rise to pain. Increased digital pulse, increased respiration, variable increase in temperature.

3. Horse adopts typical posture, hind feet well under him and, if only front feet are affected as is usual, front feet will be stretched forward, weight on the heels in an attempt to relieve the pressure.

4. Difficult to pick up feet – horse is unwilling to put weight on other affected foot or feet. Horse may appear lame or off balance in rear limbs when moved due to reluctance to put weight towards the front limbs.

5. Mares suffering from laminitis resulting from metritis (the retention of the foetal membranes, or part thereof) will have very high temperature, 104°-106°F (40°-41°C). The mucous membranes will be infected, considerable increase in pulse and respiration will be present.

6. Horse may lie down flat on his side to relieve pressure. If left lying down he must be turned frequently from side to side to avoid dangers of other diseases due to passive congestion.

7. In chronic laminitis rotation of the third phalanx (pedal bone) will occur. This may cause the toe of the third phalanx to push out through the sole of the foot.

8. Horses suffering chronic laminitis have tendency to land on heels with an exaggerated motion. The sole is dropped and flat with excessive quantities of flaky material.

9. Chronic laminitis causes heavy ring formation on the wall of the hoof – rougher and less regular than grass rings. Rings are usually present for the life of the horse and are caused by inflammation in the coronary band, and horn being produced at an inconstant level.

10. Hoof wall grows more quickly than normal at the toe because of chronic inflammation and toes may become long and curl up at the end.

Treatment

1. Acute laminitis – veterinary help will be required. In case of grain founder treatment is directed at neutralising effects of grain intake. Horse will require purgatives until all grain has been removed from intestinal tract. Thereafter, laxative diet.

2. Congestion, pressure and pain must be relieved. Methods include lukewarm soaks in warm water and Epsom salts. Standing horse in sand or deep shavings can help support the sole.

3. Antihistamines are useful and intravenous dextrose and electrolytes should be used as replacement fluids for the diarrhoea which results from both the ingestion of the grain and the purgatives, and veterinary advice is essential. Do not use corticosteroids (Azium) in laminitis. Non-steroidal anti-inflammatory drugs such as

phenylbutazone, Benamine, Ketoprofen can be useful for relieving pain.

4. Until recently it was thought that horses with laminitis benefited from being kept on the move to maintain circulation in the foot. Now that the instability of the sensitive laminae is recognised it is accepted that box rest is the preferable treatment. Pain relief is essential as is immediate veterinary advice.

5. In favourable cases, quickly treated, the foot may not suffer much – or any – deformity.

6. In chronic laminitis pressure within the foot turns the pedal bone on its horizontal axis. The toe is said to 'drop' causing the sole to lose its dome and become flat. The feet must be trimmed as near normal as possible and more frequently than is usual for unaffected horse.

7. Horse should be shod with a wide-webbed shoe to keep pressure off sole. The sole can further be protected by the use of pads.

8. Much can now be done by reshaping the foot through extensive trimming and the use of plastic to return the third phalanx to a more normal position. The fundamental principle of this treatment is to lower the heels as much as possible and to raise the toe with a layer of plastic. A shoe is incorporated in the plastic. Treatment is repeated about every 6 weeks until foot assumes a normal shape, which could be as long as 12 months. Another shoeing option is the 'heart bar' shoe – when properly used it can help return pedal bone to normal axis. Heart bar shoes must be used under veterinary advice in close consultation with farrier. Both treatments can be too painful to be possible.

9. If symptoms continue for more than 10 days prognosis is unfavourable. Horse may only be made usable again after months of careful trimming and shoeing. He will then only be useful for quiet work.

10. In cases where inflammation has not been too severe (and in grass laminitis promptly treated) the horse will become sound again.

11. Today great strides are being made in the treatment and shoeing of horses with laminitis. In every suspected case it is essential to consult your veterinarian immediately.

Grass Rings

Ridges sometimes appear in the hoof wall, particularly when horses are at grass. This condition is caused by differences in growth rate of the horn. This is not serious, and not to be confused with laminitic ridges, which are rougher and more irregular and tend to merge together towards the heel.

Navicular Disease

A disease process involving the navicular bone. In the later stages changes occur in the bone including spurring of the outside, notching on the anterior surface, discoloration and ulceration of the posterior surface. The deep flexor tendon glides over the posterior surface of the navicular bone and the roughened bone surface causes pain and lameness.

Causes

1. Poor foot balance – particularly associated with the long toe and collapsed heel conformation. This increases pressure into the back of the foot which in turn may decrease or squeeze out the blood supply to the navicular bone. Restricted blood supply can then cause bone deterioration or even necrosis (death). The bone may become pitted and roughened and pain increases as the deep flexor tendon no longer articulates over a smooth surface.
2. Hereditary predisposition – small feet, straight, upright pasterns, which subject the foot to greater concussion which can be a contributory cause.
3. Bad shoeing – trimming heel too low on horse with upright pasterns. This breaks the hoof-pastern axis and produces greater pressure of the deep flexor tendon against the navicular bone.
4. Direct injury – hard or fast work, racing, jumping, etc., especially if performed on rough or hard surfaces.

Symptoms

1. Intermittent lameness which decreases when horse is rested.
2. Hard work may make horse noticeably worse next morning but, in the early stages of the disease, rest will make lameness disappear or become very slight.
3. Horse may be restless and uneasy on his feet in the stable. Later he will point. If both forefeet are affected, he will point first one and then the other.
4. Horse travels best uphill. Lameness may show up more going downhill and over rough ground.
5. Navicular disease is often mistaken for shoulder lameness, due to the shuffling gait and shortened anterior phase of the stride typically exhibited.
6. As the disease develops the hoof gradually changes shape. Horse avoids frog pressure because of pain and tries to land on toes. Lack of frog pressure causes heels to contract and raise. Hoof becomes 'boxy' and sole and frog become more concave.

Treatment

1. Unfortunately there is no cure for this disease, but much research is under way. If recognised early and if steps are taken to relieve pressure and tension, horse may be kept workably sound for some time. Most treatments consist of different trimming and shoeing, often with an egg-bar shoe. Use of a vasodilator drug, isoxuprine, has been helpful, as circulation in the foot is increased.
2. Consult veterinarian and farrier about corrective shoeing. A graduated shoe, with thin rolled toe and thick heels will lessen the angle of the tendon and reduce pressure where tendon passes under navicular bone.
3. Branches of shoe should be as narrow as possible so that the wall bears all the weight.
4. Shoeing with hoof cushion and a thick, wedge-heeled pad has afforded relief in many cases.
5. Horse should be kept up, well fed, and given fresh grass or alfalfa and one third of a pint of cod liver oil daily, to promote a good growth of horn. Biotin supplementation also helps hoof growth.
6. Exercise should be at the walk, under saddle, to control the action. Exercise assists good circulation within the foot.
7. In long-standing cases, where the hoof has already become 'boxy', the veterinarian may decide to perform a hoof section to give immediate relief.
8. Neurectomy (de-nerving), or bilateral posterior digital neurectomy is the only means of achieving any degree of permanent relief.
9. Neurectomy does not, in most cases, deprive the foot of all sensation. It is looked on as 'dangerous' and 'dishonest' by many horsemen, but it is widely practised in certain areas and many de-nerved horses have been hunted, show-jumped and steeplechased for one or more years after the operation, free from pain and lameness. However, there are side-effects that can occur with neurectomy and it is considered a 'salvage' procedure by the veterinary profession. De-nerved horses require particular attention to hoof care.
10. If a de-nerved horse comes up for sale it must be disclosed that the operation has been performed. The horse is legally unsound.

Pedal Ostitis

Inflammation of the pedal bone. Quite common in riding horses and racehorses.

Causes

1. Continued concussion.

2. May be the sequel to corns, laminitis or punctures of the sole.
3. In some cases the laminae and sensitive sole may be involved.

Symptoms
1. Lameness – varies in degree. Similar to an early case of navicular disease in type of lameness, but differs in that it is acute, occurs suddenly and is aggravated by exercise.
2. Common in the forefeet, rare in the hind feet. Horse reacts to hoof testers at the bottom of the foot. Pain may be diffuse or localised.
3. Horse is tender on his feet – goes short.
4. Pain will be accentuated by trotting him on loose gravel and he may go very lame.
5. Heat in the foot. May be evidence of bruising of the sole.
6. X-ray will confirm the diagnosis.
7. Usually only one foot is affected.

Treatment
1. Treatment will depend on cause. Consult veterinarian.
2. Shoeing with light, wide-webbed shoe and pads will prevent pressure on the sole and may help. Frequent attention to the feet is important.
3. Turning horse out on soft land for 6 months or more may cure the condition if due to constant bruising of the sole.
4. Give plenty of walking exercise under saddle on soft ground.
5. Good feeding and green food essential.
6. Soft ground is vital, hard ground will accentuate the trouble.
7. Anti-inflammatory drugs may be prescribed.

Sandcrack

Symptoms
1. A vertical splitting of the wall of the hoof.
2. Varies in length and depth – true sandcrack extends from the upper to the lower border of the wall.
3. Usually occurs on inside quarter of the forefoot and in hind toe.
4. Begins as a small fissure close to coronet and extends upwards, downwards and inwards.
5. Does not usually cause lameness, unless deep enough to expose the sensitive laminae.

Causes
1. Weak, brittle feet.
2. Concussion (in the fore), or strain (in the hind) from heavy loads.
3. Injury (i.e. a tread) to the coronary band.

4. Rasping the wall.

Treatment
1. If sandcrack is deep and exposes the sensitive tissues, these become liable to injury. The injury may be simple pinching or more serious infection and inflammation. In this case there will be considerable pain and lameness. Consult the veterinarian and your farrier.
2. Pain and inflammation must be treated first. Poultice foot for 2-3 days. This removes foreign matter and pus.
3. Prevent movement. Crack may be immobilised by riveting the edges firmly together with a horseshoe nail driven horizontally and clenched at each end.
4. Shoe with a flat shoe. If crack is at the toe, do not use a toe clip, but draw two small clips, one on each side of the toe. This will help to prevent movement of the divided wall.
5. Remove a portion of the wall at the bottom of the crack before shoeing. This will ensure that no pressure exists between the affected part of the wall and the shoe. Such pressure would tend to force the crack open wider.
6. The growth of new, sound horn must be encouraged. The repeated application of a mild blister (Cornucrescine) to the coronet combined with good feeding, adding cod liver oil to the feed. and feeding new spring grass, will all help. A biotin supplement will also promote hoof growth.
7. Granulation tissue (proud flesh) may form and protrude from the crack if the deep sensitive tissues were the site of infection. Daily application of a caustic or astringent dressing (silver nitrate, copper sulphate, etc.) will remove this tissue apparently painlessly.
8. If the crack is discovered in the early stages and is not deep, some control can be effected by burning grooves into the wall with a hot iron. Grooves may be made transversely across the crack, or across the wall above and below the crack, and also in the shape of a V. The apex of the V may coincide with the lower limit of the crack and the sides slope up towards the coronet, or the V may be inverted so that the sides slope towards the lower border of the hoof. The grooves should be as deep as possible without damaging the inner sensitive structures. The object is to divert concussion from the weak area to a stronger area of the wall.

Split Hoof

Splits or fissures in the wall, beginning at the lower border and extending upwards, are generally the result of direct injury. They are

Split hoof.

usually superficial and shallow. Often seen in horses turned out without shoes, and when feet are neglected. Treat as for sandcrack which has not reached the coronet. Can be grooved out with a dremmel tool and filled with fibreglass or acrylic – consult your veterinarian and your farrier. Prevent splits by trimming feet regularly and providing correct diet.

CHAPTER 27

Interfering

Brushing

This may happen at any pace faster than a walk, when the horse's opposite limbs hit one another alternately, usually at the fetlock, occasionally at the coronet.

Causes
1. Bad conformation.
2. Bad action.
3. Horse is young and green, or old and weak.
4. Horse is overtired, or overworked, or underfed.
5. Prominent clench.
6. Ill-fitting shoes, or shoes which are too heavy.

Treatment
1. Discover the cause and if possible remove it.
2. If cause is youth and greenness of horse, use brushing boots or Yorkshire boots during schooling for a few weeks until horse gains more muscle tone.
3. Adjust shoeing – shoe with feather-edged shoe (inner branch very strong and built up, with no nail holes), or, in the case of a hunter, with a flat shoe fitted close under the wall on the inside, or a three-quarter shoe.

Speedy Cutting

This term is applied to injury inflicted by the opposite limb just below the knee. The blows can be severe and inflict a wound. It is rare, except in high-stepping trotters or horses being forced over heavy going when unfit or unbalanced. Treat as for brushing.

Over-reaching

An injury to the back of the foreleg (usually in the heel area) caused by the toe of the hind shoe. Damage is usually caused by the inner margin of the toe of the hind shoe and not by the front of the toe.

Causes
1. Forelimb insufficiently extended, or hind limb over-extended.
2. Galloping and jumping in heavy going.
3. Careless riding.

Treatment
1. On returning to the stable, treat as bruised wound (see Chapter 31). Wounds vary in severity from slight bruising to deep cuts.
2. The toe of the hind shoe must be made wide and square and well concaved on its inner surface. Shoe must be placed well back at the toe with the clips let into the wall and flush with it. The wall at the toe should be left on but blunted with the rasp.
3. Horses liable to over-reach should wear over-reach boots when hunting or jumping.

Forging

Occurs at trot when the toe of the hind shoe strikes the underneath surface of the corresponding front shoe.

Causes
1. Young, green horse which promises to be a 'goer'.
2. Bad riding (insufficient attention to rhythm).
3. Bad conformation – over-sloping pasterns.
4. Feet too long in the toe.

Treatment
1. If due to youth, forging will disappear when horse is older and in better condition and can be ridden up to his bit with better balance and self-carriage.
2. Shoe forefeet with concave shoes to assist horse in getting front feet out of the way quickly.
3. Hind shoes should be made with square toes and set well back under the wall at the toe.

Over-reaching.   *Forging.*

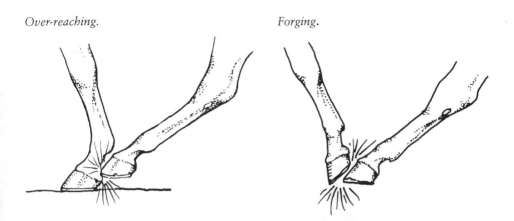

4. Flat hind shoes with heels slightly thinner than the toes will help by retarding the forward movement of the hind foot.

Undercutting

Injury to the toe of the hind foot, caused by the toe of the front foot scraping it as the front foot comes up from the ground.

Causes
1. Peculiarity of the action – perhaps caused by very compact, short-backed conformation.

Treatment
1. Shoe the front feet with square-toed, bevelled-off shoe with two clips. Set shoe well back under the wall at the toe. This causes front toe to miss toe of hind foot when horse is in action.
2. In serious cases, protect hind toe with a box clip. This added weight also retards the forward movement of the hind foot and helps to avoid contact with the forefoot.

CHAPTER 28

Diseases of the Bone

Splints

Bony enlargement on the cannon bone or the splint bones or between any of the three bones. Usually on the inside of the foreleg, but sometimes on the outside. More often on the forelimbs but occasionally on the hind.

Causes
1. Periostitis – inflammation of the bone skin – caused by:
   - Concussion – perhaps provoked by bad conformation.
   - Strenuous work too early, with too much weight inflicted on immature limbs.
   - Blows inflicted by one foot on the opposite leg.

Symptoms
1. Horse usually walks sound but trots lame.
2. Lameness increases with work.
3. Usually obvious to sight and touch – but not always,.
4. Pressure of the fingers on the seat of disease causes pain.
5. Often heat and pain and a developing 'lump' which may vary in size from barely visible to quite a prominent swelling.

Treatment
1. Once formed, splints generally cause little trouble.
2. Formation rare in horses over 6 years old.
3. Much depends on the site of the splint. If formed on the cannon bone, or splint bones, out of the way of the knee and fetlock joints and the tendons, they cause little trouble. High splints may affect the action of the knee. Splints positioned far back may interfere with the free movement of the tendons.

4. While splint is forming rest horse and put on laxative diet.
5. Hose with cold water for 15 minutes three times a day (or stand in cold stream).
6. Apply cold water bandages or cooling lotion between periods of irrigation.
7. Ensure that horse is shod so that there is pressure on the frog. Leather between the shoe and the wall will help to reduce concussion.
8. If lameness persists after 2 weeks, or if there is large swelling, an X-ray is advised to determine if splint bone is fractured (especially if trauma is cause). The fractured end of splint bone must be removed surgically.
9. If there is no fracture splint may be blistered or pin-fired usually with great success.
10. Exercise should be very light. If sound at walk, give walking exercise. If horse is worked during formation of splint, a very large splint will be the result.
11. Splint formation is very common in horses under 6 years. Young horses have more lime in bloodstream as bones are still forming. Tendons and ligaments are less able to absorb shock and concussion than in an older horse. Bad bruising slows circulation causing lime deposit to form.
12. Average cases go sound in 4 to 6 weeks and have no further trouble with the splint, unless it is so large that it causes interference. In this case it can be removed surgically.
13. Many splints are absorbed in later life and disappear.

Splint.

Bone Spavin

Bony enlargement on the lower, inner aspect of the hock.

Causes
1. Heredity – sickle hocks and cow hocks are susceptible.
2. Immaturity – working horse too hard too young.
3. Severe exertion – jumping out of heavy going, pulling up suddenly, drawing heavy loads.
4. Any undue concussion, particularly if horse is unfit or overtired.
5. Degenerative arthritis in the hock joint, which can be result of all above, or ageing.

Bone spavin.

Symptoms
1. Lameness, either slight or severe. Increases initially after short rest, but diminishes with exercise.
2. Horse takes short stride with affected leg. Marked stiffness in

affected joint which causes dragging of the toe.

3. The quarter of the affected leg drops when the foot comes to the ground.
4. Turning in a small circle with affected leg on the outside increases the lameness and horse has a jerky way of taking the foot off the ground.
5. Lameness may disappear after a few months but if the horse stands for a while, after exercise, and then is moved again, increased stiffness will be apparent.

Treatment

New treatments include Adequan or Methotrexate injections, or nutritional supplements that reduce arthritic pain and inflammation.

1. Veterinarian should decide treatment.
2. Surgery (removal of a portion of the cunean tendon) can give good results and may be indicated.
3. Initial treatment – rest and laxative diet. Hot fomentations until inflammation has subsided.
4. Follow up with cold water irrigation for a few days.
5. Blistering is useless since inflammation produced is only superficial. Pin-firing often gives good results.
6. If corrective shoeing is used an effort should be made to make foot break over the medial aspect of the toe. This can be done with a high heel (wedge heel, not calkins) and a rolled toe. This aids the horse in his way of going.

Occult Spavin

Name given to bone spavin which occurs between the articular surfaces of the bones of the hock joint. No bony enlargement is visible. Causes as for bone spavin.

Symptoms

1. As for bone spavin, but no bony enlargement visible.
2. Lameness does not diminish with exercise. Degree of lameness may vary, but horse is constantly lame and lameness may become more pronounced with exercise.
3. More heat noticeable in affected hock.

Treatment

1. As for bone spavin – nutritional supplements that reduce arthritic pain and inflammation, or Adequan or Methotrexate injections. Consult veterinarian.
2. Likely to be very long (at least 8 months) and the horse may be

permanently crippled.

3. Consult veterinarian about advisability of surgical treatment to encourage fusion, the success rate is about 70%.
4. Initially, rest in loosebox and then turn out to grass for several months more, if possible. Take advice of attending veterinarian.
5. Shoe with high-heeled shoe to rest joint.

Osselets

Traumatic arthritis of the metacarpo-phalangeal joint.

Causes
1. Concussion. Most osselets occur in young Thoroughbreds or Standardbreds in early training. Majority of cases start at 2 years of age.
2. Poor conformation – horse with upright pasterns more likely to develop osselets.
3. New bone growth is caused by the periostitis which results from pulling of the joint capsule attachments.

Symptoms
1. Swelling on the front of the fetlock joint. In most cases swelling extends at least half-way round the joint.
2. If both front fetlock joints are affected the horse moves with short, choppy gait.
3. If only one fetlock is involved horse shows obvious lameness in that limb.
4. Pressure applied to the swollen area causes horse to flinch.
5. Fibrous enlargement of the joint capsule on the anterior surface of the fetlock joint is present and is easily palpated.
6. Choppy gait may lead observer to think shoulder lameness is involved but careful examination will make the changes at the fetlock joint obvious.

Treatment
1. X-rays are essential to determine if new bone growth is present and, if so, whether it is involving joint surfaces.
2. Complete rest is absolutely essential. Horse should be removed from training at once.
3. Ice-packs or cold hosing can be used to reduce acute inflammation.
4. Antiphlogistine poultice also useful to reduce acute inflammation.
5. Injecting the inflamed joint capsule with a corticoid, if caught early enough, is often helpful in preventing new bone formation and may

be repeated weekly for three injections.

6. Fetlock should be kept bandaged for support for at least 2 weeks. The unaffected leg should also be wrapped for support.

7. After inflammation has been reduced the fetlock may be blistered.

8. After acute inflammation has receded, X-ray therapy is sometimes beneficial, but must never be combined with any other treatment.

9. Osselets in the chronic phase are sometimes fired and blistered. Firing is probably useful because it creates an acute inflammation but blistering is of little use. However, many regard firing as outdated.

10. Horse must be rested at least 6 months before being put back into training. Horses which have received corticoid therapy appear sound and are often put back into training too quickly which results in a recurrence of the disease.

11. In some cases bony tissue may have to be surgically removed.

12. If condition is only a serious arthritis and a periostitis has not resulted in new bone growth, or if new bone growth does not involve the articular surfaces of the joint, horse may be able to run normally and be workably sound.

13. If new bone growth involves the articular surfaces of the joint, or if horse has upright pasterns, prognosis is unfavourable, as permanent damage may have been caused.

14. In all cases where osselets are suspected, call in veterinarian at once.

Ringbone

Ringbone.

Bony enlargement resulting from an ostitis of the upper or lower pastern bones. Two classifications – high ringbone, involving the long pastern bone; or low ringbone, involving the short pastern bone. Either classification may, or may not, involve the joint.

Causes

1. Poor conformation – upright or over-long pasterns.
2. Concussion, sprains and blows.
3. Shoes left on too long, allowing heels to grow too long. This removes frog pressure and increases jar on the feet.
4. Shoeing with long toe, low heel, so that hoof-pastern axis is broken.

Symptoms

1. If ringbone involves a joint, the horse may come out slightly lame, and lameness will persist.
2. Heat and pain will not be present for a week or two.
3. As with other bony enlargements a horse will be more lame on hard ground than on soft.

4. Fetlock joint will lack flexion.
5. If ringbone does not involve a joint, there will be no lameness.
6. In later stages the enlargement may be felt – in the case of high ringbone, around and above the coronet.
7. Low ringbone in the later stages changes the shape of the hoof. The exostosis appears in front of the coffin bone, and in long-standing cases the wall will show a ridge.

Treatment
1. Consult veterinarian. In some cases, if diagnosed in very early stages before new bone growth starts, limiting the motion of the foot may help. This is achieved by applying a plaster cast. Cast remains in place for 4 weeks.
2. Rest and laxative diet. After cast is removed minimum 4 months rest required.
3. Reduce inflammation with cold water irrigation.
4. Shoe with thin-heeled bar shoe, if horse is going on his heels. If disease is at the toe, fit an open rocker shoe. If joint is stiff, use rocker or rocker bar shoe. Farrier will advise in conjunction with veterinarian.
5. Blistering or pin-firing may prove effective.
6. New treatments include Adequan or Methotrexate injections, or nutritional supplements that reduce arthritic pain and inflammation. Cortisone injections also may be effective. Surgery may also be possible and effective.
7. If ringbone involves a joint the horse will probably be incurably lame.

Sore Shins

Inflammation of the periostium (membrane covering the bone) in front of the cannon bone. Common in young racehorses.

Causes
1. Concussion – galloping on hard ground.

Symptoms
1. Horse goes short, usually in both forelimbs, and may or may not be lame.
2. Heat and tenderness on the front of the cannon bone.
3. Painful, diffuse swelling occurs on the front of the cannon bone.
4. Legs may become enlarged.
5. Loss of freedom of action in both forelimbs. If work continues, lameness will result.

Sore shin.

Treatment
1. Rest and laxative diet.
2. Apply hot packs or poultices (antiphlogistine or Animalintex) to relieve pain.
3. After 2 or 3 days change to cold water irrigation.
4. Continue to apply cold water bandages for a week or two, even after starting work. Helps tone up the legs.
5. In bad cases, where there is a bony deposit, the legs should be blistered.

Side Bones

Ossification of the lateral cartilages of the foot.

Causes
1. Poor conformation may predispose horse to sidebone. The faults in conformation may be hereditary.
2. Result of inflammation of the lateral cartilages caused by concussion.
3. May result from a blow or a tread.
4. Undue concussion fostered by thick-heeled shoes or calkins.

Unilateral side bone.

Symptoms
1. Can be felt. In 'partial' side bone, a portion of the cartilage remains flexible, whilst the other portion is resistant. In complete side bone there is no flexibility.
2. Lameness is not generally present unless some other condition (e.g. ringbone) is also affecting the limb.
3. The side bones may not cause lameness, but a contracted foot, causing pressure on the sensitive parts by squeezing them between the pedal bone and the ossified cartilage and the wall of the hoof, will cause pain and lameness.
4. In cases of unilateral side bone (which usually occurs on the outside) the shoes will wear more on the outside branch.

Treatment
1. If no lameness is present, none is indicated.
2. If horse is lame, rest and cold applications are indicated.
3. Special shoeing may relieve pressure, and expand hoof.
4. Blistering, and/or firing may be helpful.
5. If lameness persists, the veterinary surgeon may perform an operation known as 'grooving the wall'. This relieves the pressure which is causing the lameness.

CHAPTER 29

Sprains and Strains

Many opinions are that these are synonymous although some consider a sprain to be more severe than a strain. Sudden stress on a tendon or ligament beyond its normal range and capability causes torn fibres. The horse is more susceptible to this type of injury when muscles are tired or fatigued and therefore no longer able to fully support the less elastic tendons and ligaments. Jumping from hard into soft going, and uneven landing on rough ground can also cause similar injury.

'Bows', sprained tendons and 'broken down' are loosely applied terms which generally refer to a rupture of some of the ligamentous attachments of the tendon sheath. Tendons are part of a muscle and attach muscles to bone, but unlike the fleshy 'belly' of the muscle they are inelastic, tough white cords (see diagram of ligaments and tendons in the leg, page 114). On the rare occasions when the tendon itself is over strained or stretched it remains stretched, because, being inelastic, it cannot retract. This condition is known as a bowed tendon.

Causes
1. Pulling a horse up suddenly, as in polo.
2. All the weight of the body coming on one leg.
3. Too much galloping (e.g. a racehorse in training).
4. Galloping or jumping in heavy going, especially when the horse is tired.
5. Allowing the toes to get too long.
6. Defective conformation, e.g. long, sloping pasterns; a crooked leg; tied in below the knee.
7. Ringbone, or enlarged pasterns, which restrict the free movement of the joints. This may mechanically cause the relaxation of the tendons.
8. Rarely sprains may be caused by horse slipping or getting cast in stable.

Sprained tendon.

Symptoms – General
1. Lameness – sudden and severe.
2. Pain, heat and swelling – diffuse at first, becoming better defined later, around the tendons.
3. In case of slight strain affecting the sheath and fibres of the superficial tendon only, lameness may be very slight. There will be heat but only slight swelling.

Symptoms of Injury to the Flexor Tendons
1. Lack of flexion of the knee when in motion.
2. Inability to raise and flex the leg, resulting in dragging of the toe.
3. When standing, horse keeps knee slightly bent and heel off the ground, to relax the tendon.
4. Injury to deep flexor tendon, or check ligament, involves a great deal of pain.
5. When deep flexor tendon is involved, swelling may be at the side of the leg.
6. When injury is to the superficial flexor tendon, swelling or curve is at the back of the leg.
7. When check ligament is injured, there is little external swelling or heat. However, horse will flinch as he puts the foot to the ground, due to the weight coming suddenly on to the injured ligament.
8. When suspensory ligament is injured there is seldom much swelling.

Diagnosis of Seat of Sprain
1. Lift the foreleg and press the various tendons with finger and thumb until the horse flinches.
2. To test check ligament, apply pressure by lifting the foot and bending it right back (under elbow). In this position the ligament can be felt.
3. Test suspensory ligament in the same way as check ligament.
4. If the swelling over the tendons 'pits' on pressure from the tips of the fingers, the swelling is not due to sprain.

5. Lameness, heat, and swelling of the limb in the region of the tendons, may be due to causes other than sprains, e.g. infection and pus in the foot, compression from a rope round the limb, a blow from the opposite foot.
6. If in doubt, remove the shoe and exclude the possibility of the cause of lameness being in the foot before treating as for sprain.
7. In all cases consult veterinarian.

Treatment – General for all Sprains

1. Complete rest and laxative diet (no grain). Seek veterinary help at once.
2. There is considerable divergence of opinion over the treatment of strained tendons. Modern practice generally favours tight bandaging or putting leg into plaster cast to avoid swelling and tendon thickening.
3. Traditional treatment involved poulticing and prolonged rest. Modern methods prefer a gradual return to gentle exercise as soon as the heat and soreness have left the part, since prolonged rest will allow part to thicken.
4. If tight bandaging is favoured it must be employed as soon as possible after injury. The bandaging must be correctly applied with cotton wool or Gamgee wadding underneath to spread pressure evenly.
5. Slight strains may be relieved by cold water bandages, or support bandages over a cooling or astringent lotion.
6. If bandaging is employed the bandage should be removed after 48 hours and the leg massaged (hand rubbed) for some time to improve circulation and prevent formation of adhesions between parts by the fluid which is exuded.
7. Bandage is then replaced and massaging and rebandaging repeated morning and evening for a week.
8. Fit a wedge-heeled shoe for 10 to 14 days to relieve pressure on tendons. A patten or raised heel 'rest' shoe was traditionally used in severe cases of tendon injury. Due to more modern treatment of maintaining gentle exercise from a minimum of twice daily walking in hand initially, to gradual slow build-up of work to recovery, 'rest' shoes are now obsolete. Gentle movement ensures the new fibres are laid down in the direction they need to follow, and it helps to disperse any fluid build-up.

After-treatment for Sprains

1. Traditionally horse was rested for 6 months after a serious sprain. This procedure is not now generally recommended. Prolonged rest will allow adhesions to become permanent.
2. Modern treatment calls for a limited period of complete rest followed

by slow walking work. Consult with your attending veterinarian.

3. Hand rubbing of the tendons is beneficial.
4. Embrocation (an ointment or liniment) may be beneficial as a stimulant combined with hand rubbing.
5. Wedge heels may be used and the height gradually reduced.
6. Blistering and firing, which produce pain and destruction of tissues, led to the horse resting the part and congestion occurring. These treatments are not generally advised. Massage, bandaging, electrotherapy and short-wave therapy are preferable after treatments for strains and sprains.

Curb

Curb.

An enlargement, approximately 5ins (13cm) below the point of hock. Either a thickening of the sheath of the deep flexor tendon, or an enlargement of the ligament uniting the bones of the hock.

Causes
1. As for sprains.
2. Jumping badly, or out of deep going.
3. Weak hocks, or sickle hocks are liable to curb.

Symptoms
1. A curved, convex enlargement is visible when hock is viewed from the side. May be very slight and found only on manipulation.
2. Heat and pain are usually present.
3. Horse may or may not be lame. If lame he will go on his toe and when standing will raise heel off the ground.

Treatment
1. Rest and laxative diet.
2. Shoe with wedge-heeled shoe.
3. Treat as for sprains.
4. An embrocation or mild blister may be applied.
5. In bad cases, where conformation of hocks makes them prone to curb, your veterinarian may suggest firing as an alternative.

30

Bursal and Synovial Enlargements

Definition

Enlargements or distentions of the synovial membrane which encloses all true joints, and certain parts of all tendons and some ligaments. An increased secretion of synovia, or joint oil, nature's provision to lessen irritation, causes the enlargements. When over-exertion or strain produce irritation, the synovial membrane is excited to increase secretion of oil.

Horses with upright shoulders, fetlocks or hocks (i.e. with conformation lacking in elasticity of the joints) are most liable to synovial enlargements. Classified under this general heading are thoroughpin, bog spavin and wind galls.

Treatment – General Notes

1. Treatment must depend on cause. Those enlargements caused by work and concussion may be cured but are likely to reappear.
2. Enlargements caused by accidents, sprains of ligaments or parts of the tendons, are not so likely to reappear once they have been reduced.
3. Rest and laxative diet.
4. Friction and pressure help by stimulating the action of the blood vessels.
5. Horses showing much wear benefit from hosing with cold water, followed by brisk hand rubbing.
6. Liniments are useful for reducing enlargements.
7. Dry pressure bandages, applied after hand rubbing, are very effective.

Bog Spavin

Distension of the capsule of the true hock joint. Puffy swelling appears on the inside and a little to the front of the hock.

Causes
1. Straight hocks may predispose the horse to strain causing bog spavin.
2. Undue strain being thrown on hocks, e.g. slipping backwards, or overwork.

Symptoms
1. Small bulges are seen on the inside of the hock.
2. Swelling is usually cold, painless and fluctuating.
3. Horse is usually not lame, unless swelling is sufficiently large to interfere with the action of the joint.
4. If case is recent and acute there will be inflammation, with attendant heat, swelling and pain – i.e. lameness.
5. If lameness is present horse will carry his leg and swing it clear of the ground.

Treatment
1. If swelling is small and no lameness is present, no treatment is necessary.
2. To relax the joint a high-heeled (long, sloping wedge heel, not calkin) shoe may be applied. Shoe should be rolled at the toe and have very strong clip.
3. In acute cases, cold applications with astringent lotions are indicated. Massage will also help.
4. In chronic cases, after inflammation has subsided, blistering or firing may be tried. Acid firing is the safest and most likely to assist.

Thoroughpin

Thoroughpin.

Distension of the tendon sheath immediately above and on either side of the point of hock. Seldom causes lameness but is a technical unsoundness and can be unsightly.

Causes
1. Straight hocks – predispose the horse to possible strain which may cause thoroughpin.
2. Pulling up suddenly from a gallop, especially in soft going.
3. Rearing or kicking violently.

Symptoms
1. If recent, and due to injury, swelling will be hot, tense and painful.
2. Usually, the swelling is cold, and not tender to the touch.
3. Swelling is egg-shaped, and often goes through from one side to the other. Is usually particularly evident on the inner side of the hock.

Treatment
1. If thoroughpin is small, no treatment is necessary. Work may continue.
2. If thoroughpin is large, rest horse and apply a blister, or iodine ointment.
3. In acute cases, application of cooling, astringent lotion, followed by carefully applied pressure bandages, are often successful in reducing the swellings.
4. Some good results have been obtained by aspiration of the fluid and injection of hydrocortisone into the sac. This should be left to the veterinary surgeon.
5. In chronic cases, acid firing may be resorted to.

Wind Galls

Swellings just above the fetlock and on either side of it. Seldom give rise to lameness, except when associated with a sprain. Not a technical unsoundness.

Causes
1. Strain and overwork.
2. Toe of hoof being allowed to get too long, and heels too low.

Treatment
1. Treat as for thoroughpin.
2. Hosing with cold water, or standing horse in running stream may help.
3. Shoe with wedge-heeled shoe to relieve pressure.
4. Pressure bandages in the stable are useful, but once used they tend to become a permanent necessity.

Capped Knee

Swelling of the tendon sheath which passes over the front of the knee (extensor tendon).

Causes
Usually caused by a blow, e.g. hitting a jump.

Treatment
1. Rest.
2. Massage – iodine liniment often useful.
3. Pressure.
4. If necessary, a mild blister may be applied.

Location of common bursal and synovial enlargements.

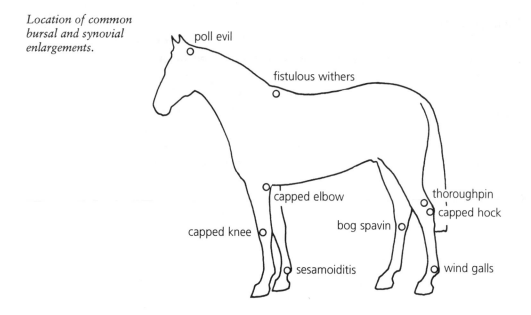

5. Condition is usually of little consequence and does not result in lameness.

Sesamoiditis

Inflammation of the sesamoid bone and/or the sesamoid sheath of the flexor tendon.

Causes
1. Pulling up suddenly.
2. Jumping – especially down a drop.
3. Faulty conformation – turned out toes.
4. Other causes – as for sprained tendons.

Symptoms
1. Lameness – usually well marked, but may be off and on.
2. Heat and usually swelling over the flexor tendons at the affected fetlock.
3. In serious cases, horse will not bring the heel to the ground.

Treatment
1. Rest.
2. Cold water treatment.
3. Blister or pin fire, or acid fire.
4. No permanent cure.

Capped Elbow

Sometimes termed a 'shoe boil'. An enlargement of the subcutaneous bursa at the point of the elbow.

Causes
1. Lack of bedding – horse bruises point of elbow, either on the ground or with the heel of his shoe, when lying down.
2. May be caused by horse kicking forwards at flies in hot weather.

Symptoms
1. A swelling appears at the elbow and extends to the arm.
2. In the early stages, swelling may be painful on manipulation.
3. Limb may be stiff and movement hampered.
4. After about 2 weeks the swelling, which was soft, becomes firm.

Treatment
1. In early stages – cold water applications, followed by massage with astringent lotions.
2. If swelling continues to increase in size, it may have to be drained. This is a job for the veterinary surgeon.

Preventive Measures
1. Ensure horse has plenty of bedding – preferably wood shavings which will not be easily displaced.
2. If horse lies down frequently and is liable to injury (and in early stages of capped elbow to avoid re-bruising swelling) fit 'stuffed sausage' boot (also called 'shoe boil' boot).
3. Shoes should be sloped off very obliquely at heels. Heels kept well rounded; or fit three-quarter shoes.

Capped Hock

Bruising and subsequent swelling of the subcutaneous bursa at the point of the hock.

Causes
1. Blows and kicks – usually self-inflicted. (Kicking back of stable or leaning on hocks during travel.)
2. Once an enlargement occurs on the point of the hock it is constantly bruised when the horse lies down.
3. Occasionally the swelling is due to thickening of the tendon. If the tendon is involved the swelling is hard – if it is the bursa, the swelling

is soft. Thickening of the tendon is more serious and may cause lameness, but it is a rare condition.

Symptoms
1. As in capped elbow, subcutaneous bursa is bruised and a soft swelling results.
2. If recent, swelling will be hot and painful to the touch.

Treatment
1. Give plenty of bedding.
2. In recent cases cold applications should be used.
3. An antiphlogistine poultice may help to reduce the swelling if it is recent.
4. Repeated, mild blistering is useful.

Preventive Measures
1. Give plenty of bedding – as for capped elbow.
2. Pad sides of loosebox.
3. Leave a light burning at night.
4. Fit hock boots as protection in stable and when travelling.

Poll Evil

Soft, painful swelling on the top of the head, just behind the ears.

Causes
1. Direct injury – i.e. a blow, either self-inflicted (striking the poll against a manger, low doorway, etc.) or by someone striking the horse on the head with a whip handle, etc.
2. Pressure – heavy bridle or tight headcollar.
3. May appear without any apparent cause.

Treatment
1. Remove the cause (if caused by pressure).
2. Treatment is the same as for acute abscess, but securing drainage is difficult owing to site of injury.
3. In time the inflammatory fibrous growth, which follows the initial swelling, goes deep and involves a portion of the ligamentum nuchae – the largest ligament in the body – and causes intense pain during any movement of the head.
4. Keep horse in loosebox and place food where horse can reach it with minimum head movement. Give laxative diet.
5. Poultice the region of the poll – antiphlogistine.

6. Most cases require surgical treatment – call the veterinary surgeon.

Fistulous Withers

Similar to poll evil but in this case the sinus is located in the region of the withers.

Causes
1. Pressure and pinching from saddle or badly fitting harness.
2. May be a sequel to a sitfast.
3. May be caused by an infectious bacteria, brucellosis. This form is difficult to cure, and discharges may be infectious to man or other livestock. Consult a veterinarian immediately with a draining abscess.

Symptoms
1. At first a small swelling appears on top of, or to either side of, the withers.
2. Swelling is sore and tender on manipulation.
3. The tissue under the skin is bruised and in time an abscess forms.
4. Horses in poor condition, or with high withers, are most liable to injury.

Treatment
1. Same as for poll evil.
2. Like poll evil, fistulous withers is a very serious condition. Veterinary advice should be sought as early as possible. Neglected cases may be impossible to cure.

CHAPTER **31**

Wounds

Types of Accidental Wound

1. Incised or clean-cut wounds. Caused by a sharp cutting edge – e.g. knife, razor, glass. The divided surfaces are smooth and regular. Bleeding is usually severe. Healing is favoured by the absence of bruising or tearing of flesh. Usually easy to stitch (suture).
2. Lacerated or torn wounds. Caused by blunt instruments entering the flesh and being forcibly torn out, e.g. barbed wire, projecting nail. Torn wounds are common. The broken surfaces are rough but bleeding can be less than in an incised wound.
3. Contused or bruised wounds. Caused by blows, kicks, falls, galls, etc. The skin is not actually broken but the vessels under the skin are ruptured and the injured parts become infiltrated with blood. Relatively common.
4. Puncture wounds. Caused by thorns, stakes, nails (in the feet), or stable forks (in the limbs). Usually such wounds have a small entrance but they may penetrate deep into the tissues. Puncture wounds are always serious. If in the foot, an abscess often forms. Unlike other wounds, where early closure is essential, puncture wounds must be kept open in order to drain. If allowed to close too soon, dirt may be trapped inside and infection will quickly develop.

Treatment of Wounds

1. Stop the bleeding.
   ▪ If only small vessels are involved, exposure to the air will generally suffice. If not, the edges of the wound should be brought together with gentle pressure. Irrigate with clean water, preferably flowing (e.g. hose) followed by application of pressure bandage. Apply direct

pressure to the wound especially to help arrest bleeding. Consult the veterinarian if:

(a) bleeding is profuse

(b) the wound may need stitching

(c) an anti-tetanus booster is required.

2. Clean wound thoroughly.
   - Clip away hair in vicinity of wound.
   - Wash thoroughly. Trickle constant stream of water very gently on the wound for 15 minutes Use hosepipe if available. Otherwise a saline solution is best to cleanse wounds – use contact lens saline or 2 tbs table salt in 1 gallon (4.5 litres) lukewarm water and apply with cotton wool. Avoid sponges and use of disinfectants.
   - Remove any foreign matter but do not probe.
   - If wound is a puncture, the veterinary surgeon must gently probe it but no unqualified person should try. If wound is near joint, there is danger of rupturing the joint oil sac.

3. Dress the wound.
   - Render broken surfaces clean.
   - If wound is small, simply cover liberally with antibiotic wound powder or ointment.
   - Bring divided parts together as closely as possible and keep them in that position. If wound is large, sutures may be necessary.
   - Prevent movement of the injured part so far as possible.
   - Protect from flies. Bandaging is not always necessary but if a bandage is used the wound should be covered with surgical lint and then bandaged lightly – to allow room for any subsequent swelling.

4. Additional measures.
   - Give anti-tetanus injection. If horse has permanent anti-tetanus protection, give booster.
   - Keep loosebox, or stall, scrupulously clean to avoid possible reinfection.
   - Rest horse and put on a laxative diet.
   - Avoid raising dust when a wound is exposed.
   - If swelling is excessive, hot fomentations may be necessary.
   - Antibiotics – penicillin, trimethoprim-sulfa, etc. – have superseded disinfectants. Antibiotic treatment should always be given in cases of puncture wounds near joints, into tendon sheaths and in the foot.

Some Common Wounds

Bit Injuries
   - Show on bars of mouths, tongue, cheeks, or in chin groove.
   - Caused by badly-fitting or worn bit, rough hands, or ragged molars.

- Treatment – discontinue work for a few days. After feeding, wash out mouth with warm water and salt. Remove cause, adjust bit.

Girth Galls
- Show on soft skin behind the elbow.
- Caused by too tight, too hard, or too loose girth on horse in soft condition.
- Treatment – do not use saddle for a few days. Then use a Balding, 'Cottage Craft' or string girth or encase girth in sheepskin or non-chafing tube.
- If skin is not broken, harden skin by applying salt and water, methylated spirit or witch hazel, several times a day.
- In severe cases inflammation can be reduced by applying a cortisone ointment.

Saddle Sores and Sore Back
- Any injury – from slight rub to severe swelling – caused by friction or pressure from badly-fitting saddle.
- Stop work under saddle. Exercise in hand.
- Treat open wounds by fomentation.
- Later harden with salt and water or methylated spirit.
- Trace and remove cause of injury.

4. Broken knees.
- Injury to the surface of one or both knees caused by stumbling and falling. Varies in severity from slight abrasion to exposure of the knee bones.
- Any injury to a joint is a job for the veterinary surgeon.
- Treatment – complete rest. Irrigate continuously with cold water. Do not probe wound.
- With an open joint, the main danger is inflammation which may result in disease of the bone. An exostosis is formed, resulting in a permanently stiff joint.
- Protect the wound by putting on a knee cap lined with clean surgical lint. Do not bandage the knee.

Antiseptics and Antibiotics

Most antiseptics retard healing by killing healing cells as well as harmful organisms.

Safe Antiseptics
1. Saline solution (salt and water – 1 teaspoon salt to 1 pint (0.5 litre) of water).

2. Potassium permanganate – enough just to turn the water purple.
3. Hydrogen peroxide.
4. Tamed iodine solution (Betadine or Pevidine), dilute 1:4 with water.
5. If using any other antiseptic on wounds, use in a very dilute solution (usually just one or two drops to a pint of water).
6. When disinfecting surgical equipment, use a strong solution of disinfectant.
7. Sulphanilamide and nitrofurazone are good wound dressings. Do not use blue lotion, scarlet oil, or caustic substances on a fresh wound that exposes tissue beneath the skin, as they cause more damage and slow healing.

Antibiotics
1. Penicillin and other antibiotics, used under the guidance of a veterinary surgeon, are excellent and now generally replace disinfectants.
2. Some horses suffer allergic reactions to antibiotics and to some antiseptics. Watch all treated animals carefully.

CHAPTER 32

Warbles, Bots and Biting Flies

Warbles (*Hypoderma bovis* and *Hypoderma lineatum*)

Occur in cattle-raising areas of the northern hemisphere between 25° and 60° North latitude. The adult fly is about ¼in. (6mm) long and looks rather like a bee. These flies do not bite but make a distinctive whirring sound which alerts horses and cattle to their presence and sets them running for shelter.

The adult flies lay their eggs from May to August, chiefly on the hairs of horses' (or cows') legs. In 4 to 5 days the eggs hatch and the larvae burrow through the skin, then through the connective tissue, and by the following January to May they begin to appear as small lumps just under the skin, generally on the horse's back. Each 'warble' lump has a small hole at its summit to which the posterior spiracles of the larva are pressed to obtain air. Here the larva grows much larger. When it emerges, or is extracted, from the warble the larva (also called a warble) is about ½in. (12mm) long and whitish to light brown in colour.

When the larva reaches maturity, having fed on the fluid exuded from the inflamed flesh, it works its way out through the hole, falls to the ground, and about 6 weeks later a new warble fly emerges.

Treatment
1. Warbles which are not under the saddle or harness should be left alone to ripen naturally.
2. If a warble is under the saddle, the saddle must be left off until the warbles have been removed.
3. Encourage warble to ripen by application of heat – hot fomentations or poultice.
4. When ripe, a small hole can be felt in the centre of the lump. The larva can be squeezed out by gentle pressure of the thumbs at the base of the lump.

5. Do not press with thumbs until larva is ready to emerge. There is a danger of bursting it under the skin and turning the lump septic.
6. After the warble has been squeezed out, or broken out of its own accord, wash out the cavity with diluted disinfectant and dress with iodine.

Bots (*Gasterophilus* spp.)

These are the larvae of gadflies (botflies). The gadfly, a brownish yellow, hairy fly about 2/3in. (16mm) long, lays its eggs during late summer and autumn on the hair of horses. The little yellow eggs are attached to the hairs, generally on the front parts of the horse, in reach of the tongue.

The eggs hatch in 10 to 14 days and the horse licks them off his coat and takes them into his mouth, where they penetrate the mucous membrane of the gums, lips and tongue. They remain there for a short growing period and later pass on to the stomach and intestine, where they remain attached to the walls for almost a year. Finally they release their grip and pass out with the faeces to pupate in the soil. Adult botflies emerge from the pupal cases in 3 to 9 weeks, depending on the temperature.

Symptoms
1. If present in large quantities, there may be a loss of condition – dry, staring coat.
2. May be a rise in temperature and quickened pulse rate.
3. Horse may become restless and kick at belly.
4. Bots have differing effects on digestive system, horse may have intermittent diarrhoea or constipation.
5. The presence of larvae in the stomach has an inflammatory effect. The stomach wall rises and swells around the bots.
6. Bot larvae are about 3/4in. (19mm) long and may be expelled in the dung, usually in the spring.
7. In small quantities they are not injurious.

Prevention
1. Keep horses away from pastureland during season when gadfly (botfly) lays its eggs. (Turn horses out after dark and bring in early in the morning.)
2. Pick or clip the eggs off the skin when seen.
3. Frequent grooming removes some eggs.
4. Weekly application of a 2% carbolic dip to those parts of the horse on which eggs are deposited destroys them.
5. When the eggs are found in quantity on the legs rub them over with

a cloth dipped in paraffin.

6. Provide darkened shelters for horses at pasture during the gadfly (botfly) season. This will give horses protection against the attacks of the flies.

Treatment

1. Gasterophilus control can be achieved with dichlorvos or trichlorfon, administered by stomach tube. (Best done in early spring when larvae are in stomach and before they pass out of horse.)
2. Ivermectin paste and mebendazole-trichlorfon (Telmin B) paste are also effective against stomach bots and the earlier stages migrating in the tissues of the mouth. Administer at 0.2mg per kg. Use ivermectin in late autumn after frost has killed the adult gadflies, to prevent stomach bots from wintering over inside the horse.
3. Consult your veterinarian to work out an effective worming programme rotating different drugs for the best results.

Biting Flies

Biting flies (stable flies, mosquitoes, horse and deer flies, and occasional horn flies) attack horses on warm days throughout the summer.

Prevention

1. Regular applications of insecticidal preparations (e.g. pyrethrins, dichlorvos or lindane) are indicated in buildings.
2. Fly repellents, sprays, liquids, etc. which can be safely applied to horse may also help.
3. Keep horses in stable during hours of peak fly activity.

3 3

Loss of Condition

Obvious Reasons for Loss of Condition
1. Improper feeding.
2. Excessive work.
3. Lack of water.

Less Obvious Reasons for Loss of Condition
1. Worms.
2. Teeth.
3. Lampas.
4. Quidding.
5. Bolting food.
6. Parasites.
7. Stable vices.

Intestinal Parasites
Various types of intestinal parasites affect horses. See Chapter 17, Preventive Medicine, and Chapter 32, Warbles, Bots and Biting Flies for information about common internal parasites and their control.

Teeth
1. Upper molars grow downwards and outwards.
2. Lower molars grow upwards and inwards.
3. Therefore, the outside of the upper molars and the inside of the lower molars get uneven wear. They grow sharp points and lacerate the cheeks and tongue.
4. Pain stops horse from eating normal amount of food. Also prevents him from chewing food.
5. Teeth should be floated (rasped) periodically – once or twice a year.
6. Bad or decaying tooth may also stop horse from eating or chewing properly. Horse will probably hold his head on one side.

7. Check teeth regularly.

Lampas

1. Not considered a pathological condition. Gums and lips may become irritated and congested.
2. Gives a 'dropped' appearance to the roof of the mouth, where an inflamed fleshy lump may be visible.
3. In young horses, usually associated with cutting of permanent teeth.
4. In old horses caused by sharp molars, indigestion, blood disorders and bit injuries.
5. Grass awns or foxtails which stick in gums and lips from grazing grasses gone to head or from hay cut late and gone to head. Very painful and can cause horse to go off feed completely.

Treatment
- Inspect molars – rasp if necessary.
- Put horse on laxative diet. If horse is completely off feed consult veterinary surgeon.
- If due to grass awns or foxtails, remove offending forage. Pick visible awns out of mouth.
- Rinse mouth with witch hazel or alum in 2% solution twice daily.
- Rest horse for a few days and allow only soft foods.

Quidding

The food, after partial mastication, is rolled and shifted in the mouth and finally ejected.

Causes
- Dental irregularities which cause pain when horse tries to chew.
- May be associated with sore throat.
- Lampas.
- Some acrid substance in food.

Treatment
Remove the cause.

Bolting Food

Horse swallows food without proper mastication.

Causes
- Lampas.
- Dental irregularities – sharp teeth.
- Parasites.
- Stable vices.
- Greed.

Treatment
- In first three cases – remove cause.
- If cause is greed, it is usually greed for corn. Add chaff, bran, horse cubes, etc., in higher proportion to grain.
- Put bar across manger.
- Feed from the ground.
- Put salt block in manger.

Ringworm

Contagious skin disease caused by a fungus. Easily transmitted from one animal to another by saddlery, grooming kit, or by occupying the same loosebox or stall as an infected horse.

Causes
1. Contagion – from strange stable, during transportation, pre-infected clothing, tack or grooming kit.
2. Dirty horses more prone to attack.
3. Horses in low condition also prone to attack.
4. Inferior forage – musty hay and oats – may be cause of transmitting the disease round the stable.

Symptoms
1. Raised, circular patches of hair on neck and shoulders.
2. Patches grow in size and scab off leaving greyish-white crusts on the bare skin.
3. Spreads rapidly. Horse loses condition.

Treatment
1. Isolate. Pay strict attention to disinfection of tack and grooming kit. Keep separate tack-cleaning materials for the infected horse. Veterinary advice is essential.
2. If coat is long, clip horse. Burn hair at once. Disinfect clippers after use.
3. As the fungi infect the skin, a specific oral antibiotic can be most effective. Griseofulvin is often used, under the trade name 'Fulcin',

and can be given in the feed for a 7-day course.

4. It is also possible to treat ringworm topically with appropriate lotions or sprays. Iodine can also be usefully applied to each patch.

5. Keep horse well groomed and disinfect kit often. After grooming, go over horse with stable rubber damped with a mild disinfectant.

6. Burn all litter and disinfect loosebox thoroughly.

7. Wear overalls when grooming infected horse. Keep sleeves rolled down and wear rubber gloves, or wash hands thoroughly afterwards. Ringworm can be passed from the horse to his attendant.

8. Thoroughness in treating all ringworm patches is vital. The disease will spread if just one spot is neglected. Repeat treatment of all spots until they appear dead.

9. Successful treatment of ringworm requires skilled veterinary attention. Treatments are constantly changing and the veterinary surgeon will advise the most up-to-date and effective treatment.

10. Keep horse isolated and under observation for some time, in case of further outbreak.

Canadian Pox

Very similar to ringworm in appearance, but eruption usually in clusters of pimples, most frequently near the girth or behind the elbow. Highly contagious disease due to a bacillus.

Treatment
1. As for ringworm.
2. After treating the sores with iodine (or a solution of 1 part carbolic acid to 40 parts water) apply boracic acid and flour – or other dressing recommended by veterinary surgeon.
3. Put horse on laxative diet.
4. Precautions should be taken as for ringworm to avoid spread of the disease, both to other horses and to attendant.

Acne

Skin eruption similar to Canadian pox but the pimples are scattered and do not occur in clusters. Generally occurs near the withers. Much less common than Canadian pox.

Treatment
Same as Canadian pox.

Mange

There are three main types of mange parasite:
1. Sarcoptic. Most serious – now rare. Caused by a burrowing mite. The parasite generally attacks near the withers but is harboured in infected harness and often also attacks the face.
2. Soroptic. Similar to sarcoptic but less serious. In this case the mite does not burrow but is a scavenger upon the skin surface (caused by a different mite). Seeks the cover of long hair and most often found in the mane and tail.
3. Symbiotic. Caused by a different mite again and is confined to the legs and heels – especially in horses with a lot of 'feather'.

Symptoms
1. Itchiness.
2. In symbiotic mange, stamping of feet, often rapidly repeated.
3. Affected parts become thicker and wrinkled and hair eventually falls off leaving skin covered with a thin crust.

Causes
1. Contagion.
2. Dirt and lack of grooming.

Treatment
1. Isolation.
2. Put on laxative diet.
3. Clip and burn all hair.
4. There are many new parasiticides, which give better control than old remedies containing sulphur, which itself may cause dermatitis. Treat as instructed by the veterinary surgeon.
5. Precautions must be taken to kill all parasites sheltering outside the body, otherwise re-infection will occur. Use a blow lamp (with care) to kill parasites sheltering in woodwork, etc.

Ticks

Similar to those found on dogs.

Treatment
1. Search out ticks and dab with mineral oil or turpentine, or paraffin or touch with a singeing lamp. Take care not to burn the horse.
2. When tick relaxes its hold it will fall off, or can be removed quite easily between the finger and thumb or with tweezers. Be careful to

remove the head as well as the body. Pull straight out, do not twist.
3. Crush ticks as you remove them and drop bodies into paraffin or turpentine or burn immediately.
4. Do not try to pull ticks off without applying something to make them relax or a small wound on the skin will result where tick was clinging.
5. Do not snip off with scissors or the head will remain embedded in the skin and could cause inflammation.
6. Tick dip preparations used for dogs can be applied bi-weekly to lower legs, mane and tail hairs to help prevent infestation. Do not apply dip to underside of dock of tail or it will cause skin irritation.

Lice

Found on horses in poor condition or worm infested and pastured with cattle. Also picked up by horses at grass. They are blood-sucking and soon pull horse down in condition.

Symptoms
1. Give blotchy appearance to the coat.
2. Itchiness – horse will rub against any convenient object.
3. Lice and nits (eggs) can be seen on close examination.

Treatment
1. Clip horse and groom thoroughly.
2. Apply a preparation such as pyrethrin-based powder or shampoo to kill lice.
3. Repeat treatment in 10 days to catch the eggs which have hatched since first application.
4. Disinfectants are useless against lice. They only blister the skin.
5. Ivermectin, which is an effective horse wormer, will also kill lice. However, its swift elimination from the body may not ensure that all lice are effectively eradicated.

CHAPTER 34

Non-Parasitic Skin Diseases

Cracked Heels

Cracks in the heel region, running crossways, sometimes extending from one side of the heel to the other.

Causes
1. Exposure to wet and cold.
2. Irritation from mud.
3. Injuries from ropes and hobbles.
4. Bad stable management (standing in dirty, wet bedding; ammonia fumes aggravate the condition).
5. Washing horse's legs and failing to dry properly. This removes natural oils which keep skin supple, and makes horse prone to chill.
6. Sweat running down the legs to the heels (common in racehorses).

Symptoms
1. Skin in the hollow of the pastern on one or more legs becomes tender, reddened and scaly.
2. Small vesicles form and then rupture, causing a crack over the point where vesicle developed.
3. If not treated, crack extends and deepens, its edges becoming thickened and calloused.
4. Horse is lame – goes on toes.
5. Limb may become swollen.

Treatment
1. Wash with warm water and medicated soap. Dry thoroughly.
2. Clip off all hair in hollow of pastern.
3. In mild cases, in the early stages, apply zinc and caster oil ointment.
4. In advanced cases it may be necessary to dress wounds with

sulphanilamide pads and bandages to restrict movement, and keep clean and dry.

5. Veterinary advice should be sought. A course of antibiotics is very useful. Rest, laxative diet.
6. When healing starts, keep heels soft with Vaseline.

Prevention

1. If possible, do not clip legs. Hair protects them.
2. Do not wash muddy legs. Bandage lightly (over straw) until dry and then brush off mud.
3. If legs are washed, always dry carefully.
4. In wet, muddy country, oil heels, or apply Vaseline, before taking horse out.
5. Keep legs warm at night with stable bandages.

Mud Fever

Excessive exposure to mud can cause the skin to become infected by bacteria. The superficial layers of skin are damaged by the bacteria and the area becomes inflamed with some swelling, then raw with a crusting scab. The legs and sometimes the belly are affected.

Causes

1. Similar to cracked heels. Washing legs is a prime cause.
2. Wetting or chapping by water and mud sensitise the skin and cracks, oozing and swelling occur. White-haired areas of legs, and horses with sensitive skin, are often more susceptible.

Symptoms

1. Limbs swell, heat and tenderness of the skin.
2. Skin becomes thickened, rough, and covered with little scabs.
3. When scabs are detached, hair falls off with them and a red base is exposed.
4. Lameness, depending on degree of the disease.

Treatment

1. If there is a fever present, give mild dose of Epsom salts in horse's water or in bran mash. Use 1/4lb or 113g Epsom salts.
2. Keep horse on laxative diet, and rest.
3. Wash legs with warm water, rinse and dry thoroughly. It is important to soften and remove all scabs so that air can reach the exposed skin. The bacteria will then dry out. Antibiotic ointment will then kill the bacteria.

4. If infection has become deep-seated then oral antibiotics may also be necessary.
5. Veterinary advice may be required.

Prevention
1. As for cracked heels.
2. Do not wash mud off – allow it to dry and then brush it off.
3. If legs are washed, dry thoroughly.
4. Apply grease or Vaseline to vulnerable legs before exposure to mud and wet.

Nettlerash (Urticaria, Hives)

A skin disorder in which round swellings appear on various parts of the body.

Causes
1. Sudden change in diet. Error of diet – i.e. too much grain, too little work, too much protein. Overheated blood.
2. Occurs most frequently in young animals.
3. Often seen when young animals are first turned out on to lush pasture.
4. May be an allergic reaction to some plants or insect bites and stings.

Symptoms
1. Round lumps appear very suddenly on the body. Vary in size from very small to several inches across.
2. Swellings are flat on the surface and elastic on manipulation.
3. Rarely is there any irritation.
4. In mild cases, lumps may appear on the neck only. Otherwise they occur either in patches, or all over the body.

Treatment
1. Keep horse at rest in loosebox. Laxative diet.
2. Call veterinary surgeon. An antihistamine should be administered, and dose repeated for 2 days.
3. Swellings may be dressed with a cooling lotion (e.g. witch hazel or calamine) if they persist.
4. Swellings usually disappear spontaneously.
5. Remove the cause if this can be isolated.

Sweet Itch (Mane and Tail Eczema)

This skin disease is now thought to be due to an allergic reaction to biting flies, particularly midges. Often found in small ponies but also affects other classes of horses and is most common when they are at pasture. Liable to recur annually in spring and summer.

Causes
1. Most probably an allergic reaction to flies or biting insects.

Symptoms
1. Areas of skin at root of mane, tail and on the neck and withers, become thickened, inflamed and scaly.
2. Animal rubs against any convenient object.
3. Upper layer of skin is damaged and serum leaks out and collects on surface.
4. The hair falls out leaving moist, bare patches.
5. Later, the skin becomes thickened, hard, wrinkled and scaly.

Treatment
1. As sweet itch is thought to be an allergic reaction to flies or biting insects, keep horses stabled in spring and summer during hours of dawn and dusk, when these insects are most active.
2. Treatment with parasiticide benzyl benzoate to cool and soothe the inflamed area, which should be kept clean.
3. Consult veterinarian. Local treatment consists of clipping hair from affected parts, washing with warm water and mercurial soap, drying well and applying dressing, e.g. zinc and castor oil ointment, or salicylic acid ointment, or propamidine cream.
4. Antihistamine may be required in some cases.
5. Epsom salts in drinking water or in feed are helpful.
6. If horse is sufficiently badly affected to be off work, feed no grain. Substitute extra hay with bran or linseed mashes.

CHAPTER 35

Internal Diseases

Lymphangitis (Monday Morning Disease)

Constitutional blood disorder causing inflammation of the lymphatic system and glands. Most frequently affects a hind limb.

Causes
1. Any factor which prevents the proper flow of lymph – particularly infection.
2. Bacteria entering through an infected wound in the lower part of the limb may set up infection in the lymphatic system.
3. Lack of exercise, combined with no reduction of the usual grain ration. Reduce grain on workless days, increase hay to compensate.
4. Over-nutritious feeding.
5. Sudden changes of diet.

Symptoms
1. Extreme lameness.
2. At onset of attack, quickened pulse, heavy breathing, and often a shivering fit.
3. A limb, or limbs (usually one or both the hind limbs) become swollen, hot and painful.
4. The swelling may extend from foot to stifle. Leg may be twice normal size.
5. Due to pain, the leg is constantly moved and held up.

Treatment
1. Horse should be put in a loosebox and either led out or made to move round the box for a few minutes two or three times a day.
2. Put on a laxative diet. Grain ration should be cut out completely, replace with extra hay.

3. The old treatment was to give full dose of aloes in a ball. This practice still has something to recommend it and is sometimes followed.

4. Call the veterinary surgeon. Modern treatment is sulphonamide drugs and antibiotics in the early stages of an attack.

5. If no aloes ball has been given, add 2-4oz (57-113g) Epsom salts to feed or water two or three times daily.

6. Apply hot fomentations to swollen leg for up to an hour two or three times a day. Dry leg carefully afterwards.

7. Later, give walking exercise for 10 minutes several times a day.

8. Turn horse out on sparse pasture to encourage him to move around and so reduce swelling.

Prevention

1. Horses prone to attack should be exercised every day.

2. On the rest day, bran should be substituted for the grain ration, and quiet walking exercise should be given, or the horse turned out for a short period.

3. Recurrence of the disease may cause a permanent thickness of the leg.

Azoturia (Myohaemoglobinuria, also called 'Tying up')

A peculiar disease of horses closely related to and similar in cause and symptoms to lymphangitis. May be met in any type of animal at any time of year, especially horses in training for competitive events or hunting fit. It is a degenerative condition of muscle, especially over the loins and in the hindquarters.

Causes

1. Exact cause not known. Disease often follows enforced idleness of horse in hard condition – particularly if grain ration is not reduced.

2. Accumulation of glycogen in the muscles of resting horse which, on sudden activity, is used up quickly, creating a marked increase in production of lactic acid which causes swelling and degeneration of muscle fibres.

3. Deficiency of vitamin E is thought to have a contributory effect.

4. Putting a horse straight back to hard work after an enforced period of rest.

Symptoms

1. Horse goes out sound but later slackens and shows muscular stiffness. This may occur after 10 to 15 minutes of exercise or after a phase of work followed by a rest and then when the horse is asked to

move again.
2. Horse starts to stagger and roll in his gait. Shows marked lameness in a hind limb.
3. Profuse sweating, and quickened breathing.
4. Muscles over the loins may be seen quivering.
5. Horse may collapse if forced to proceed.
6. Temperature rises to about 103°F (39.4°C).
7. Muscles over loins may become very hard, tense and painful.
8. If urine is passed, it is coffee-coloured, opaque and may be blood-streaked.

Treatment
1. Get horse home and into loosebox, if possible. Do not try to make him walk – transport him in a trailer or horsebox.
2. Apply hot blankets to his loins.
3. Call the veterinary surgeon.
4. Mild cases recover quickly, but severe cases may be followed by death in a few days.
5. During recovery, keep horse on laxative, easily assimilated diet, i.e. bran mashes, gruel, green food and hay.

Prevention
1. Sensible diet.
2. Whenever possible, give some exercise (if only turning into paddock) every day.
3. When horse is not worked, or if work is greatly reduced, adjust diet immediately.
4. A vitamin E supplement to the diet may be helpful.
5. A form of myositis caused by excessive fatigue can occur in hard worked horses (i.e. endurance, eventing, hunting). Symptoms are often seen shortly after exercise ceases and horse is at rest. Treatment is much the same, but in addition, fluid and electrolyte losses must be dealt with. A veterinarian should be consulted immediately.
6. Vigilance for prevention is essential. One onset predisposes the horse towards another.

Strangles

An acutely contagious disease caused by bacteria – a specific strangles streptococcus (*Streptococcus equi*) – which is inhaled and sets up catarrh of the upper air passages, and fever. The germ enters the lymphatic vessels and is caught in the lymph glands (usually those of the head and neck) where it breeds and eventually causes abscesses.

Symptoms

1. Dullness and apathy.
2. Rise in temperature – to between 103° and 105°F (39.4° and 40.6°C).
3. Mucous membrane of the eye changes from healthy light pink to an unhealthy red colour.
4. Thin watery discharge from one or both nostrils will turn to a thick yellowish discharge.
5. Sore throat and coughing.
6. The glands under the jaw swell and become hot and tender.
7. The head is held stiffly extended. The horse has difficulty in swallowing.
8. After a few days an abscess forms and then bursts.
9. After the abscess breaks, the horse's temperature quickly falls.
10. Strangles most frequently attacks horses under 6 years of age.

Treatment

1. Isolate horse in roomy, airy loosebox with plenty of fresh air.
2. Carefully disinfect the old box and all clothing, saddlery and equipment which may have been in contact with the sick horse.
3. Keep horse warm with rugs and flannel bandages.
4. The strangles bacteria is killed by most antibiotics. Early diagnosis is important – to prevent spread of the disease – so call veterinary surgeon at the earliest signs. Veterinary opinion sometimes varies as to whether to administer antibiotics at initial diagnosis, or to encourage the abscess to burst and disgorge its pus before using antibiotics.
5. Give inhalations of eucalyptus.
6. Cleanse nostrils frequently with warm water and keep them smeared with eucalyptus ointment.
7. Encourage abscesses to mature by application of stimulating liniment, hot fomentations or poultices.
8. When abscess is mature (or pointing) it will burst, discharging a thick pus. If it does not burst it should be lanced by the veterinary surgeon.
9. After abscess bursts, destroy matter and treat as an ordinary wound.
10. Horse should be fed soft food – damp bran mash, boiled oats, etc. If food is not soft the horse will have difficulty eating due to sore throat.
11. Good nursing is essential. Strangles usually runs its course in 6 weeks.
12. Convalescence is long, from 2 to 3 months. An additional long period of conditioning is necessary before normal work can be resumed. This will prevent the risk of secondary respiratory infections occurring.

Prevention
1. Strict stable management and hygiene, combined with fresh air, suitable food and adequate exercise help prevent occurrence of strangles.
2. Infection usually occurs from contaminated food, drinking water (drinking troughs), utensils, clothing or litter.
3. Infection sometimes occurs during transit, or while staying in strange stables. Ensure proper disinfection of all premises and equipment.
4. Avoid conditions favouring development, e.g. chills, debility, etc.
5. Recovery tends to convey a lengthy if not lifetime immunity.
6. Strangles vaccine is available and advised in some circumstances.

Tetanus (Lock Jaw)

A disease caused by the tetanus bacillus which gets into the bloodstream via a wound. The disease is more prevalent in some districts than others. Fatal in nine cases out of ten.

Symptoms
1. Rise in temperature to between 103° and 105°F (39.4° and 40.6°C).
2. General stiffening of the limbs.
3. Membrane of the eye will extend over eyeball
4. Horse becomes highly nervous.
5. Horse stands with nose and tail stretched out, and as disease progresses, jaw becomes set.

Treatment
1. Call veterinary surgeon immediately. If disease is seen in early stages, before jaw becomes set, there is a chance of recovery.
2. Keep horse absolutely quiet, in a dark box.
3. Feed only soft, laxative foods. Withhold hay, as it may cause choking.
4. Keep plenty of fresh water within easy reach.
5. Treatment consists of administering very large doses of concentrated tetanus anti-toxin both intravenously and subcutaneously, every day until definite improvement sets in.
6. If infected wound can be found, treat with antiseptic.

Prevention
1. Immunise all horses against tetanus, and give annual booster shots.
2. If horse has not been immunised, or if in any doubt, anti-tetanus serum, which will give temporary immunity only, should be given as early as possible after any injury. Most dangerous injuries are puncture wounds – tetanus germs are destroyed by contact with the air, but thrive in deep, puncture wounds.

Pneumonia

Inflammation of the lungs (frequently following strangles, or influenza).

Causes
1. Invasion by virulent organisms. Often following contagious diseases such as strangles, glanders, influenza.
2. Colds or chills.
3. Long exposure or over-exertion.
4. A drench going down the 'wrong way', or a stomach pump entering the windpipe by mistake.

Symptoms
1. Rapid, shallow breathing.
2. Dullness and loss of appetite.
3. High fever, accompanied by muscular weakness and staggering.
4. The head is outstretched, and the nostrils dilated.
5. A short, soft cough appears at times.
6. There is usually a scant, rusty-coloured nasal discharge This later becomes greyish and more abundant.
7. The pulse is rapid but weak. The temperature is very high up to 107°F (41°C).
8. Horse will rarely lie down. He may have shivering attacks.
9. If disease progresses favourably, the temperature will gradually sub-side after 7 or 8 days. The horse appears brighter and feeds better.
10. Complete recovery takes place in 2 or 3 weeks.
11. In unfavourable cases, the breathing becomes more rapid and laboured. The pulse weakens and is irregular.
12. Any sudden drop in temperature is a bad sign.

Treatment
1. Good nursing, combined with plenty of fresh air. Keep horse in loosebox with rugs and stable bandages for warmth.
2. Antibiotics and sulphonamide drugs are given.
3. Give inhalations of eucalyptus or Friar's Balsam.
4. Take the chill off drinking water. Epsom salts may be put in drinking water to keep the bowels open.
5. Do not drench.
6. Laxative diet – linseed tea, bran mashes, carrots, etc.
7. Pneumonia is a very serious illness – call the veterinary surgeon as soon as possible.

Colic

A set of symptoms indicating abdominal pain.

Causes

1. Too much food – over-taxing the stomach.
2. Unsuitable or unsuitably prepared foods – too much new green grass, new oats, mouldy hay, too much boiled grain.
3. Stoppage between the stomach and the small intestine.
4. Digestive trouble – bolting food, sudden change of diet.
5. Watering and working immediately after feeding. Watering when overheated.
6. Crib biting and wind sucking.
7. Sand in the stomach.
8. Parasites.
9. Twisted gut.
10. Stones in the kidneys or bladder.

Symptoms

There are several types of colic: spasmodic, flatulent or tympanic colic, impaction or blockage colic, and twisted gut.

Spasmodic Colic

- Pain is intermittent. It is due to spasmodic contractions of the muscular wall of the bowel arising most often from local irritation, or an overactive gut wall.
- Spasms are usually violent.
- Horse kicks at belly and paws the ground.
- Horse may lie down and roll.
- Horse may look round at his flanks, stamp, and break out in cold, patchy sweat.
- Temperature does not rise at first but may do so later due to excitement as pain becomes more frequent and intervals of rest are shortened.
- Breathing may become hurried and 'blowing'.
- After a time the pain subsides and horse begins to feed and drink normally. But the symptoms may recur after an interval.

Flatulent (Wind Colic) or Tympanic Colic

- Caused by over-production of gas during digestion. If more is produced than can be absorbed or passed out naturally then it is trapped, causing distension of the gut wall and ensuing pain.
- Symptoms are similar to those of spasmodic colic, but usually the pain is more continuous, and less severe.

▪ Belly is inflated. Horse appears uneasy. He wanders round his loose-box and may crouch and 'tuck up' but rarely lies down.

Impaction or Blockage Colic

Blockage can be caused most commonly by a build-up of fibrous material restricting the normal passage of digestion (e.g. a horse over-eating its straw bed). It may occur as a result of dietary change or insufficient mastication. It can occur as a result of worms blocking the alimentary tract. Often the pain initially is low grade and continuous. Bowel movement and gut noise slows down or stops, and if the blockage remains then pain will gradually become more intense.

Twisted Gut

The mesentery (membrane) supporting the alimentary canal becomes torn and the gut may twist over on itself. This form of colic may be caused by a stumble or fall or by too strenuous work after a heavy feed. It is sometimes thought to be caused by rolling – but equally it may cause rolling. In cases of twisted gut the temperature rises to 105°F (40.6°C) – higher than in other forms of colic. Deterioration of the horse's condition will be swift. Veterinary advice must be sought urgently. Surgery may be the only treatment. Modern surgery for colic has a high success rate but is expensive.

Treatment

1. Seek veterinary advice.
2. If outside, bring horse in to nearest stable and encourage him to stale.
3. Keep horse warm. Bed loosebox down well. Horse may lie down but should be watched in order to avoid injury if he rolls.
4. Gentle walking exercise may be beneficial.
5. Safest procedure is to keep horse walking gently for half an hour or so and to try to persuade him to eat a small bran mash with Epsom salts. Await the veterinary surgeon's visit for further advice.
6. Hot blankets rolled up and applied to the belly underneath and well back may help relieve pain and stimulate the bowels.
7. Walking may help to stimulate bowels also but it is not a cure for colic and horse should not be walked for an extended period. He may be walked slowly when pain is acute and rested when pain subsides; this will avoid him throwing himself about and sustaining injury.

Whistling and Roaring

Whistling and roaring are different degrees of the same affliction of the larynx.

Whistling

A high-pitched noise generally heard at fast paces. A whistler is usually better able to carry out hard work than is a roarer, but whistling may lead to roaring.

Roaring

A deep noise heard on inspiration at fast paces. A horse may become so distressed at fast paces that he must be pulled up. May lead to heart trouble.

Causes of Whistling and Roaring

1. Direct cause is the partial or total destruction of the nerve controlling the muscles which move the cartilage on the left side of the larynx. Damage to this nerve can be caused by:
   - Sudden and excessive exertion – galloping when at grass or work too early in horse's preparation – which causes increased blood flow and sudden dilation of main artery at the base of the heart around which the left nerve winds.
   - Strangles – insufficient recovery time given after an attack of strangles is commonly believed responsible for causing whistling and roaring.
   - An attack of pharyngitis, bronchitis, pneumonia, influenza or pleurisy may also be responsible for causing the damage.
   - Heredity may play a part – animals may not show symptoms until they are 3 or 4 years old or even later.
   - The vocal chord and its neighbouring cartilages are not drawn back sufficiently, due to the damaged nerve, and the whistling noise is caused by air passing the obstruction as it is breathed in.

Symptoms

1. Unless both sides of the larynx are paralysed, no abnormal sound is heard when the horse is at rest.
2. Whistling may be heard at trot, canter or gallop.
3. Roaring is usually heard in the faster paces, but is sometimes also heard at trot.
4. The sound in both cases may be scarcely perceptible or quite noticeable, according to the gravity of the case.
5. A fit horse will make less noise than an unfit one.
6. The noise is always heard on inspiration (breathing in).

Treatment

The only treatment is surgical. A simple operation consists of removal of the obstruction lining the laryngeal pouches. Consult your veterinarian. This operation is known as a 'hobday' operation.

Prevention
1. Do not breed from affected horses.
2. Rest sufficiently after attacks of strangles, bronchitis, etc.

Broken Wind (Heaves)

Breakdown of the air vesicles (alveoli) of the lungs.

Causes
1. Too much strain on lungs due to chronic cough, or after bronchitis, asthma, pleurisy or pneumonia.
2. Excessive feeding, particularly of bulky foods, before exercise.
3. Feeding dusty hay.
4. Over-galloping an unfit horse.
5. Allergic reactions to mould spores, pollens, or dust in pasture or hay.

Symptoms
1. Harsh, dry cough, gets worse with exercise.
2. Slight discharge from the nose.
3. Cough later becomes short and weak.
4. Breathing is laboured after any exertion.
5. Double effort at exhalation: watch flanks – horse appears to heave twice on breathing out.

Treatment
1. Treatment is palliative; there is no cure for broken wind.
2. Special feeding can help keep horse in work, particularly in early stages.
3. All food should be damped. Linseed oil should be mixed with food three times a week.
4. Hay is best avoided or fed damp or in the form of haylage. Many horses are successfully fed prepared feed, containing grain and also sugar-beet pulp, fed wet, and pelleted grass or hay.
5. Some horses thrive best if kept outside.
6. Bed on shavings, paper, Aubiose or peat to prevent horse eating too much bulk in form of straw.
7. Do not allow the horse to become too unfit or overweight.

High Blowing

Not an unsoundness. A noise made by horse during exhalation only. It is caused by an abnormality of the false nostril which vibrates as horse breathes out. Quite common among well-bred horses. High blowers are said to be very sound-winded horses.

Cold in the Head

Similar to a head cold in man, and brought about by infection or exposure. Not serious in itself but serious complications may result if horse is worked with a cold.

Symptoms
1. Sneezing. Horse is dull and lethargic.
2. Rise in temperature which may remain above normal for 2 or 3 days.
3. Thin nasal discharge. Later becomes thick.
4. Horse may have a cough.
5. Eyes may water.
6. Coat will be dull and staring.

Treatment
1. Isolate to prevent spread.
2. Keep horse warmly clothed but allow plenty of fresh air.
3. Feed laxative diet.
4. Give inhalations of Friar's Balsam to assist discharge.
5. Give electuary to relieve cough.
6. Do not work the horse.

Coughs

Coughs are symptoms of several troubles.

Causes
1. Horse brought up from grass may cough due to impure air in the stable, or indigestion, or too sudden change from soft to hard food.
2. Sore throat – laryngitis.
3. Irritants, e.g. some of a drench going down the windpipe instead of the gullet; something stuck in the throat; dusty stables or riding arenas.
4. Indigestion. May be due to discomfort in stomach and intestines but if no improvement after removing any apparent cause, suspect worms.
5. Broken wind.
6. Teething.

Treatment
1. Treatment consists of correct diagnosis and removal of the cause.

2. If due to coming up from grass – keep top of stable door open night and day to allow fresh air. Make change of food gradual.

3. In cases of laryngitis, keep horse warm in well-ventilated stable. Give inhalations of eucalyptus. Smear electuary on tongue frequently. Massage throat with liniment. Feed gruel, hay tea, grass, bran mashes.

4. Coughs due to indigestion – check horse's worming record. If in doubt, have horse dosed for worms.

5. Coughs due to irritants generally right themselves in a short time. If considerable amount of fluid gets into lungs the irritation may cause pneumonia.

6. Teething cough will disappear as soon as the cause disappears. Feed laxative diet and add Epsom salts to food.

Influenza

Highly infectious disease.

Causes
1. Equine influenza is caused by a virus.
2. It is spread via the atmosphere, as well as contact, e.g. clothing, food, bedding, grooming kit, infected stables.

Symptoms
1. Two types.
   - Mild type runs its course in 6 to 8 days.
   - Severe type or 'pink eye' – most critical period is fifth to eighth day.
2. In both types – high temperature, 103°-106°F (39.4°-41.1°C), and exhausted condition.
3. Catarrhal discharge from eyes and nostrils.
4. Coughing and great depression.
5. Severe type is recognised by bright red colour of the eye as opposed to yellowish colour in mild type.
6. In severe type, swellings may develop on legs, muzzle and belly.
7. Pneumonia may develop.
8. Severe type can be fatal. If cured there may be permanent respiratory trouble.

Treatment
1. Prevention is better than cure. Healthy horse is less liable to the disease than one in poor condition.
2. If an outbreak occurs in the stable, take the temperature of every horse before work. A rise in temperature is the earliest symptom of

mild cases. Call veterinarian. Take care to prevent chilling by covering horse with anti-sweat sheet and sheet or rug.

3. Good stable management, isolation of new horses, and care when travelling will help to prevent the disease.
4. If influenza occurs, isolate the patient at once.
5. Keep warm in airy, draught-free loosebox. Bandage legs for extra warmth.
6. Careful nursing is vital. Feed soft food, little and often.
7. Steam head frequently with Friar's Balsam or eucalyptus.
8. Call the veterinary surgeon.
9. Maintain a sound system of vaccination against equine flu.

Prevention

Horses can, and should, be immunised annually against the known influenza viruses prevalent in the UK.

Glossary of Terms

Abscess Localised collection of pus in a cavity made by disintegration of tissues in any organ or part of the body. Chronic abscess – one which may have been in existence for some time. Acute abscess – one which forms quickly and is often accompanied by pain.

Absorbent Medicines which suck or draw off dead tissues in the system. Vessels which absorb or take up various fluids of the body. Draws moisture, as in bedding.

Acute An ailment or disease with brief and severe symptoms which terminates in a few days with relief, cure or death.

Anaemia A deficiency of the blood.

Anterior At or near the front.

Astringents Medicines which restore the tone of muscular fibres and check morbid discharge by their power to contract muscular fibres and coagulate certain fluids.

Bog Spavin A soft swelling on the inner front surface of the hock joint. It is caused by strain.

Bone Spavin Bony enlargement on the inside, lower aspect of the hock.

Caudal Pertaining to the tail.

Cervical Of the neck.

Chronic A disease of long duration (as opposed to acute).

Curb Enlargement of the ligament or tendon just below the point of hock. Due to sudden strain.

Cyst A closed cavity containing either liquid or semi-solid secretions of the lining membrane.

Distal Farthest from a pont of reference; at the end; away from the body.

Dorsal Situated on or near the back of the body or the front of a leg.

Drench Liquid medicine administered orally by means of a drenching bottle. (Rarely used today.)

Effusion Out-pouring of the watery part of the blood through the walls of overloaded vessels.

Ewe-Necked A neck which is concave from withers to poll instead of convex. An upside-down neck.

Exostosis Abnormal deposit of bone.

Forelegs Out of One Hole Very narrow chest. Little room for the lungs to function properly so horses with this conformation are usually non-stayers, often winded. Horses built this way will often knock themselves.

Gamgee Non-sterile cotton encased in gauze. Excellent for use under leg bandages.

Good Bone Cannon bone and tendons measuring 8½ to 9 inches (21 to 22.5cm) in circumference just below the knee. A horse with good bone will be better able to carry weight

Goose Rumped Tail set on too low and quarters dropping away to the hocks.

Herring Gutted Horse with barrel too narrow compared to legs – too much daylight underneath. Horse runs up light.

Hogging Clipping off entire mane. (American – Roaching.)

Jumping Bump Pronounced point of croup.

Jute Coarse material (burlap) used for night rugs.

Lateral At or near the side.

Ligaments Bands of white (inelastic) and yellow (elastic) fibrous tissue. Ligaments hold tendons and joints in place – join bone to bone. Check ligaments, for example, join bone to deep flexor tendon (below knee) and (above knee) to the superficial flexor tendon.

Medial At or near the midline; towards the inside of the leg.

Mucus Fluid substance secreted by the mucous membrane.

Muscle Bundle Bundle or sheet of contractile fibres which produce movement in the animal body. Muscles are attached to bones by tendons or ligaments.

Palmar Relating to the back of a front leg.

Plantar Relating to the back of a hind leg; opposite to dorsal.

Posterior At or towards the rear.

Proximal Nearest to a point of reference or point of origin; towards the body.

Pus A liquid of creamy colour and consistency, secreted in sores or abscesses, formed by dead bacteria and white blood cells.

Serous Cyst Inflammation of the skin covering a bony projection, e.g. capped hock.

Short of Rib Horse with big gap between the last rib and the point of the hip. (Short back but long loin.)

Splints Bony enlargements which arise on the splint bone, the cannon bone or both.

Stale Urinate.

Stockinette   Knitted material commonly used to make support or exercise bandages.

Tendons   Tough, white, inelastic cords which connect muscles to bones.

Tucked Up   Refers to a horse whose belly looks tight and drawn up towards the backbone. (Usually occurs after a hard day's work.)

Well Ribbed Up   Rib cage extends well back, only room for a clenched fist between the last rib and the point of the hip.

Ventral   Towards the abdominal surface of the body.

Vesicles   Small blisters or vessels containing fluid.

Wind Galls   Swelling of the synovial membrane of the fetlock joint (joint sac), or the sheath of the tendon. Caused by strain.

Index

Page numbers in **bold** denote illustrations.